MW01055574

Working with People at High Risk
of Developing Psychosis

Working with People at High Risk of Developing Psychosis
A Treatment Handbook

Edited by

Jean Addington
Department of Psychiatry
University of Toronto, Canada
PRIME Clinic, Centre for Addiction and Mental Health

Shona M. Francey
PACE Clinic, Orygen Research Centre, Victoria, Australia

and

Anthony P. Morrison
School of Psychological Sciences
University of Manchester, UK
Psychology Services, Bolton, Salford and Trafford Mental Health Trust

John Wiley & Sons, Ltd

Copyright © 2006   John Wiley & Sons Ltd, The Atrium, Southern Gate, Chichester,
West Sussex PO19 8SQ, England

Telephone   (+44) 1243 779777

Email (for orders and customer service enquiries): cs-books@wiley.co.uk
Visit our Home Page on www.wiley.com

Other Wiley Editorial Offices

John Wiley & Sons Inc., 111 River Street, Hoboken, NJ 07030, USA

Jossey-Bass, 989 Market Street, San Francisco, CA 94103-1741, USA

Wiley-VCH Verlag GmbH, Boschstr. 12, D-69469 Weinheim, Germany

John Wiley & Sons Australia Ltd, 42 McDougall Street, Milton, Queensland 4064, Australia

John Wiley & Sons (Asia) Pte Ltd, 2 Clementi Loop #02-01, Jin Xing Distripark, Singapore 129809

John Wiley & Sons Canada Ltd, 22 Worcester Road, Etobicoke, Ontario, Canada M9W 1L1

Wiley also publishes its books in a variety of electronic formats. Some content that appears in print may not be
available in electronic books.

Library of Congress Cataloging-in-Publication Data

Working with people at high risk of developing psychosis : a treatment handbook / edited by Jean Addington,
 Shona M. Francey and Anthony P. Morrison.
     p.   cm.
  Includes bibliographical references and index.
  ISBN-13: 978-0-470-01162-1 (cloth : alk. paper)
  ISBN-10: 0-470-01162-9 (cloth : alk. paper)
  ISBN-13: 978-0-470-01163-8 (pbk : alk. paper)
  ISBN-10: 0-470-01163-7 (pbk : alk. paper)
  1. Psychoses—Handbooks, manuals, etc.   2. Psychoses—Treatment—Handbooks, manuals, etc.
 I. Addington, Jean.   II. Francey, Shona M.   III. Morrison, Anthony P., 1969–
  [DNLM: 1. Psychotic Disorders—diagnosis.   2. Psychotic Disorders—therapy.   3. Risk Factors.
 WM 200 W926 2006]
 RC512.W67   2006
 616.89—dc22   2005018265

British Library Cataloguing in Publication Data

A catalogue record for this book is available from the British Library

ISBN-13 978-0-470-01162-1 (hbk)   978-0-470-01163-8 (pbk)
ISBN-10 0-470-01162-9 (hbk)   0-470-01163-7 (pbk)

Typeset in 10/12pt Times by TechBooks Electronic Services, New Delhi, India
Printed and bound in Great Britain by Antony Rowe Ltd, Chippenham, Wiltshire, UK
This book is printed on acid-free paper responsibly manufactured from sustainable forestry
in which at least two trees are planted for each one used for paper production.

Contents

About the Editors

Jean Addington completed her PhD at the University of Calgary, Alberta. She is currently Director of the PRIME Clinic and Director of Psychosocial Treatments in the First Episode Psychosis Program at the Centre for Addiction and Mental Health in Toronto, Canada. She is also an Associate Professor in the Department of Psychiatry, University of Toronto. The Toronto PRIME Clinic is a research-based clinic for individuals who have an 'at risk mental state'. Her clinical and research interests lie in the understanding and management of this 'at risk mental state' and of early psychosis. She has published widely in this area: including psychosocial interventions, cognition, social functioning and substance use in early psychosis and the development of early intervention services. Her current work includes the development of risk assessment models for the conversion to psychosis and cognitive behaviour therapy in the ultra high risk period.

Shona M. Francey is a clinical psychologist with 20 years' experience in public mental health. She began working in the field of early intervention for psychosis when the Early Psychosis Prevention and Intervention Centre (EPPIC) was first established in 1992 in Melbourne, Australia. Within the EPPIC programme she worked as a case manager, COPE therapist and Group Programme leader. COPE is a cognitively oriented psychotherapy that was developed at EPPIC to promote recovery from first episode psychosis. Shona has also been involved in education and training about early psychosis, and the establishment of the PACE Clinic for young people thought to be at risk of developing psychosis. At PACE she has contributed to the development and evaluation of psychological therapy for this at risk group. She completed her PhD examining neurocognitive indicators of risk for psychosis in the PACE population and is currently the Clinical Coordinator of the PACE Clinic.

Anthony P. Morrison is a Reader in Clinical Psychology at the University of Manchester and is also a Consultant Clinical Psychologist in a specialist programme of care for people with early psychosis in Salford and Trafford. He has published a number of articles on trauma and psychosis, cognitive therapy for psychosis and experimental studies of cognitive processes in psychosis, and has been involved in a number of treatment trials for cognitive therapy for early psychosis and the prevention of psychosis. He has also published several books on the topic of psychological approaches to the understanding and treatment of psychosis. Unkind observers have suggested his interest in both trauma and losing touch with reality stem from his support of Manchester City Football Club.

List of Contributors

Jean Addington, *Associate Professor, Department of Psychiatry, University of Toronto, Director, PRIME Clinic, Director, Psychosocial Treatments, First Episode Psychosis Program, Centre for Addiction and Mental Health, 250 College Street, Toronto, Ontario M5T 1R8, Canada.*

Andreas Bechdolf, *Consultant Psychiatrist, Early Recognition and Intervention Centre for Mental Crisis – FETZ, Department of Psychiatry and Psychotherapy, University of Cologne, Joseph-Stelzmann-Str. 9, 50924 Cologne, Germany.*

Max Birchwood, *Director, Birmingham and Solihull Early Intervention Service, Birmingham and Solihull Mental Health Trust. Professor of Mental Health, University of Birmingham, 97 Church Lane, Aston, Birmingham B6 5UG, UK.*

Samantha E. Bowe, *Clinical Psychologist, Psychology Services, Bolton, Salford and Trafford Mental Health NHS Trust, Bury New Road, Prestwich, Manchester M25 3BL, UK.*

April A. Collins, *Deputy Administrative Director, Schizophrenia Program, Centre for Addiction and Mental Health, 1001 Queen Street West, Toronto, Ontario M6J 1H4, Canada.*

Shona M. Francey, *Clinical Coordinator, PACE Clinic, ORYGEN Research Centre, Department of Psychiatry, University of Melbourne, Locked Bag 10, Parkville, 3052, Australia.*

Paul French, *Coordinator, EDIT Service, Bolton, Salford and Trafford Mental Health NHS Trust, Salford Psychology Services, Bury New Road, Prestwich, Manchester M25 3BL, UK.*

Andrew I. Gumley, *Senior Lecturer in Clinical Psychology, University of Glasgow, Department of Psychological Medicine, Gartnavel Royal Hospital, 1055 Great Western Road, Glasgow G12 0XH, UK.*

Henry J. Jackson, *Professor and Head of School of Behavioural Science, Department of Psychology, Redmont Barry Building, University of Melbourne, Parkville, 3010, Victoria, Australia.*

Joachim Klosterkötter, *Professor of Psychiatry and Director, Department of Psychiatry and Psychotherapy, University of Cologne, Joseph-Stelzmann-Str. 9, 50924 Cologne, Germany.*

Steven Leicester, *Psychologist, PACE Clinic, ORYGEN Research Centre, Department of Psychiatry, University of Melbourne, Locked Bag 10, Parkville, 3052, Australia.*

Shôn Lewis, *Professor of Psychiatry, School of Psychiatry, and Behavioural Sciences, University of Manchester, Education and Research Centre, Wythenshawe Hospital, Manchester M23 9LT, UK.*

Anthony P. Morrison, *Reader in Clinical Psychology, University of Manchester, Manchester M13 9PL, UK.*

Paul Patterson, *Project Manager, Early Detection & Intervention Team (ED:IT), Harry Watton House, 97 Church Lane, Aston, Birmingham B6 5UG, UK.*

David Penn, *Associate Professor, Department of Psychology, Adjunct Associate Professor, Department of Psychiatry, University of North Carolina-Chapel Hill, Department of Psychology, Davie Hall, CB#3270, Chapel Hill, NC 27599-3270, USA.*

Lisa Phillips, *Clinical Psychologist and Research Co-ordinator, PACE Clinic, ORYGEN Research Centre, Department of Psychiatry, University of Melbourne, Locked Bag 10, Parkville, 3052, Australia.*

Amanda Skeate, *Clinical Psychologist/Clinical Lead, Early Detection & Intervention Team (ED:IT), Harry Watton House, 97 Church Lane, Aston, Birmingham B6 5UG, UK.*

Verena Veith, *Clinical Psychologist, Early Recognition and Intervention Centre for Mental Crisis – FETZ, Department of Psychiatry and Psychotherapy, University of Cologne, Kerpener Str. 62, 50924 Cologne, Germany.*

Alison R. Yung, *Associate Professor and Principal Research Fellow, PACE Clinic, ORYGEN Research Centre, Department of Psychiatry, University of Melbourne, Locked Bag 10, Parkville, 3052, Australia.*

Foreword

Most people who develop a psychotic disorder, such as schizophrenia, do so gradually with initially rather subtle changes in experience, emotional state and behaviour. These changes are usually distressing and impact insidiously on relationships, cognitive capacities and daily functioning. This frequently unfolds during the critical period of adolescence or young adulthood, at a time when such changes may be difficult to distinguish from normal developmental vicissitudes, but also when they can derail and constrain the pathways to fulfilment of one's potential. Even when the young person, their family, teachers or the family doctor may be aware that 'something is not quite right', the problem is difficult to characterise and diagnose. This undifferentiated clinical state has been termed the 'at risk mental state', a label that underlines the change in mental state and implies that the person is at risk for something more serious. If the person progresses to a fully fledged psychotic episode because the positive symptom dimension has become more severe and sustained, then and only then are we able to use the term 'prodromal' (retrospectively) for this preceding sub-threshold stage.

Even though people in this 'at risk mental state' are below the diagnostic threshold for an Axis 1 psychotic disorder, they are often clinically unwell with distress and functional impairment. They may meet criteria for other syndromes such as depression. Frequently they or their families do seek help. What are we to offer them? Whatever we offer should ideally be not only helpful, but safe. We are on firm ground when we offer needs-based intervention, e.g. treating their depression, improving their relationships, tackling comorbid substance abuse and/or monitoring risk. Less secure is the attempt, based on the fact that between 20 and 50% of these young people will progress to first episode psychosis within a year if something more specific is not offered, to try to prevent progression to psychosis. Recent landmark studies, conducted by the authors of this handbook and their colleagues, have shown that cognitive-behaviour therapy is effective in reducing the risk of early transition and at least delaying the onset of frank psychosis. In contrast to antipsychotic medication, also effective in this regard, cognitively based therapies are appealing in that they are essentially safer and better accepted by most patients, at least as a first line therapy. The authors of the various chapters are international experts and pioneers of the psychological approach in the earliest phases of psychotic illness, and have much accumulated clinical wisdom and ongoing innovative techniques to impart to the reader. This book forms part of the renaissance of the psychological interventions in the psychotic spectrum and focuses on a phase where, at least for some patients, psychological approaches may be not only necessary but sufficient.

Patrick McGorry MD, Professor, University of Melbourne,
Director, ORYGEN Youth Health (incorporating EPPIC),
and President, International Early Psychosis
Association (IEPA)

Acknowledgements

Many people have been supportive, encouraging and helpful in the development of this book. I would first like to acknowledge Jane Edwards from EPPIC for 'encouraging' me to put this book together. I would like to thank the research staff of the PRIME Clinic, in particular Amanda McCleery, Maria Haarmans, and Huma Saeedi, for all of their work in editing and proof reading chapters. Last but certainly not least I would like to thank Diane Kirsopp for her tremendous effort and work involved in developing the idea of this book until its final completion.

Jean Addington

CHAPTER 1

Introduction

Shôn Lewis

AT RISK MENTAL STATES IN PSYCHOSIS: AN INTRODUCTION

The idea that a set of subjective experiences exist which, in many cases, herald imminent psychosis has a long history in psychiatry. However, the operational delineation of these features, often coupled with alterations in functioning and a background of demographic risk factors, was only developed to the extent that it was reliably definable and therefore useable in research, by Alison Yung, Patrick McGorry and colleagues in the mid 1990s (Yung et al., 1998). These criteria, which comprise four sub-sets, have given rise to a paradigm of research which promises much in terms of early detection and secondary, or even primary, preventions. The closest previous attempt at a set of reliable criteria was made by the Bonn group in the 1970s (Huber & Gross, 1989).

Terminology in this area continues to be confusing. The term 'prodrome' to describe this collection of subjective features is widely used, although it is technically wrong and possibly misleading to the sufferer. Epidemiologists define a prodrome as a set of symptoms, which in all cases will lead on to the full syndrome. This is not the case with this set of features described by Yung and colleagues (1998). Only a proportion of such cases go on at follow-up to develop psychosis, which means that the epidemiologically correct term is that this set of features is a 'precursor'. This term has not caught on, perhaps because it lacks clinical immediacy. Instead, the terms 'at risk mental state' (ARMS) or 'ultra-high risk mental state' (UHR mental state) have been applied in an attempt to convey the message that nothing is inevitable.

The descriptive epidemiology of ARMS, how common they are, who gets them, how long they last and so on, is still in its infancy. We have little reliable data about the incidence and prevalence of this constellation of symptoms in the general community. Part of the reason for this is that studies which have set out to identify such cases are often in the context of treatment studies or clinical trials where, for ethical reasons as well as reasons of convenient ascertainment, clients are seeking help for these symptoms. Factors which cause an individual to seek help on the basis of these symptoms are not well understood. Community surveys, especially in Europe, have shown that a surprisingly high proportion of apparently healthy individuals, perhaps 5–15%, will report isolated psychosis-like phenomena for which most will not seek help. Presumably, the decision to seek help is partly

Working with People at High Risk of Developing Psychosis: A Treatment Handbook.
Edited by J. Addington, S.M. Francey and A.P. Morrison. © 2006 John Wiley & Sons, Ltd.

driven by the subjective distress and this will vary from one individual to another. On top of that, individuals will vary in the extent to which they seek help for a given level of distress, which will depend on a range of internal and external trait and state factors, including health beliefs, perceptions that the abnormalities constitute a threat to health and might be amenable to intervention, availability of health care and so on.

These currently unmeasured factors will inevitably mean that sample structure will be very sensitive to social context and thus collected samples will differ from one another in ways which are likely to be important, and influence final transition rates to psychosis, but are essentially unknown. Nonetheless, follow-up studies are in general agreement that the risk of developing an operationally defined Axis 1 psychosis over the next 12 months is massively increased. Rates of transition to psychosis in follow-up studies published so far vary between 10% and 50%. While some commentators see this five-fold variation as a weakness in the field, it is small in comparison to the increased risk this represents over the base population. An age-matched community sample of young adults would show an incidence rate of new cases of no more than five per 10 000 per year. Even a 10% risk of psychosis in the year following detection of an ARMS will therefore represent a 200-fold increased risk. This huge increase in risk, particularly in a population of young people, immediately raises the prospect of intervention to head off the psychosis.

INTERVENTION STUDIES: GENERAL METHODOLOGICAL ISSUES

Two plausible treatment modalities present themselves straight away, by inference from the treatment of psychosis: antipsychotic drug treatment and specifiable psychological treatment, specifically cognitive behaviour therapy. The evidence base for the effectiveness of antipsychotic drug treatments in psychosis is incontrovertible. The evidence base supporting the effectiveness of cognitive behaviour therapy in psychosis is more recent and smaller. However, several systematic reviews and meta-analyses have supported its effectiveness (Cormac, Jones & Campbell, 2002; Pilling et al., 2002), although only as an adjunct to antipsychotic drug treatment: it has not formally been assessed in the absence of drug treatment.

Three randomised controlled trials of interventions have now published interim or final data. The first was the Personal Assessment and Crisis Evaluation (PACE) trial by McGorry and colleagues (2002) in Melbourne, which evaluated the effectiveness of a six-month combined intervention of low dose risperidone, a second generation antipsychotic drug, plus cognitive behaviour therapy in addition to case management, compared to case management alone. This was an open trial. The second trial by McGlashan and colleagues (2003) at Yale was a double-blind randomised placebo controlled trial of low dose olanzapine, another second generation antipsychotic drug, versus placebo, for 12 months. The third trial, the Early Detection and Intervention Evaluation (EDIE) trial by Morrison and colleagues (2004) in Manchester, compared the effectiveness of a six-month (26 sessions) package of cognitive behaviour therapy versus monthly monitoring. The trials had important similarities. Each used the Melbourne criteria for defining cases; had a 12-month follow-up after commencement of treatment; randomised about 60 subjects and had rates of transition to psychosis as the primary outcome. The trials had important differences too, particularly in case-finding strategies. Assessment measures at baseline differed too: the PACE trial used the Comprehensive Assessment of At Risk Mental States (CAARMS) structured assessment tool (see Chapter 2), the Prevention through Risk Identification Management and Education (PRIME) trial used the Structured Interview for Prodromal States (SIPS: Miller et al., 2003), and the EDIE trial used the Positive and Negative Syndrome Scale (PANSS).

Results showed that each of the interventions had some therapeutic effect in terms of reducing transition rate, although this tailed off after treatment was discontinued. Differences between the results of the trials appeared in other areas. One important finding to emerge was that consent rates from eligible subjects differed between these studies and were lowest for the double-blind drug study and highest for the psychological treatment study. This is in no way surprising given the way that subjects themselves tend to formulate their problems, often not in the framework of a medical model. It does have implications for the generalisability of any findings and for considerations about how useful any treatment might be. Even if a treatment is highly effective, if it is not acceptable to the target population it is of little use. This difference in ascertainment is the most likely reason that the three trials reported differences in final transition rates, regardless of randomised treatment group. Transition rates at one year were highest for the double-blind trial (27%) and lowest for the psychological treatment trial (15%). One explanation for this is that only those people who are most distressed and urgently seeking help will elect to go into a double-blind placebo controlled trial, whereas a higher proportion of the eligible population, including less distressed cases, will consent to an open psychological treatment trial. That this is the case appears to be supported by data from the PACE trial, which usefully followed up subjects who declined to go in to the trial (McGorry et al., 2002). Surprisingly, those subjects did better than the clients overall who consented to the treatment trial. In almost all other clinical trial contexts, refusers do worse than those consenting to go in to the trial: presumably the explanation here is that the non-consenters did not feel sufficiently distressed or in need of urgent treatment that they wished to go in to the trial.

One of the still unanswered issues which is important from the public health viewpoint when trying to judge the potential impact of an effective preventive intervention is not 'How many help-seeking ARMS cases go on to develop psychosis?' but 'What proportion of new cases of psychosis came through the prior route of help-seeking ARMS?' From this, the population attributable fraction can be estimated: what proportion of new cases of psychosis would be prevented by an effective intervention for people with ARMS? These are difficult data to collect accurately since they involve retrospective accounts by people with first episode psychosis.

ETHICAL ISSUES

There are particular ethical dilemmas thrown up by research and the possibility of treatment in this area. The first, and in some ways the most obvious, concerns the giving of treatment to a group of at risk individuals where most of whom (60% or more) will not, even without treatment, develop the disorder. To what extent is it justified to expose all the at risk group to treatment in that case? Not surprisingly, any answers in this area are not black and white but rather a matter of degree. What is the level of risk of transition at which it becomes acceptable to treat the whole group? To give a related real-life example, we know that about 20% of individuals following a first episode of psychosis will not have a subsequent episode, even without treatment. Yet we make the judgement clinically that treating all individuals with maintenance drug treatment after the first episode is justified, since 80% will benefit. It is not possible currently to predict accurately who will be in the 20% who will not need ongoing treatment, in the same way that it is not currently possible to predict who are the 60% or more of ARMS who will not go on to develop psychosis. The assumption implicit with the relapse prevention example is that 80% is a sufficiently large number to justify intervention across the board. Clearly, a judgement is also being made about the undesirability of the outcome: one can argue that a first episode of psychosis (or a first relapse) is a sufficiently severe outcome to warrant intervention in all cases. Further dimensions are the effectiveness of the intervention (will it reduce transition rates from 30% to 0%, or merely to 20%) and the risk of adverse effects, which is clearly specific to the type of intervention used. For drug treatments the risk of adverse effects may be relatively high and the effects themselves serious. For psychological interventions it is assumed that risk is lower and this may indeed be the case, although there are plausible risks inherent in psychological treatments too, including stigmatisation.

The central ethical dilemma here can be circumvented if the main therapeutic target is defined differently. Currently, the debate circles on the issue of prophylaxis: how many cases of a psychotic disorder can be prevented is weighed against the cost of treating unnecessarily a majority who will not go on to get the disorder in any event. However, other outcomes may be at least as appropriate. Delaying the onset of psychosis or ameliorating its severity once it begins would also be important therapeutic gains from an intervention. The primary outcome of most immediate relevance to people seeking help for ARMS is reducing the severity and functional impact of the symptoms themselves. If the primary therapeutic target is to alleviate these current sub-threshold symptoms rather than explicitly to prevent future psychosis, then all those who receive an experimental treatment may expect benefits. Current models of how symptoms develop in early psychosis are still at an early stage, but it seems inherently likely that reducing current symptoms will lessen the risk of future transition, so as a therapeutic target it makes sense. Severity of baseline sub-clinical symptoms was one of two predictors of outcome, the other being treatment allocation in the EDIE trial. Furthermore, transition to psychosis sounds as if it is an all or nothing phenomenon. In fact, the operational definitions used are rating scales with continuously distributed properties and the definition of transition is based on passing an essentially arbitrary threshold of severity. Again, this makes it less clear that one is best off dealing with a binary or categorical outcome.

WHAT THE FUTURE HOLDS

Research in this emerging area of at risk mental states is only just beginning. On the epidemiological front, more clarity is needed about base rates and the natural history of ARMS. The role of external factors such as street drug use is still unclear. Biological issues have begun to be explored. Potentially important is the issue of progression with preliminary longitudinal evidence suggesting progressive regional structural abnormalities during this early phase can be replicated (Pantelis et al., 2003). The role of normal genetic variants in mediating risk, perhaps via particular cognitive traits and styles, is likely. Connected to this are two interfaces which require more exploration if models for psychological interventions are to be refined. One is the interface between ARMS and full psychosis. The other is the presumed interface between isolated psychotic symptoms in the general community and the constellation of these symptoms, coupled with distress, which constitute ARMS.

The future role of psychological treatment seems certain to be important. There are good theoretical reasons why psychological interventions might be particularly appropriate at this early, transitional phase and they are certainly more acceptable for this help-seeking client group than drug treatments. However, the relative effectiveness of drug treatments and psychological treatments will at some stage need to be evaluated. It is entirely likely that clinical guidelines emerging from this area will see psychological treatments, particularly cognitive behaviour therapy, as first line treatments, with drug treatments indicated for clients whose symptoms do not respond to psychological intervention.

REFERENCES

Cormac, I., Jones, C. & Campbell, C. (2002). Cognitive behavior therapy for schizophrenia. *The Cochrane Database of Systematic Reviews*, **2**, 1–46.

Huber, G. & Gross, G. (1989). The concept of basic symptoms in schizophrenic and schizoaffective psychoses. *Recenti Progressi in Medicina*, **80**, 646–652.

McGlashan, T.H., Zipursky, R., Perkins, D.O., Addington, J., Miller, T.J., Woods, S.W. et al. (2003). The PRIME North America randomized double blind clinical trial of olanzapine vs placebo in patients at risk for being prodromally symptomatic for psychosis: I. Study rationale and design. *Schizophrenia Research*, **61**, 7–18.

McGorry, P.D., Yung, A.R., Phillips, L.J., Yuen, H.P., Francey, S.F., Cosgrave, E.M. et al. (2002). Randomized controlled trial of interventions designed to reduce the risk of progression to first-episode psychosis in a clinical sample with subthreshold symptoms. *Archives of General Psychiatry*, **59**, 921–928.

Miller, T.J., McGlashan, T.H., Rosen, J.L., Cadenhead, K., Ventura, J., McFarlane, W. et al. (2003). Prodromal assessment with the structured interview for prodromal syndromes and the scale of prodromal symptoms: Predictive validity, interrater reliability, and training to reliability. *Schizophrenia Bulletin*, **29**, 703–715.

Morrison, A.P., French, P., Walford, L., Lewis, S.W., Kilcommons, A., Green, J. et al. (2004). Cognitive therapy for the prevention of psychosis in people at ultra-high risk: randomised controlled trial. *British Journal of Psychiatry*, **185**, 291–297.

Pantelis, C., Velakoulis, D., McGorry, P.D., Wood, S., Suckling, J., Phillips, L. et al. (2003). Neuroanatomical abnormalities before and after onset of psychosis: A cross-sectional and longitudinal MRI comparison. *Lancet*, **361** (9354), 281–288.

Pilling, S., Bebbington, P., Kuipers, E., Garety, P., Geddes, J., Orbach, G. et al. (2002). Psychological treatments in schizophrenia: I. Meta-analyses of family intervention and cognitive behavior therapy. *Psychological Medicine*, **32**, 763–782.

Yung, A.R., Phillips, L.J., McGorry, P.D., McFarlane, C.A., Francey, S., Harrigan, S. et al. (1998). Prediction of psychosis: A step towards indicated prevention of schizophrenia. *British Journal of Psychiatry*, **172** (Suppl.), S14–20.

CHAPTER 2

Identification of the Population

Alison R. Yung

A common goal, in both general and psychological medicine, is to identify individuals 'at risk' of a particular disorder and to intervene in those 'at risk' to prevent the disorder from becoming manifest. For example, methods are being tested for detecting people at risk of diabetes with the aim of detecting and intervening early in the course of the disease (Barker et al., 2004), and for detecting individuals at high risk of breast cancer with the aim of providing some prophylactic treatment to prevent onset (Bouchard et al., 2004; Metcalfe, 2004; Prichard, Hill, Dijkstra, McDermott & O'Higgins, 2003). One strategy used in early detection within general medicine is genetic testing. With this technology, 'at risk' status can be diagnosed before any symptoms of disorder are present. This is possible even *in utero* or before implantation in the case of *in vitro* fertilisation. These techniques are possible for a range of diseases including achondroplasia, Huntington's disease and Duchenne's muscular dystrophy.

But what of identifying individuals 'at risk' of psychotic disorders such as schizophrenia? There are no genetic tests for these disorders, nor even any aetiopathological diagnostic investigations. How can 'at risk' status for psychotic disorders be recognised? What are the implications of such 'at risk diagnoses' for treatment and prevention of disorder? A number of attempts have been made to define certain groups as 'at risk' either of schizophrenia or to psychotic disorders more generally. Different strategies have been used each with different meanings of 'at risk', including different implications for intervention. These will be briefly summarised, followed by a detailed discussion of our own approach.

FAMILY HISTORY APPROACHES

The traditional approach to identifying individuals at risk of schizophrenia is to study family members of patients with the disorder (Asarnow, 1988; Cornblatt & Obuchowski, 1997). Thus a group with presumably an increased genetic risk is identified, and then additional risk factors, which make the transition to a frank psychotic disorder more likely, can be examined. This is known as the 'high risk' approach. Assessments usually begin when subjects are children, with follow-up continuing over many years. The aim is to detect the

Working with People at High Risk of Developing Psychosis: A Treatment Handbook.
Edited by J. Addington, S.M. Francey and A.P. Morrison. © 2006 John Wiley & Sons, Ltd.

development of psychotic disorder at some stage in the person's life span. Researchers using the high risk family history approach acknowledge that the transition rate to a psychotic disorder is not likely to be large and results may not be generalisable beyond the genetically defined high risk group (Asarnow, 1988; Cornblatt & Obuchowski, 1997). Furthermore, intervention in these 'at risk' individuals is not practical or at least not ethical, as the degree of risk is low and the timing of onset of psychotic disorder not known. Indeed, these genetic high risk studies have never claimed early intervention as a goal, focusing instead on investigating causal pathways into schizophrenia and other psychotic illnesses.

Mednick, Parnas, Schulsinger and Mednick (1987) modified the genetic high risk strategy by focusing on adolescent offspring who were entering the peak age of risk (i.e. by adding age as a risk factor). This approach made the high risk paradigm more practical. However, the number developing a psychotic disorder from this cohort is still not expected to be large, and the number of false positives is too high to make any intervention practical.

Similarly, the Edinburgh high risk project (Hodges, Byrne, Grant & Johnstone, 1999; Johnstone et al., 2000; Miller, Byrne, Hodges, Lawrie & Johnstone, 2002) studies individuals with presumed high genetic liability for schizophrenia, including both first and second degree relatives of schizophrenia probands. Like the Mednick approach, this study also recruits young adults (aged 16–25) who will pass through the period of maximum risk of developing schizophrenia during the planned 10 years of the study. Recently reported data revealed that 13 out of 162 subjects (approximately 8%) have developed schizophrenia to date, six years after study commencement (Johnstone, Cosway & Lawrie, 2002). Although this rate of onset of schizophrenia is well above expected community rates, recruitment of large numbers is needed in order to clarify other risk factors for the development of schizophrenia, and to eventually identify a group for whom preventive treatment is justified.

PSYCHOPATHOLOGICAL (SYMPTOMATIC) APPROACHES

An alternative to the genetic high risk approach is to focus on individuals who report symptoms that are known to occur prior to the onset of a psychotic disorder; that is, symptoms found in psychotic prodromes. This is in contrast to the genetic high risk strategies which study asymptomatic individuals. There are different ways of approaching the recruitment of possibly prodromal individuals, but a first step in all approaches is to identify prodromal features of the psychotic disorders such as schizophrenia.

Characterising the Prodrome

The most common method for investigating prodromal features is the examination of a case series of patients with established psychotic disorders. Thus, a retrospective description of the symptoms and signs which led up to the defining first psychotic episode is gained. A particularly sound example of such research is that done by Häfner's group in Germany (Häfner, Maurer, Loffler & Riecher, 1993; Häfner et al., 1998). Data on prodromal features were collected using a standardised structured instrument, the Interview for the Retrospective Assessment of the Onset of Schizophrenia (IRAOS) (Häfner et al., 1992). Several other researchers have also studied psychotic prodromes by retrospective case series. Much of this literature is summarised in the review paper by Yung and McGorry (1996b).

Another German group, led by Huber, also used retrospective descriptions to characterise psychotic prodromes, but approached this from a different theoretical perspective. Its emphasis has been on the importance of 'basic symptoms' as precursors to the onset of the psychotic phase of schizophrenia (Gross, 1989; Huber & Gross, 1989; Klosterkötter, Ebel, Schultze-Lutter & Steinmeyer, 1996). Basic symptoms are subjectively experienced abnormalities in the realms of cognition, attention, perception and movement. They have also been described as 'self-experienced neuropsychological deficits' (Klosterkötter, Schultze-Lutter, Gross, Huber & Steinmeyer, 1997b). The development of the Bonn Scale for Assessment of Basic Symptoms (BSABS) (Klosterkötter et al., 1997a) and, more recently, the Schizophrenia Prediction Instrument – Adult Version (SPI-A) (Schultze-Lutter et al., 2004) has enabled the assessment of these symptoms to be operationalised.

Aside from retrospective descriptions, a different approach is to prospectively follow up patients with already diagnosed schizophrenia and examine the prodromal features leading up to a psychotic relapse. Thus the **relapse prodrome** rather than the **initial prodrome** is the subject of investigation in these studies. In some studies of relapse prodrome, antipsychotic medication is ceased in order to observe emerging psychosis (Donlon & Blacker, 1973) and others follow a more naturalistic design (Birchwood et al., 1989; Heinrichs & Carpenter, 1985; Subotnik & Nuechterlein, 1988). Besides any ethical issues, the problem with this method is that it has not been established exactly how the signs and symptoms of a relapse prodrome in schizophrenia relate to the prodromal features of a first psychotic episode. Some symptoms may be modified by such factors as medication, the fear of relapse and hospitalisation, and the family's changing perception of the patient (Yung & McGorry, 1996b). In fact, in one study of relapse prodrome, concern about the possibility of relapse is mentioned as an early symptom by patients who were taken off maintenance medication and were being observed (Donlon & Blacker, 1973).

Through a review of the literature of both the retrospective case series and the prospective studies of relapse prodromes (Yung & McGorry, 1996b) and a case series of consecutive referrals of patients with a first episode of psychosis (Yung & McGorry, 1996a), our group theorised that features of psychotic prodromes could be divided into eight main sub-types: (1) Neurotic symptoms, (2) Mood-related symptoms, (3) Changes in volition, (4) Cognitive changes, (5) Physical symptoms, (6) Other symptoms, (7) Behavioural changes and (8) Attenuated (sub-threshold) psychotic symptoms or isolated psychotic symptoms. Typical features of each category are shown in Table 2.1.

This last category, attenuated or isolated psychotic symptoms, refers to psychotic-like experiences which differ from frank psychotic symptoms in their intensity, frequency and/or duration. An example is a persecutory idea that is held with less than delusional conviction. This has less **intensity** than a fully formed persecutory delusion. In contrast, if an individual fleetingly holds a persecutory belief with delusional conviction but for only one hour, this is distinguished from a threshold psychotic symptom on the basis of **duration**: the abnormal experience has not been present for long enough. Similarly, if someone had a hallucination only twice in a month, these may be considered to be isolated psychotic experiences, and therefore below the threshold for full-blown psychosis on the basis of **frequency**: they are not happening often enough.

Of course, not all symptoms will be found in all individuals or even at any one point in time in a particular individual. There is a great deal of variability between individuals and across time in the one person. In fact, the process of development of a psychotic episode has been described as a 'moment to moment march of psychological changes' (Docherty, Van

Table 2.1 Prodromal features of schizophrenia – modified from Yung et al., 2004a. *Treating Schizophrenia in the Prodromal Phase* – London: Taylor and Francis

(1) Neurotic symptoms	Anxiety Restlessness Anger, irritability
(2) Mood-related symptoms	Depression Anhedonia Guilt Suicidal ideas Mood swings
(3) Changes in volition	Apathy, loss of drive Boredom, loss of interest Fatigue, reduced energy
(4) Cognitive changes	Disturbance of attention and concentration Preoccupation, daydreaming Thought blocking Reduced abstraction
(5) Physical symptoms	Somatic complaints Loss of weight Poor appetite Sleep disturbance Suspiciousness Change in sense of self, others or the world
(6) Other symptoms	Obsessive compulsive phenomena Dissociative phenomena Increased interpersonal sensitivity
(7) Behavioural changes	Deterioration in role functioning Social withdrawal Impulsivity Odd behaviour Aggressive, disruptive behaviour
(8) Attenuated or sub-threshold versions of psychotic symptoms	Perceptual abnormalities

Kammen, Siris & Marder, 1978, p. 420). Typically, non-specific 'neurotic' type symptoms seem to be followed by symptoms which are attenuated or sub-threshold forms of full-blown psychotic symptoms just prior to the development of the frank psychotic disorder (Yung & McGorry, 1996b). Because of the degree of variability between patients, it is useful to try to discern some commonly occurring prodromal features which seem to occur in most individuals. These are shown in Table 2.2.

Identifying the 'Prodrome' Prospectively

Having characterised the prodrome of a first psychotic episode, the next challenge is to identify psychotic prodromes prospectively, thus enabling intervention and research into

Table 2.2 Most frequent prodromal symptoms described in retrospective studies

Reduced concentration and attention
Reduced drive and motivation
Depression
Sleep disturbance
Anxiety
Social withdrawal
Suspiciousness
Deterioration in role functioning
Irritability

Source: From Yung & McGorry (1996b). The Prodromal Phase of First Episode Psychosis: Past and Current Conceptualisations. *Schizophrenia Bulletin*, **22**, 353–370.

this important phase. Just knowing which symptoms typically occur in a psychotic prodrome does not provide any information about the degree of risk conferred by particular prodromal features or syndromes. As can be seen in Table 2.2, the most frequently occurring prodromal features are non-specific and could be the result of a number of conditions, such as major depression, substance abuse, and physical illness, as well as a psychotic prodrome or even a frank psychotic disorder itself. Even attenuated or isolated psychotic symptoms may not necessarily progress to a frank psychotic disorder. It is becoming increasingly clear from large scale population studies that attenuated and frank psychotic symptoms are quite common in the community. For example, van Os, Hanssen, Bijl and Vollebergh (2001) found a lifetime prevalence of 17.5% for 'psychotic experiences' in the general population (n = 7076). The majority reporting such symptoms were not distressed by them and did not seek help. Similar rates of psychotic-like experiences have been found in other epidemiological studies (Eaton, Romanoski, Anthony & Nestadt, 1991; Tien, 1991).

This problem of lack of specificity and its implications for using prodromal features as indicators of risk for onset of psychotic disorder is an important one. Focusing on individuals with apparently prodromal symptoms and signs and identifying them as those likely to develop a psychotic disorder will lead to the problem of a large number of false positives: most people with these features would not make the transition to a full-blown psychotic disorder. Thus, the syndrome which seems like, or could be, a prodrome should be thought of, not as a disease entity, but as a state risk factor for a full-blown psychotic disorder. That is, the presence of the syndrome implies that the affected person is at that time more likely to develop psychosis in the near future than someone without the syndrome. Instead of being labelled as 'prodromal' the person should be thought of as having an 'at risk mental state' (Yung et al., 2003). This terminology highlights the risk factor approach, suggesting that the syndrome is a risk factor for incipient onset of full-blown psychosis in the near future (Yung, Phillips, Yuen & McGorry, 2004b; Yung et al., 1998a, 1998b, 2003). The term 'near future', of course, needs clarification. Research on the duration of prodromes in psychotic disorders suggests that this time period could be thought of as about two years (Loebel et al., 1992), although this needs investigation, and would depend on the course of the apparently 'prodromal' syndrome, or at risk mental state, over this time.

Three broad methods have used the symptomatic approach to identify at risk individuals: the 'psychosis proneness' method of Chapman and Chapman et al. (Allen, Chapman,

Chapman, Vuchetich & Frost, 1987; Chapman & Chapman, 1987; Chapman, Chapman, Kwapil, Eckblad & Zinser, 1994), the basic symptoms method of the Bonn and Cologne groups (Klosterkötter, Hellmich, Steinmeyer & Schultze-Lutter, 2001; Klosterkötter et al., 1997b) and the Ultra High Risk method developed by our group from Melbourne, Australia (Yung et al., 1998a, 1998b, 2003, 2004b).

Psychosis Proneness

Chapman and Chapman and colleagues (Allen et al., 1987; Chapman & Chapman, 1987; Chapman et al., 1994) attempted to identify individuals at risk of psychosis, or what they called 'hypothetically psychosis-prone', by focusing on attenuated and isolated psychotic symptoms. They hypothesised that these symptoms confer a predisposition or diathesis to psychotic disorder. In addition to these 'positive' psychotic phenomena, they also theorised that people who displayed physical and social anhedonia and impulsive non-conformity were also at risk. They developed questionnaires to measure these psychopathological symptoms (Chapman & Chapman, 1980; Chapman, Edell & Chapman, 1980).

Chapman and Chapman et al. (Allen et al., 1987; Chapman & Chapman, 1987; Chapman et al., 1994) also noted the need to focus on people at or near the age of greatest risk for schizophrenia, that is late adolescence and early adulthood, so they studied college students. One sample of college students with high levels of self-reported 'psychotic-like' symptoms were followed longitudinally over time and compared with a group of controls. At 10- to 15-year follow-up, students who scored highly on scales of perceptual abnormalities and magical thinking were more likely to have developed a psychotic disorder than comparison subjects. Social anhedonia, physical anhedonia and impulsive non-conformity were not predictive of psychotic disorder at follow-up, although high scores on the Social Anhedonia scale correlated with high levels of psychotic-like experiences at follow-up. However, the actual numbers of students who developed a psychotic disorder after 10- to 15-year follow-up was low: 11 out of 375, or 2.9%. This was not significantly higher than in the control group (2 out of 159, or 1.3%). However, there was a trend for those in the group with high scores on the Perceptual Aberration and Magical Ideation scales to differ significantly from controls, with 10 subjects out of 193 making the transition (5.2%) (p = 0.06) (Chapman et al., 1994). That is, those students with sub-threshold forms of delusions and hallucinations seemed to be more at risk of subsequent full-blown psychotic disorder than those without these symptoms.

However, many students with high levels of magical ideation and perceptual abnormalities did not develop a psychotic disorder. This finding is perhaps to be expected, given the seemingly large number of people in the general population who report psychotic-like experiences, as noted previously (van Os et al., 2001). The implications are similar for a longitudinal epidemiological study from New Zealand (Poulton et al., 2000). This study found that children at age 11 with psychotic-like experiences had an increased risk of schizophreniform disorder at age 26 compared to children who did not have such experiences. However, most of the children with psychotic-like experiences did not develop a psychotic disorder.

To date, because of the low numbers developing a psychotic disorder, the high number of false positives and the long time frame of the follow-up, the psychosis-proneness research has not been able to be used as the basis for any preventive intervention.

Table 2.3 High risk criteria based on basic symptoms

At least two out of nine of the following basic symptoms:
Inability to divide attention
Thought interference
Thought pressure
Thought blockages
Disturbance of receptive speech
Disturbance of expressive speech
Disturbances of abstract thinking ('concretism')
Unstable ideas of reference ('subject-centrism')
Captivation of attention by details of the visual field

Source: From Schultze-Lutter et al. (2004). The Schizophrenia Prediction
Instrument, Adult Version (SPI-A). *Schizophrenia Research*, **70**, 76–77.

Basic Symptoms as Predictors

A study by the Bonn group in Germany examined the predictive capacity of the basic symptoms in a cohort of non-psychotic patients attending a tertiary referral psychiatric setting. Presenting diagnoses were mainly mood, anxiety, somatoform and personality disorders (Klosterkötter et al., 1997b, 2001). Thus this research represents a major shift in focus from the work by Chapman and Chapman as the population studied is a clinical one. Subjects were followed up on average eight years after initial assessment, and over this period over 50% of them had developed schizophrenia. Certain basic symptoms – disturbances of receptive speech, blocking of thoughts, visual perceptual disturbances, olfactory, gustatory and other sensory disturbances – were found significantly more often in the group which developed schizophrenia compared to the group which did not, suggesting that these symptoms may be predictors of schizophrenia.

This study used an enriched sample of tertiary referred patients, most of whom had high levels of basic symptoms. The study's authors regarded them as being 'susceptible to schizophrenia' on the basis of their psychopathology. Thus it is difficult to translate the findings from this study cohort to the wider population. This is particularly so since there are no studies reporting the prevalence and stability of basic symptoms in non-psychotic psychiatric disorders.

From this study, the authors developed a check-list of nine symptoms suggestive of a schizophrenia prodrome (see Table 2.3), as measured by the BSABS (Klosterkötter et al., 1997a). High risk criteria were then developed requiring the presence of at least two of these symptoms. The predictive validity of these criteria are currently being examined in a multi-site European study.

The Ultra High Risk Approach

As has been found with the Chapman and Chapman research, there are problems with using prodromal symptoms and signs alone to identify people thought to be at incipient risk of onset of psychotic disorder, even psychotic-like experiences. Particularly in a non-clinical sample, the false positive rate would be far too high and any intervention provided may be done so unnecessarily. One possible solution to this problem of false positives is a sequential screening approach or 'close-in strategy' (Bell, 1992). This involves putting in place a number of different screening measures to concentrate the level of risk in the selected sample to create an enriched cohort. In other words, an individual must meet a number of conditions to be included in the high risk sample. Thus to identify people at high risk of onset of psychotic disorder in the near future, symptoms and signs are combined with other risk factors. One risk factor is age. It is known that the age of highest incidence of psychotic disorder is adolescence and young adulthood (Häfner et al., 1993). As noted previously, this risk factor has been used in the Mednick approach (Mednick et al., 1987), the Edinburgh High Risk study (Johnstone et al., 2002) and the psychosis-proneness research (Chapman et al., 1994). Other risk factors which could be added are family history of psychotic disorder, schizotypal personality disorder, deterioration in psychosocial functioning and distress or a perceived need for psychiatric help by the person or people close to him or her.

Our research group used combinations of these risk factors to describe three samples considered to be at 'ultra high risk' (UHR) of psychotic disorder. The addition of the qualifier 'ultra' is to distinguish these individuals from subjects in traditional high risk studies who are identified on the basis of genetic risk alone. These studies use one measure of risk and the period of risk is considered to be a lifetime. The UHR approach attempts to identify individuals at risk for a brief period (one to two years). That is, they are considered to be potentially in a state of incipient psychotic disorder or possibly prodromal. The other main difference is that the UHR group is symptomatic and presenting for clinical care, in contrast to the asymptomatic but genetically liable individuals included in the other genetic high risk studies. Similarly, the UHR approach also contrasts with that of Chapman and Chapman (Allen et al., 1987; Chapman & Chapman, 1987; Chapman et al., 1994) by its use of a clinical population. The UHR criteria are applied to young people being referred to a psychiatric service for help. Thus a two-stage screening procedure is applied: recognition of need for care, then recognition of UHR criteria within the help-seeker. This method reduces the chance that a well person who happens to have psychotic-like experiences but who is otherwise functioning adequately will be identified as UHR.

Three UHR sub-samples have been defined. These are: (1) presence of attenuated (sub-threshold) psychotic symptoms, (2) history of brief self-limited psychotic symptoms and (3) positive family history of psychosis, plus persistent low functioning (Yung et al., 2003). For example, individuals in Group One have sub-threshold psychotic symptoms in terms of the intensity or frequency of their experiences. Group Two subjects have a history of frank psychotic symptoms that spontaneously resolve within seven days. Finally, Group Three includes young people with a presumed genetic vulnerability to psychosis who have had a recent and marked deterioration in functioning. The genetic vulnerability includes those with either a schizotypal personality disorder (as defined by the *Diagnostic and Statistical Manual of Mental Disorders*, DSM IV) (American Psychiatric Association, 1994) or a first degree relative with a history of any psychotic disorder.

The criteria for each of the UHR groups were originally operationalised using the Brief Psychiatric Rating Scale (BPRS) (Overall & Gorham, 1962) and the Comprehensive Assessment of Symptoms and History (CASH) (Andreasen, 1987), which could be used to specify the intensity of a psychotic symptom. Additionally, criteria specifying the frequency and duration of the experiences were needed, as this degree of fine detail in relation to sub-threshold symptoms is missing from the BPRS and CASH. Prospectively, the recency of these symptoms also needed to be assessed as degree of risk may fluctuate depending on current or recent symptomatology. That is, after a self-limited episode of sub-threshold psychotic symptoms (perhaps stress induced), how long should the individual be considered to be at UHR for frank psychotic disorder?

In addition to the UHR criteria being operationalised, a clear definition of frank psychosis was required as the outcome point in assessing the predictive validity of the criteria. This was based on the presence of clear-cut threshold level psychotic symptoms (delusions, hallucinations and formal thought disorder) occurring several times per week for at least one week. This threshold is essentially that at which neuroleptic medication would probably be commenced in common clinical practice. This definition of onset of threshold psychosis is, of course, somewhat arbitrary, but does at least have clear treatment implications and applies equally well to substance-related symptoms, symptoms that have a mood component – either depression or mania – and schizophrenia spectrum disorders.

Testing the UHR Criteria

Having defined the UHR criteria, the next step was to test their ability to identify individuals likely to develop a psychotic disorder within a brief follow-up period. A study was conducted from 1995–1996 to test the criteria in this manner (Yung et al., 2003). In order to do this, a specially designed clinical research centre, the Personal Assessment and Crisis Evaluation (PACE) Clinic, was established (Yung et al., 1996). The aims of the PACE Clinic were to assess, manage, and follow up putatively UHR ('prodromal') subjects. PACE was located at a community adolescent service for general medical as well as psychological problems. Its location was intended to promote access and avoid stigma. PACE attendees received supportive counselling and case management in addition to treatment of target symptoms, such as depression. They may have received antidepressant or anxiolytic medication but no neuroleptic medication was used (Yung et al., 2003).

This study also aimed to investigate which if any other demographic or symptomatic measures were predictive of onset of a psychotic disorder within the UHR group. Participants in the study were assessed at baseline with the following measures: the Psychotic Disorders section of the Structured Clinical Interview for DSM IV (SCID) (First, Spitzer, Gibbon & Williams, 1997) to establish that none was psychotic at study entry, the Family Interview for Genetic Studies (FIGS) (Maxwell, 1992) to determine if there was any family history of psychotic disorder, the Quality of Life Scale (QLS) (Heinrichs, Hanlon & Carpenter, 1984) and Global Assessment of Functioning (GAF) (American Psychiatric Association, 1994) to assess functioning and disability. A structured interview was performed to assess the duration of symptoms and decline in functioning.

Monthly interviews were also conducted to monitor mental state. The following instruments were used: the Brief Psychiatric Rating Scale (BPRS) (Overall & Gorham, 1962), the Scale for the Assessment of Negative Symptoms (SANS) (Andreasen, 1983), the Hamilton Rating Scale for Depression (HRSD) (Hamilton, 1960), the Hamilton Rating Scale for Anxiety (HRSA) (Hamilton, 1959), and the Young Mania Rating Scale (YMRS) (Young, Biggs, Ziegler & Myer, 1978), as well as the new instrument, the Comprehensive Assessment of At Risk Mental States (CAARMS) (Yung et al., in press). A full SCID was administered to subjects after the development of psychosis to determine the DSM IV diagnosis.

As hypothesised, meeting the UHR criteria was associated with a high rate of onset of psychotic disorder (Kaplan-Meier estimate of 0.41 with 95% confidence interval of 0.25–0.53 within 12 months) (Yung et al., 2003), a rate several hundred-fold above that expected in the general population. Belonging to both the genetic high risk group and the attenuated symptoms group, long duration of symptoms, poor functioning, poor attention as assessed by the SANS and depression significantly increased the risk of development of psychosis in the UHR sample (Yung et al., 2003, 2004b).

THE CAARMS: ASSESSING UHR STATUS AND THE AT RISK MENTAL STATE

As well as developing the UHR criteria, our group also developed an instrument for assessing them which could incorporate all of the relevant dimensions. The CAARMS (Yung et al., in press) is a semi-structured interview which includes scales for assessing in detail threshold and sub-threshold psychotic phenomena and other symptoms and signs which occur in the psychotic prodrome, including negative, dissociative and 'basic' symptoms (Klosterkötter et al., 1996).

Rationale for a New Instrument

There were three main reasons for developing a new instrument:

1. To enable UHR criteria to be applied using the one instrument

As noted above, prior to the development of the CAARMS, assessing UHR status required the application of two separate instruments, the BPRS and the CASH, as well as a separate assessment of the recency of symptoms. The CAARMS measures all these aspects and includes its own operationalised criteria for UHR status. CAARMS cut-offs for UHR status and frank psychotic disorder were developed based on the previous criteria, see Table 2.4.

2. Rating the subjective experience

It is thought that changes in subjective experience, such as the basic symptoms, may precede overt and objectively perceived phenomena such as delusions, hallucinations, thought disorder and blunted affect (Chapman, 1966; Gross, 1989; Huber, Gross, Schuttler & Linz, 1980). Hence another focus of the CAARMS is to assess subjectively experienced phenomena, which may be present in the absence of any behavioural abnormalities. For example, the subject may complain of the feeling of having no feelings or altered emotions, but present with an intact affect with no evidence of blunting. These subjective experiences can be rated on the CAARMS. Similarly, the CAARMS includes items exploring the subjective experience of conceptual disorganisation and concentration difficulties.

3. Recording sequence of events, including fluctuations

Documenting the first ever change from premorbid state and the evolution of symptoms over time is another aim of the CAARMS. It has an introductory overview section which records this 'graphically' on a time line and documents first noted symptoms with their dates of onset. The CAARMS also measures fluctuations in symptoms, recording onset and offset dates of symptoms and whether or not the phenomena have been present continuously since last assessed. This detail of rating has been included as we have found, from our experience working with UHR young people, that the intensity and frequency of abnormal experiences fluctuate and the transition to psychosis from premorbid state, through the prodromal phase,

Table 2.4 CAARMS defined Ultra High Risk and Psychotic Disorder Threshold Criteria (reproduced with permission of Taylor and Francis publishing)

Group 1: Attenuated Psychosis Group *This criterion identifies young people at risk of psychosis due to a sub-threshold psychotic syndrome. That is, they have symptoms which do not reach threshold levels for psychosis due to sub-threshold intensity (the symptoms are not severe enough) or they have psychotic symptoms but at a sub-threshold frequency (the symptoms do not occur often enough).*

1(a) Sub-threshold intensity:

- **Severity Scale Score of 3–5** on *Disorders of Thought Content* subscale, **3–4** on *Perceptual Abnormalities* subscale **and/or 4–5** on *Disorganised Speech* subscales of the CAARMS

PLUS

- **Frequency Scale Score of 3–6** on *Disorders of Thought Content, Perceptual Abnormalities* **and/or** *Disorganised Speech* subscales of the CAARMS for **at least a week**
- **OR Frequency Scale Score of 2** on *Disorders of Thought Content, Perceptual Abnormalities and Disorganised Speech* subscales of the CAARMS **on more than two occasions**

1(b) Sub-threshold frequency:

- **Severity Scale Score of 6** on *Disorders of Thought Content* subscale, **5–6** on *Perceptual Abnormalities* subscale **and/or 6** on *Disorganised Speech* subscales of the CAARMS

PLUS

- **Frequency Scale Score of 3** on *Disorders of Thought Content, Perceptual Abnormalities* **and/or** *Disorganised Speech* subscales of the CAARMS

PLUS (for both categories)

- **Symptoms present in past year** and for not longer than five years

Group 2: BLIPS Group *This criterion identifies young people at risk of psychosis due to a recent history of frank psychotic symptoms which resolved spontaneously (without antipsychotic medication) within one week.*

- **Severity Scale Score of 6** on *Disorders of Thought Content* subscale, **5 or 6** on *Perceptual Abnormalities* subscale **and/or 6** on *Disorganised Speech* subscales of the CAARMS

PLUS

- **Frequency Scale Score of 4–6** on *Disorders of Thought Content, Perceptual Abnormalities* **and/or** *Disorganised Speech* subscales

PLUS

- **Each episode of symptoms is present for less than one week** and symptoms spontaneously remit on every occasion

PLUS

- **Symptoms occurred during the last year** and for not longer than five years

(Continued)

Table 2.4   *(Continued)*

Group 3: Vulnerability Group *This criterion identifies young people at risk of psychosis due to the combination of a trait risk factor and a significant deterioration in mental state and/or functioning.*

- **Family history of psychosis** in first degree relative <u>or</u> **Schizotypal Personality Disorder** in identified patient

PLUS

- **30% drop in GAF** score from premorbid level, sustained for a month

PLUS

- **Change in functioning** occurred within last year and maintained for at least a month

Psychotic Disorder threshold

- **Severity Scale Score of 6** on *Disorders of Thought Content* subscale, **5 or 6** on *Perceptual Abnormalities* subscale **and/or 6** on *Disorganised Speech* subscales of the CAARMS

PLUS

- **Frequency Scale Score of greater than or equal to 4** on *Disorders of Thought Content, Perceptual Abnormalities* **and/or** *Disorganised Speech* subscales

PLUS

- Psychotic symptoms present for **longer than one week**

Source: From Yung, Phillips & McGorry (2004a). *Treating Schizophrenia in the Prodromal Phase.* London: Taylor and Francis.

seems not to be a smooth or relentlessly progressive one. Fluctuations may be related to person's coping resources, life circumstances, stress level, substance use and non-specific interventions such as counselling.

Scoring and Structure of the CAARMS

The CAARMS is a semi-structured interview schedule designed for use by mental health professionals who are already able to assess and evaluate subjects' information. It requires the interviewer to make judgements about what interviewees say and to follow up and explore possible symptoms, if necessary. Objective assessment of certain mental state features is also required, such as of blunting of affect and formal thought disorder. Ratings are documented on the CAARMS Score Sheet, which accompanies the interview schedule.

The CAARMS includes the following subscales: Disorders of Thought Content (assessing obsessions, delusional mood, over-valued ideas and delusions), Perceptual Abnormalities (assessing distortions, illusions and hallucinations), Conceptual Disorganisation (assessing subjectively experienced difficulties with forming thoughts as well as objectively assessing degrees of formal thought disorder), Motor Changes (assessing subjectively experienced difficulties with movement as well as objective signs of catatonia), Concentration and Attention (again assessing both the subjective experience and objective rating), Disorders of Emotion and Affect (assessing subjective sense of change in emotions and objective rating of blunting of affect), Subjectively Impaired Energy (a basic symptom) and Impaired Tolerance to Normal Stress (a basic symptom). An intensity and frequency rating for each of these subscales is recorded separately.

The CAARMS has two functions: (1) to provide a comprehensive assessment of psychopathology thought to indicate imminent development of a first episode psychotic disorder and (2) to determine if an individual meets UHR status or has crossed the threshold for a psychotic disorder based on criteria derived from the CAARMS assessment.

Testing the CAARMS

Inter-rater Reliability

Inter-rater reliability of the CAARMS was assessed by joint interviews of 34 UHR subjects at baseline (Yung et al., in press). Both researchers were in the room with the subject, one as interviewer and one as observer. There were four pairs of raters, with the role of interviewer rotating between them. Raters were either psychiatrists or trained clinical research psychologists. Table 2.5 shows the intra-class correlation coefficients (ICC) of each of the eight main domains. As can be seen, good to excellent agreement was found with all scales, with only the Energy domain displaying an ICC lower than 0.7. The overall agreement (total CAARMS score) was 0.85.

The predictive validity of the CAARMS was assessed by examining the predictive power of the CAARMS domains scores and overall score for psychosis onset within the follow-up period in the sample of 49 UHR young people. This was done by comparing scores in the group which became psychotic with scores in the group which did not. High CAARMS overall score was significantly associated with development of psychotic disorder. CAARMS measures of disorders of Concentration and Attention (CA), Emotion and Affect (EA), Impaired Energy (E) and Impaired Tolerance to Stress (S) were highly predictive of psychotic disorder. Disorders of Thought Content (TC), Perceptual Abnormalities (PA), Conceptual Disorganisation (CD) and Motor Changes (M) were not predictive. Dividing the subscales

Table 2.5 Intra-class correlation coefficients of the eight CAARMS subscales

CAARMS subscale	All raters*
Disorders of Thought Content	0.79
Perceptual Abnormalities	0.83
Conceptual Disorganisation	0.89
Motor Changes	0.93
Concentration and Attention	0.72
Disorders of Emotion and Affect	0.83
Energy	0.62
Impaired Tolerance to Normal Stress	0.82
Overall	0.85
n	34

* There were four pairs of raters.

Table 2.6 Cox regression results examining associations between CAARMS measures and risk of psychosis

	p-values
Thought Content	0.088
Perceptual Abnormalities	0.260
Conceptual Disorganisation	0.600
Motor Changes	0.370
Concentration and Attention	0.004
Emotion and Affect	0.038
Impaired Energy	0.031
Impaired Tolerance to Stress	0.034
Positive Symptoms	0.380
Negative Symptoms	0.001
Overall Score	0.007

into Positive (TC, PA, CD, M) and Negative (CA, EA, E and S) symptoms showed the Negative symptoms to be highly and consistently predictive of psychotic disorder, whereas the Positive symptoms were not predictive (Yung et al., in press), see Table 2.6.

OTHER SCALES FOR IDENTIFYING UHR INDIVIDUALS

Another interview and scale, similar to the CAARMS, has been developed by the PRIME group in North America. The Structured Interview for Prodromal Symptoms (SIPS) and the Scale of Prodromal Symptoms (SOPS) (Miller et al., 2003) provide question probes, rating scales and anchor points which allow the rater to make a decision about whether the criteria for 'prodrome' are met. The SPI-A (Schultze-Lutter et al., 2004), noted previously, assesses basic symptoms and is used to determine whether the basic symptom criteria for inclusion are met. It is beyond the scope of this chapter to go into detail about these other scales, but readers are referred to the paper by Addington (2004) in which these instruments are compared.

CONCLUSIONS

Several methods of identifying groups of people at risk for psychotic disorders have been discussed. Some of these suffer from high rates of false positives and low predictive power, making their application to the field of preventive treatment unsuitable. The UHR approach has been successful to date in identifying a cohort with a high rate of transition to frank psychosis. Thus intervening in this group in an attempt to prevent onset of full-blown psychotic disorder may be justifiable. However, the decision to treat, and with what, depends on the individual's presentation and circumstances. Issues of stigma and labelling, as well as unnecessary intervention, must be taken into account. An added caveat is that the risk of transition in someone meeting UHR criteria depends on the population from which they are drawn. Thus the UHR criteria cannot and should not be applied to a healthy population as a screening measure, as the expected rate of transition within this population would be much lower than in a clinical group presenting for help. Nonetheless, the development of reliable and valid criteria for identifying the UHR population has laid the groundwork from which preventive treatment can develop. Obviously research needs to continue into further increasing our ability to predict who will develop psychotic disorder, even from within the UHR group. With such research underway in a number of centres throughout the world, the exciting possibility of delaying, reducing the severity, or even preventing the onset of a first psychotic episode arises.

REFERENCES

Addington, J. (2004). The diagnosis and assessment of individuals prodromal for schizophrenic psychosis. *CNS Spectrums*, **9**, 588–594.

Allen, J.J., Chapman, L.J., Chapman, J.P., Vuchetich, J.P. & Frost, L.A. (1987). Prediction of psychotic-like symptoms in hypothetically psychosis-prone college students. *Journal of Abnormal Psychology*, **96**, 83–88.

American Psychiatric Association (1994). *Diagnostic and Statistical Manual of Mental Disorders*. Washington, DC: Author.

Andreasen, N. (1987). *The Comprehensive Assessment of Symptoms and History (CASH) Interview*. Iowa City, IA: University of Iowa Press.

Andreasen, N.C. (1983). *The Scale for the Assessment of Negative Symptoms (SANS)*. Iowa City, IA: University of Iowa Press.

Asarnow, J.R. (1988). Children at risk for schizophrenia: Converging lines of evidence. *Schizophrenia Bulletin*, **14**, 613–631.

Barker, J.M., Goehrig, S.H., Barriga, K., Hoffman, M., Slover, R., Eisenbarth, G.S. et al. (2004). Clinical characteristics of children diagnosed with type 1 diabetes through intensive screening and follow-up. *Diabetes Care*, **27**, 1399–1404.

Bell, R. (1992). Multiple-risk cohorts and segmenting risk as solutions to the problem of false positives in risk for the major psychoses. *Psychiatry*, **55**, 370–381.

Birchwood, M., Smith, J., Macmillan, F., Hogg, B., Prasad, R., Harvey, C. et al. (1989). Predicting relapse in schizophrenia: The development and implementation of an early signs monitoring system using patients and families as observers: A preliminary investigation. *Psychological Medicine*, **19**, 649–656.

Bouchard, L., Blancquaert, I., Eisinger, F., Foulkes, W.D., Evans, G., Sobol, H. et al. (2004). Prevention and genetic testing for breast cancer: Variations in medical decisions. *Social Science and Medicine*, **58**, 1085–1096.

Chapman, J. (1966). The early symptoms of schizophrenia. *British Journal of Psychiatry*, **112**, 225–251.

Chapman, L.J. & Chapman, J.P. (1980). Scales for rating psychotic and psychotic-like experiences as continua. *Schizophrenia Bulletin*, **6**, 476–489.

Chapman, L.J. & Chapman, J.P. (1987). The search for symptoms predictive of schizophrenia. *Schizophrenia Bulletin*, **13**, 497–503.

Chapman, L.J., Chapman, J.P., Kwapil, T.R., Eckblad, M. & Zinser, M.C. (1994). Putatively psychosis-prone subjects 10 years later. *Journal of Abnormal Psychology*, **103**, 171–183.

Chapman, L.J., Edell, W.S. & Chapman, J.P. (1980). Physical anhedonia, perceptual aberration, and psychosis proneness. *Schizophrenia Bulletin*, **6**, 639–653.

Cornblatt, B. & Obuchowski, M. (1997). Update of high-risk research: 1987–1997. *International Review of Psychiatry*, **9**, 437–447.

Docherty, J.P., Van Kammen, D.P., Siris, S.G. & Marder, S.R. (1978). Stages of onset of schizophrenic psychosis. *American Journal of Psychiatry*, **135**, 420–426.

Donlon, P.T. & Blacker, K.H. (1973). Stages of schizophrenic decompensation and reintegration. *Journal of Nervous and Mental Disease*, **157**, 200–209.

Eaton, W.W., Romanoski, A., Anthony, J.C. & Nestadt, G. (1991). Screening for psychosis in the general population with a self-report interview. *Journal of Nervous and Mental Disease*, **179**, 689–693.

First, M.B., Spitzer, R.L., Gibbon, M. & Williams, J.B. (1997). *Structured Clinical Interview for DSM-IV Axis I Disorders*. Washington, DC: American Psychiatric Press.

Gross, G. (1989). The 'basic' symptoms of schizophrenia. *British Journal of Psychiatry*, **155** (Suppl. 7), 21–25.

Häfner, H., Maurer, K., Loffler, W., an der Heiden, W., Munk-Jørgensen, P., Hambrecht, M. et al. (1998). The ABC Schizophrenia Study: A preliminary overview of the results. *Social Psychiatry and Psychiatric Epidemiology*, **33**, 380–386.

Häfner, H., Maurer, K., Loffler, W. & Riecher, R.A. (1993). The influence of age and sex on the onset and early course of schizophrenia. *British Journal of Psychiatry*, **162**, 80–86.

Häfner, H., Riecher, R.A., Hambrecht, M., Maurer, K., Meissner, S., Schmidtke, A. et al. (1992). IRAOS: An instrument for the assessment of onset and early course of schizophrenia. *Schizophrenia Research*, **6**, 209–223.

Hamilton, M. (1959). The assessment of anxiety states by rating. *British Journal of Psychiatry*, **32**, 50–55.

Hamilton, M. (1960). A rating scale for depression. *Journal of Neurology, Neurosurgery and Psychiatry*, **23**, 56–62.

Heinrichs, D., Hanlon, T. & Carpenter, W. (1984). The Quality of Life Scale: An instrument for rating the schizophrenia deficit syndrome. *Schizophrenia Bulletin*, **10**, 388–398.

Heinrichs, D.W. & Carpenter, W.T. (1985). Prospective study of prodromal symptoms in schizophrenic relapse. *American Journal of Psychiatry*, **142**, 371–373.

Hodges, A., Byrne, M., Grant, E. & Johnstone, E.C. (1999). People at risk of schizophrenia: Sample characteristics of the first 100 cases in the Edinburgh High-Risk Study. *British Journal of Psychiatry*, **174**, 547–553.

Huber, G. & Gross, G. (1989). The concept of basic symptoms in schizophrenic and schizoaffective psychoses. *Recenti Progressi in Medicina*, **80**, 646–652.

Huber, G., Gross, G., Schuttler, R. & Linz, M. (1980). Longitudinal studies of schizophrenic patients. *Schizophrenia Bulletin*, **6**, 592–605.

Johnstone, E.C., Abukmeil, S.S., Byrne, M., Clafferty, R., Grant, E., Hodges, A. et al. (2000). Edinburgh high risk study – findings after four years: Demographic, attainment and psychopathological issues. *Schizophrenia Research*, **46**, 1–15.

Johnstone, E.C., Cosway, R. & Lawrie, S.M. (2002). Distinguishing characteristics of subjects with good and poor early outcome in the Edinburgh High-Risk Study. *British Journal of Psychiatry*, **181**, s26–s29.

Klosterkötter, J., Ebel, H., Schultze-Lutter, F. & Steinmeyer, E.M. (1996). Diagnostic validity of basic symptoms. *European Archives of Psychiatry and Clinical Neurosciences*, **246**, 147–154.

Klosterkötter, J., Gross, G., Huber, G., Wieneke, A., Steinmeyer, E.M. & Schultze-Lutter, F. (1997a). Evaluation of the 'Bonn Scale for the Assessment of Basic Symptoms – BSABS' as an instrument for the assessment of schizophrenia proneness: A review of recent findings. *Neurology, Psychiatry and Brain Research*, **5**, 137–150.

Klosterkötter, J., Hellmich, M., Steinmeyer, E.M. & Schultze-Lutter, F. (2001). Diagnosing schizophrenia in the initial prodromal phase. *Archives of General Psychiatry*, **58**, 158–164.

Klosterkötter, J., Schultze-Lutter, F., Gross, G., Huber, G. & Steinmeyer, E.M. (1997b). Early self-experienced neuropsychological deficits and subsequent schizophrenic diseases: An eight-year average follow-up prospective study. *Acta Psychiatrica Scandinavica*, **95**, 396–404.

Loebel, A.D., Lieberman, J.A., Alvir, J.M., Mayerhoff, D.I., Geisler, S.H. & Szymanski, S.R. (1992). Duration of psychosis and outcome in first-episode schizophrenia. *American Journal of Psychiatry*, **149**, 1183–1188.

Maxwell, M.E. (1992). *Manual for the FIGS*. Unpublished manuscript, Clinical Neurogenetics Branch, Intramural Research Program, National Institute of Mental Health.

Mednick, S.A., Parnas, J., Schulsinger, F. & Mednick, B. (1987). The Copenhagen high-risk project, 1962–1986. *Schizophrenia Bulletin*, **13**, 485–496.

Metcalfe, K.A. (2004). Prophylactic bilateral mastectomy for breast cancer prevention. *Journal of Women's Health*, **13**, 822–829.

Miller, P.M., Byrne, M., Hodges, A., Lawrie, S.M. & Johnstone, E.C. (2002). Childhood behaviour, psychotic symptoms and psychosis onset in young people at high risk of schizophrenia: Early findings from the Edinburgh high risk study. *Psychological Medicine*, **32**, 173–179.

Miller, T.J., McGlashan, T.H., Rosen, J.L., Cadenhead, K., Ventura, J., McFarlane, W. et al. (2003). Prodromal assessment with the structured interview for prodromal syndromes and the scale of prodromal symptoms: Predictive validity, interrater reliability, and training to reliability. *Schizophrenia Bulletin*, **29**, 703–715.

Overall, J.E. & Gorham, D.R. (1962). The Brief Psychiatric Rating Scale. *Psychological Reports*, **10**, 799–812.

Poulton, R., Caspi, A., Moffitt, T.E., Cannon, M., Murray, R. & Harrington, H. (2000). Children's self-reported psychotic symptoms and adult schizophreniform disorder: A 15-year longitudinal study. *Archives of General Psychiatry*, **57**, 1053–1058.

Prichard, R.S., Hill, A.D., Dijkstra, B., McDermott, E.W. & O'Higgins, N.J. (2003). The prevention of breast cancer. *British Journal of Surgery*, **90**, 772–783.

Schultze-Lutter, F., Wieneke, A., Picker, H., Rolff, Y., Steinmeyer, E.M., Ruhrmann, S. et al. (2004). The Schizophrenia Prediction Instrument, Adult Version (SPI-A). *Schizophrenia Research*, **70**, 76–77.

Subotnik, K.L. & Nuechterlein, K.H. (1988). Prodromal signs and symptoms of schizophrenic relapse. *Journal of Abnormal Psychology*, **97**, 405–412.

Tien, A.Y. (1991). Distributions of hallucinations in the population. *Social Psychiatry and Psychiatric Epidemiology*, **26**, 287–292.

Van Os, J., Hanssen, M., Bijl, R.V. & Vollebergh, W. (2001). Prevalence of psychotic disorder and community level of psychotic symptoms: An urban-rural comparison. *Archives of General Psychiatry*, **58**, 663–668.

Young, R.C., Biggs, J.T., Ziegler, V.E. & Myer, D.A. (1978). A rating scale for mania: Reliability, validity and sensitivity. *British Journal of Psychiatry*, **133**, 429–435.

Yung, A.R. & McGorry, P.D. (1996a). The initial prodrome in psychosis: Descriptive and qualitative aspects. *Australian and New Zealand Journal of Psychiatry*, **30**, 587–599.

Yung, A.R. & McGorry, P.D. (1996b). The prodromal phase of first episode psychosis: Past and current conceptualisations. *Schizophrenia Bulletin*, **22**, 353–370.

Yung, A.R., McGorry, P.D., McFarlane, C.A., Jackson, H.J., Patton, G.C. & Rakkar, A. (1996). Monitoring and care of young people at incipient risk of psychosis. *Schizophrenia Bulletin*, **22**, 283–303.

Yung, A.R., Phillips, L.J. & McGorry, P.D. (2004a). *Treating Schizophrenia in the Prodromal Phase*. London: Taylor and Francis.

Yung, A.R., Phillips, L.J., McGorry, P.D., Hallgren, M.A., McFarland, C.A., Jackson, H.J. et al. (1998a). Can we predict the onset of first-episode psychosis in a high-risk group? *International Clinical Psychopharmacology*, **13** (Suppl. 1), 523–530.

Yung, A.R., Phillips, L.J., McGorry, P.D., McFarlane, C.A., Francey, S., Harrigan, S. et al. (1998b). Prediction of psychosis: A step towards indicated prevention of schizophrenia. *British Journal of Psychiatry*, **172**, 14–20.

Yung, A.R., Phillips, L.J., Yuen, H.P., Francey, S.M., McFarlane, C.A., Hallgren, M. et al. (2003). Psychosis prediction: 12-month follow up of a high-risk ('prodromal') group. *Schizophrenia Research*, **60**, 21–32.

Yung, A.R., Phillips, L.J., Yuen, H.P. & McGorry, P.D. (2004b). Risk factors for psychosis in an ultra high-risk group: Psychopathology and clinical features. *Schizophrenia Research*, **67**, 131–142.

Yung, A.R., Yuen, H.P., McGorry, P.D., Phillips, L., Kelly, D., Dell'Olio, M. et al. (in press). Mapping the onset of psychosis – the Comprehensive Assessment of At Risk Mental States (CAARMS). *Australia and New Zealand Journal of Psychiatry*.

CHAPTER 3

Assessment and Developing a Formulation

Shona M. Francey and Henry J. Jackson

Young people identified as being at ultra high risk for the development of psychosis (UHR) present to services seeking help for a number of issues, ranging from attenuated psychotic symptoms to depression, substance use and relationship difficulties. They are accepted into a clinical service for treatment by meeting predetermined criteria for high risk that may vary somewhat among different services for theoretical or practical reasons. These issues are explored in Chapter 2. However, by presenting to clinics, young people are signalling that they are requesting assistance for their problems. The essential first step in providing treatment for psychological problems is to conduct a thorough assessment and develop an individual case formulation.

This chapter focuses on the assessment of all presenting problems that are seen as troubling to the client, including those that potentially increase the risk of the development of psychosis in a person already somewhat vulnerable. A range of assessment tools that may be appropriate for this population to help identify targets for treatment is discussed. Finally, the development of idiosyncratic case formulations is described. It is assumed that the reader is already familiar with psychopathology, psychological assessment and mental state examination, when their application to the unique UHR client group is discussed in this chapter.

ASSESSMENT

The Central Role of Assessment

A comprehensive assessment is crucial for both treatment planning and the engagement of clients in collaborative therapy, especially therapy that is based on cognitive-behavioural principles. Cognitive Behaviour Therapy (CBT) is the therapeutic orientation applied by the different groups who have begun to work psychotherapeutically with the UHR population (French & Morrison, 2004; McGorry et al., 2002; Morrison et al., 2004) and used throughout this chapter. A thorough and skilled assessment of current psychological symptoms, their

Working with People at High Risk of Developing Psychosis: A Treatment Handbook.
Edited by J. Addington, S.M. Francey and A.P. Morrison. © 2006 John Wiley & Sons, Ltd.

development and course over time and a comprehensive knowledge of psychopathological syndromes is essential in establishing targets for therapy and selecting relevant and efficacious treatments. An individualised case formulation assembles all of the facts gathered through the assessment process into a coherent and plausible explanation of the client's situation and outlines an appropriate plan for therapy.

Young people defined as being at high risk of developing psychosis seek help for a wide range of symptoms and these are not limited to attenuated or brief psychotic symptoms (McGorry et al., 2002; Yung & McGorry, 1996b). Therefore, a comprehensive psychiatric assessment that addresses both the nature of psychotic-like experiences (if any) and the presence of other co-morbid conditions, such as anxiety, substance use and depressive disorders, is required. The importance that the client places on each symptom or syndrome, as well as their personal interpretation of the significance of the problems, needs to be carefully considered in order to engage the client and develop a formulation that is acceptable.

A high level of clinical skill and commitment is required from the therapist in order to develop the type of rapport with the client that will allow essential personal and detailed information to be elicited. Both the assessment process and the therapy itself are not possible without the establishment of a collaborative, mutually respectful relationship between the client and therapist. This forms the foundation for the rest of the therapy and generally is a key issue in youth mental health. The quality of the relationship between client and clinician has been found to impact on the outcome of treatment for patients with psychotic disorder (Frank & Gunderson, 1990; Goerung, Stylianos & Stavely, 1988) thus making this stage of the therapy process crucial. The therapist must demonstrate empathy and understanding so that the client feels secure in disclosing intimate and at times frightening material. This is especially important for the UHR young person for a number of reasons. First, it may be the first time the young person has been in a counselling or therapeutic situation and been under such close scrutiny; they may be unsure what to expect. Second, the experience of psychotic-like symptoms is often very frightening, especially the first time. Finally, this contact with mental health services may be the first of many if the young person makes the transition to a psychotic illness and requires ongoing care. Therefore, it is extremely important for the therapist to work hard at appropriately engaging the UHR client in order to instil hope and cooperativeness, and to facilitate an assertive, respectful, collaborative relationship between the client and helping services for the present and future. These issues are explored in more detail in Chapter 4; however, it is important to note here that engagement issues must be considered from the very beginning of the assessment phase.

Assessment as Introduction to Therapy

Assessment forms the first part of therapy and is essential in promoting engagement and setting the agenda for the course of the therapy. It provides the opportunity for the therapist and client to get to know each other, and allows the therapist to gain an understanding of the expectations of the client and to set ground rules for the rest of the therapy. Through the assessment process clients learn about the collaborative and active nature of therapy: the client is expected to be an active participant in therapy by monitoring behaviours, experimenting with new behaviours and reporting on homework tasks.

During the initial sessions the client learns that the goal of therapy is for the client to develop skills and strategies to overcome both current and future problems. Information about the structure of therapy, including the duration, location and expected number of sessions, as well as the rationale for treatment approaches, is provided during this assessment and formulation phase. It is explained that therapy is aimed at building client self-efficacy, by enabling clients to deal with emotional problems, and to use homework tasks to practise and test strategies discussed in therapy sessions.

Through the process of conducting a comprehensive psychological assessment, the therapist is also educating the client about the nature and likely causes of their symptoms and developing a rationale for the treatment that will be proposed following the assessment. The fundamental explanatory model used to explain the onset of psychosis is the stress-vulnerability model (Gottesman & Shields, 1972; Meehl, 1962, 1989; Spring & Zubin, 1977) which is an appropriate and useful model for UHR clients. This model posits that there is an underlying vulnerability in individuals who develop psychosis and that environmental factors or stressors are implicated in the expression of this vulnerability as an episode of illness. For UHR clients, the symptoms for which they are seeking help can be explained as evidence of vulnerability to mental illness, and therapy can be presented as an opportunity to reduce stress and vulnerability and thus reduce the risk of the onset of psychosis. This stress-vulnerability model must be explained to clients and then applied to their particular situation to develop a formulation that both explains the development of symptoms and offers hope for their resolution with targeted therapy. The process of conducting the assessment and developing the formulation provides an important introduction to therapy by demonstrating the collaborative, hopeful and client-centred approach to therapy for UHR that has been developed in a number of centres around the world.

Assisting clients to carefully and behaviourally define their problems can often reduce the problems to more manageable entities and introduce the possibility of change. Monitoring symptoms and problem behaviours increases understanding and is often empowering and normalising for clients. Measurement of symptoms can have a therapeutic effect by challenging negative distortions and highlighting improvements over time. This process leads to reduction of fear and stigma, and enhances engagement and compliance with therapy. Further, the use of appropriate assessment techniques promotes the setting of reasonable goals for therapy and reduces the chances of unrealistic expectations for change (e.g. never to feel low again), which would result in therapy being viewed as a failure.

It is important that the assessment process is carefully tailored for each client and thus flexibility is required with regard to the duration of the assessment phase and the rate at which information is gathered. For the UHR group, both level of cognitive development and attenuated psychotic symptoms can influence the assessment process and require careful consideration. For example, an individual who experiences brief periods of auditory hallucinations may have occasional concentration difficulties. Similarly, an individual who experiences persistent perplexity associated with intermittent paranoid thoughts may suffer marked social anxiety. During the assessment phase the therapist should pay attention to the client's level of motivation and ability to concentrate, as these may influence both the information received and the development of a therapeutic alliance. Other factors such as any previous experiences with health workers and counselling, personality, family and developmental issues should also be considered by the therapist at this early stage. For these reasons a flexible approach to the assessment is advocated whereby a number of sessions may be required in order to achieve the twin aims of engaging the client and gaining a thorough understanding of their situation.

Table 3.1   Assessment methods for UHR clients

Assessment interview and Mental State Examination
Semi-structured clinical interview scales
Clinician-rated symptom scales
Self-report scales
Self-monitoring
Informant interview
In vivo observation
Role-play tests

Types of Assessment

The principal method of assessment for all types of mental health issues is a detailed inter-view and history taking, and the case of UHR clients is no exception. However, additional important information can be obtained by using a variety of other assessment methods. The range of assessment methods that can be used is displayed in Table 3.1.

Each of these methods of assessment is discussed below using examples relevant to UHR young people, with the major emphasis on the essential assessment interview.

The Assessment Interview

It is assumed that the reader is experienced with psychological assessment and interviewing, and thus the discussion that follows highlights the special issues relevant to conducting an assessment with UHR clients.

At the beginning of the assessment interview, it is imperative that the therapist informs the client of the purpose and structure of the assessment process. This is especially important for UHR clients who are likely to be new to the counselling situation. One way to begin the process is to make a statement to the following effect:

> In order to help me understand your problems, I need to learn something about how
> your problems began, and under what circumstances. I am especially interested in **your
> understanding of how and why these problems began**. I also need to have a fuller
> understanding about what difficult issues you have had to deal with over the years. I am
> interested in gaining some appreciation of you as a person, your life experiences, your
> family of origin, your schooling, your connections and interests. So, if it's OK with you,
> we will spend the next couple of sessions getting a lot of information about your history
> and current worries and then we will discuss what we think would be best for us to do
> together in order to help you get on top of these problems.

In many ways the assessment process follows the typical psychiatric history-gathering format and mental state examination but it also differs in a number of important ways, due to the nature of this particular client group. Since the eventual aim is to devise a formulation and treatment plan, greater focus is given to examining various parameters of the symptoms and behaviours. The therapist does not merely tick off symptoms as being present or absent but, rather, tries to examine frequency and intensity of symptoms, and the degree of preoccupation and distress, as well as precipitating and maintaining factors. This can be assisted by the use of other types of assessment such as those described below.

Table 3.2   Content of assessment interview

Referral:	source and information supplied is reviewed with the client
History of presenting problem:	detailed description, onset and course
Past psychological history:	previous problems, significant events and treatments
Developmental history:	pregnancy, birth, developmental milestones, motor, language, social development
Medical history:	illnesses and operations, current illnesses and prognoses
Forensic history:	previous offences and penalties and any current orders or pending charges
Substance use:	past and present, relationship between use and symptoms
Family:	structure, functioning, medical and psychiatric history
Personal history:	education, occupation, social and sexual functioning, current life circumstances and supports, goals and aspirations
Risk assessment:	history of suicide attempts and triggers, current suicidal ideation and intent, risky behaviours, vulnerability to abuse and exploitation, homicidal thoughts, anger, impulsivity
Personality:	self-perception, how others see client
Mental state examination:	assessment of current presentation and reported symptoms (see Table 3.3)
Coping strategies:	history of strategies used and results, current tactics

Table 3.2 presents an outline of the essential areas that must be covered in conducting a comprehensive assessment interview.

For UHR clients it is important to place particular emphasis on the features of the assessment that are relevant to their high risk status. Some of these may become targets for treatment (e.g. attenuated psychotic symptoms, substance use), while others cannot be changed but are nevertheless crucial to the assessment and formulation (e.g. a positive family history of psychosis, early developmental delays). Further, some symptoms will require ongoing assessment and monitoring over the course of the client's involvement with the service, in particular psychotic symptoms, to determine if the threshold for a diagnosis of psychotic disorder has been reached.

UHR defining criteria include attenuated psychotic symptoms, reduction in functioning and family history of psychosis. These are described in detail in Chapter 2. These areas need to be carefully assessed using all sources of information available. This part of the assessment process can represent a significant divergence from some common practices in which longitudinal and family information is de-emphasised in favour of a focus on current behaviours. However, for UHR clients detailed developmental and personal history are required in order to establish a typical level of functioning over time against which a drop in functioning can be noticed. Similarly, greater detail about family history of mental illness must be elicited in order to determine whether there is a family history of psychosis that contributes to the young person's level of vulnerability to psychosis.

It is also important in the assessment of UHR clients to get an understanding of their beliefs about psychosis and their interpretation of the meaning of their experiences or symptoms. This is often related to the views about mental illness held by the particular culture to which the young person identifies. The young person may also hold strong beliefs and fears that have developed as a result of experiences with a mentally ill relative. Does the client expect to develop a psychotic illness and to become like them? What outcomes does the young person believe are possible for people who develop psychosis? What does the client believe are the chances that he or she will develop psychosis and what will be the likely consequences and outcomes? It is important to understand the stereotypes that a UHR client holds with respect to psychosis and other mental illnesses and how these relate to fears and expectations that he or she may have. This knowledge is essential for developing a formulation that is salient for the young person and to engage the client in treatment aimed at reducing their risk of psychosis. These issues are illustrated in the following case example.

Case example

Nick was a 15-year-old high school student who lived with his mother and older sister, both of whom had schizophrenia. His mother had had a severe and treatment-resistant illness since before he was born, frequently requiring hospitalisation due to exacerbations of paranoid symptoms focused on neighbours. Nick's sister had functioned well until she developed psychosis with paranoid symptoms at 18 and experienced severe negative symptoms with impaired functioning for the four years since her onset of illness. Nick attributed his sister's poor functioning to the medication that she was prescribed for her paranoid symptoms, but believed that she needed to take the medication so that she could remain out of hospital.

Over the past year, Nick's school performance had deteriorated and he had become increasingly isolated. He had been having difficulties concentrating on his school work, sleeping badly and had lost a significant amount of weight. His school counsellor had made many attempts to discuss things with Nick, but he maintained that he was 'OK'. The school counsellor finally arranged for the UHR service to meet Nick at school. It was crucial that the UHR service workers explained the nature of their service, gained an understanding of Nick's experience and understanding of psychosis in his relatives and educated Nick about the wide range of treatment options and possible outcomes for young people with some risk factors. After several assessment sessions it emerged that Nick had experienced some infrequent attenuated psychotic symptoms, including mild paranoid thoughts, and moreover had been terrified that seeking help would result in him being forced to take medication that would mean that he could no longer attend school or achieve any of his long-term goals. Learning that he would not be required to take antipsychotic medication and that there were other treatments available for his current situation enabled Nick to engage with the service and begin to address his problems.

Assessment of risk is important in all psychological assessment and is especially crucial for UHR clients. These young people may be experiencing frightening symptoms, experiencing changes in themselves, and may be very worried about what is happening to them, and are by definition new to UHR services. This can potentially put UHR clients at increased risk of dangerous and suicidal behaviours. The assessment of UHR clients must include questions about suicidal ideation and other responses that the young person may have considered in reaction to their symptoms. Issues of stereotypes along with either optimism or pessimism with regard to likely personal outcome are relevant here and need to be considered when attempting to estimate level of risk. The importance of monitoring risk in UHR clients is illustrated in the following case example.

Case example

Shelley was an 18-year-old who had been unemployed since leaving school a year previously. She had a long history of social anxiety that had made it difficult to attend school. Her mother also had problems with social anxiety and her father was a heavy drinker. Since leaving school, Shelley had developed an interest in devil-worship and witchcraft, which she researched on the Internet. She was particularly interested in ritual sacrifice and had begun to believe that human blood had protective powers and that it could be used to help her to overcome her social anxiety.

Shelley was referred to the UHR service by her GP and her unusual beliefs were revealed during the assessment. When questioned about what she had thought of doing in relation to these ideas, Shelley reported that she had begun to cut herself once each day to collect her blood and that she had been thinking of better ways to acquire the larger quantities of blood that she thought she needed. Although she had thought of cutting other people or stealing from a hospital, she did not think that she would do either of these things because she did not want to get into trouble. It was clearly important for the UHR service to monitor Shelley's unusual beliefs and her plans in relation to them, and to respond appropriately if dangerousness increased. At the same time, the therapist provided Shelley with education about the nature and treatment of social anxiety and used a range of methods to challenge the veracity of her unusual beliefs, whilst ensuring that Shelley continued to be engaged with the service.

The assessment of current symptoms is the central and most important part of the assessment and the traditional Mental State Examination provides essential information that can be supplemented by more detailed questioning about attenuated psychotic symptoms. The areas of enquiry in the Mental State Examination are displayed in Table 3.3.

In the case of UHR young people, more detail is usually required about the frequency and intensity of the symptoms, the degree of preoccupation and distress associated with the symptoms and the initial onset and duration of any attenuated psychotic experiences. This can be obtained using the CAARMS or similar instruments as described below and in Chapter 2.

Semi-structured Interview Schedules

Semi-structured interview schedules are useful adjuncts to the assessment interview and can assist clinicians in making diagnostic decisions. Typically they are administered by experienced clinicians and consist of suggested questions and prompts to elicit information about the presence of the specific cluster of psychiatric symptoms required in order to make a particular diagnosis. The interviewer uses clinical judgement and skill to formulate

Table 3.3 Mental State Examination

Appearance and behaviour:	description and appropriateness of dress and behaviour during interview
Attitude:	co-operativeness, rapport
Mood and affect:	subjectively reported mood and objectively noted range and appropriateness of emotional responses
Form of thought:	speech – spontaneity, rate, amount, continuity
Content of thought:	themes and preoccupations – depressed, grandiose, bizarre, anxious, perplexed
Perception:	unusual experiences not perceived by others
Cognition:	consciousness, orientation, attention, concentration, short- and long-term memory
Insight:	perception of the problem and desire for help

questions suggested by the instrument, to follow up information given by the client and to rate the presence or absence of symptoms on the basis of answers given by the client. Two examples of semi-structured interview schedules that are pertinent to the UHR population are the Comprehensive Assessment of At Risk Mental States (CAARMS) (Yung, Yuen, Phillips, Francey & McGorry, 2003) and the Structured Clinical Interview DSM-IV Axis I Disorders (SCID-IV) (First, Spitzer, Gibbon & Williams, 1996).

- The CAARMS, as described in Chapter 2, is an instrument specifically designed to prospectively measure the psychopathology of the At Risk Mental State (ARMS). It was empirically developed and consists of subscales that measure symptoms thought to be characteristic of psychotic prodromes. These subscales were developed following a re-view of relevant literature and a retrospective study of prodromes in cases of first episode psychosis (Yung & McGorry, 1996a, 1996b). The subscales measure positive, negative, basic (Gross, 1989) and dissociative symptoms. The CAARMS is designed for repeated use over time, for example each month, with young people who are thought to be at high risk of developing a first episode of psychosis within a brief time period. The CAARMS has two major uses with the UHR population: (1) to determine whether an individual meets predefined criteria for UHR and is thus eligible for particular clinical services or research programmes, and (2) to establish whether an individual's symptoms exceed the UHR crite-ria and are thus defined as having crossed the threshold into a first psychotic episode. This is often the point at which an individual would be transferred to a specialist early psychosis treatment service. Clearly this depends on the way in which the local service network is structured. The CAARMS is also an ideal tool for use in assessing outcomes in studies of young people at high risk of psychosis.
- The Structured Clinical Interview for DSM-IV (SCID: First et al., 1996) is a semi-structured interview used for assessing the presence of major Axis I DSM-IV (American Psychiatric Association, 1994) diagnoses. It was developed for use in research by trained clinicians. The SCID contains obligatory questions, operational criteria from DSM-IV, uses a categorical rating system for symptoms and provides an algorithm for making a final diagnosis. Interviewers are encouraged to use all available sources of information in rating symptoms and arriving at diagnoses. The SCID has a modular construction that permits tailoring for particular disorders under consideration. It may be appropriate and helpful for clinicians conducting assessments with UHR clients to use parts of the SCID to confirm the presence of co-morbid Axis I conditions. Although co-morbid diagnoses do not confer high risk status on their own, they are clearly an important part of the overall clinical picture that needs to be included in the formulation and treatment plan.

Clinician-rated Symptom Scales

Clinician-rated symptom scales are standardised instruments comprising lists of symptoms. The interviewer rates the severity of the client's experience of each symptom based on either direct observation or responses to specific questions. Such scales can be used to document the presence of specific symptoms and track changes in response to treatment. Two examples that have a long tradition of use in mental health settings are the Hamilton Rating Scale for Depression (Hamilton, 1960) and the Hamilton Rating Scale for Anxiety (Hamilton, 1959). A more recently developed instrument is the Calgary Depression Scale (Addington,

Addington & Maticka-Tyndale, 1993) that was specifically designed for use with individuals with a psychotic illness. Each of these instruments can be useful with the UHR group due to the high frequency of depression and anxiety disorders in this population.

- Hamilton Rating Scale for Depression (HRSD). This is an observer-rated scale used to assess level of depression. It consists of 24 items about symptoms of depression such as feelings of guilt, insomnia, level of activity and depressed mood. Items are rated on either a five-point or a three-point scale and the total scale score can range from 0 to 74.
- Hamilton Rating Scale for Anxiety (HRSA). This is a widely used clinician administered assessment of anxiety. The original version comprised 13 items, but a 14-item version has come into common use (Guy, 1976). The severity and intensity of the 14 symptoms of anxiety, such as anxious mood, fears and cardiovascular symptoms, are rated on a five-point (0–4) scale. The total scale score can range from 0 to 56.
- Calgary Depression Scale (CDS). This scale, which can also be described as a semi-structured interview schedule, consists of nine items that are symptoms of depression and was originally derived by factor analysis of two well-established depression instruments (i.e. the Present State Examination: Wing, Cooper & Sartorius, 1974; and the HRSD, described above). It was designed specifically for use with populations with psychosis and to address the problem of overlap between depressive and negative psychotic symptoms present in other scales. Items one to eight are rated by the interviewer from zero (absent) to three (severe), based on responses to questions and follow-up prompts; item nine (observed depression) is rated on the basis of observation over the entire interview. The scale has demonstrated good reliability and validity and is useful for assessing changes in depression because it is relatively quick to administer and is sensitive to change.

Self-report Scales

These are questionnaires completed by the client that provide information about symptoms and severity. There are obvious advantages (time savings, ease of disclosure of difficult information early in the course of engagement) and disadvantages (loss of opportunity to clarify details, problems for clients with poor literacy) to this method of assessment. Self-report scales can be a very useful adjunct to clinical interviewing for both the assessment and monitoring of progress. In addition, instruments that have been properly developed with acceptable psychometric properties will often have normative data against which the client can be compared. A frequently used example which is again useful for high risk clients is the Beck Depression Inventory (Beck, Ward, Mendelson, Mock & Erbaugh, 1961).

- The Beck Depression Inventory (BDI). This is the most widely used self-report scale in the assessment of the severity of depressive symptoms. It consists of 21 items, each containing four or five statements ranked in order of severity, scored from 0 to 3. A total score of 0–63 is simply the sum of the individual item scores. The BDI has been used in more than 2000 empirical studies (Richter, Werner, Heerlein, Kraus & Sauer, 1998) and its psychometric properties have been extensively investigated and supported. It is frequently used in the cognitive-behavioural treatment of depression to monitor progress over the course of therapy and follow-up.

Self-monitoring

Self-monitoring is an important tool for collecting information about idiosyncratic problems for individual clients and monitoring improvements following the commencement of treatment. Typically, clients are asked to observe the occurrence of problem behaviours (or cognitions or emotions) and to record information about their frequency, intensity and duration. Introducing self-monitoring early in the course of assessment reinforces the active, collaborative and individually tailored nature of therapy.

Although at face value asking clients to record instances of problems may seem easy, clients often struggle to comply with the requests of the therapist. Success and accuracy in self-monitoring is enhanced by applying a few key principles. Firstly, it is important to be very clear about the behaviour to be monitored, to specifically define what is to be observed, and how it is to be recorded. It is usually best for the therapist to draw up a monitoring record for the client to use, to list instructions and to work through an example of how to use the record. It is optimal for the client to record the target behaviour as soon as it occurs in order to rely less on memory. Finally, it is better to obtain explicit agreement from the client that the monitoring exercise is a good idea, has the potential to provide important information for the therapy, and that they are prepared to make a commitment to complete the task.

For UHR clients, self-monitoring is often about the occurrence of attenuated psychotic symptoms such as hallucinations. In such cases the use of a diary form of self-monitoring, which also defines the context (place, preceding events) of the symptoms, can provide important information for the development of coping strategies.

INFORMANT INTERVIEW

Interviewing informants who know the client well can provide additional information pertinent to the assessment and development of a formulation for UHR clients. There may be information about family history of mental illness that the referred young person is unaware of, as well as early developmental issues and temporal links between significant life events and the onset of symptoms which can be revealed by discussions with informants, usually a parent. However, it is important to be sensitive to any issues that the young person may have regarding the use of family members as informants, as these may jeopardise engagement with the service. The young person should be asked for his or her permission to interview a parent with regard to important background information about his or her presenting problems and developmental history.

In Vivo Observation

Direct observation of clients in situations that they find difficult or in which problem behaviours tend to occur is another useful assessment tool. Information gathered through direct behavioural observation can be useful in understanding precipitating and maintaining factors, and in testing the reality of the client's recollection and interpretation of events. Although time-consuming, demonstrating a willingness to leave the office to gain a greater understanding of the client's situation can be very beneficial to engagement and is particularly useful for clients who find talking difficult. For young UHR clients, issues along the continuum of social anxiety to paranoia are frequently seen as presenting problems. *In vivo* observation of social interactions provides the therapist with accurate information about the client's level of social skills, the reactions of others to the client and events that generate anxiety in the client, and is thus very useful for defining targets for therapy and assessing progress over time.

Role-play Tests

Role-play tests can also be used to enhance the therapist's understanding of the client's reactions to particular situations that cause them difficulties, and determine the associated cognitions that may be appropriate targets for treatment. For example, a client may worry that whenever a teacher enquires about progress on an assignment he or she is criticising the client for being slow to complete tasks. The therapist could role-play this situation using a range of behaviours, ask the client to articulate his or her thoughts in response to the different examples and later in therapy discuss the evidence supporting the different interpretations.

THE CASE FORMULATION

Formulation – What is it?

A comprehensive case formulation is essential for most forms of psychological therapy and is particularly emphasised in CBT approaches. It is the culmination of the pre-therapy assessment and engagement phases and provides the framework for organising the important facts of the case. The formulation is developed by the therapist, in collaboration with the client, from the information gathered during the assessment, and proposes possible links between aspects of the presenting symptoms and the developmental history, which in turn suggest the agenda for therapy. The therapist draws on his or her knowledge and experience of psychiatric syndromes, individual symptoms, personality styles and developmental influences to explain the timing of onset and maintenance of key presenting symptoms and to provide a rationale for the subsequent therapy. The presentation of the formulation to the client is an important opportunity to enhance the therapeutic alliance by demonstrating significant interest and insight into the client's situation and transmitting optimism about the possibilities for improvement.

Case Formulation for UHR Clients

Obviously, the formulation must be based on the key presenting symptoms for which the client has sought help. However, it is equally important to consider the meaning or interpretation of these symptoms for each client. For the UHR group, the presenting symptoms are often attenuated psychotic symptoms or brief psychotic episodes. Thus, both personal history around the time of first onset of symptoms and the client's pre-existing ideas about the meaning of psychotic symptoms need to be considered when developing a formulation to be presented to the client. It is essential that the stress–vulnerability model of psychosis is presented during the assessment phase as the overarching explanation for the onset of psychotic symptoms, and is then used as the framework for each individualised case formulation. This explanatory model can be flexibly applied to the wide variety of UHR cases. Furthermore, such a model allows negative stereotypes of psychosis to be challenged and fosters the optimistic setting of attainable goals for therapy.

It is well known that UHR clients present with a wide range of symptoms and problems and that the vast majority of clients have other (non-psychotic) DSM-IV diagnoses, principally mood and anxiety disorders, when first seen in specialist clinics. Accordingly, the case formulation will incorporate these other conditions and an explanation of the interactions between these and the specific UHR symptoms where they are present.

Although derived from a comprehensive and hopefully accurate assessment of the client's situation, the formulation is actually a working hypothesis about the cause, maintenance and appropriate treatment of the client's problems and should be presented as such. The client's understanding of their problems is included from the beginning of the assessment. This means that the resulting formulation is likely to be acceptable to the client. It is important that the client is aware that the formulation will be constantly informed and updated by experiences during therapy, and that the collaborative nature of the therapy ensures that their ongoing feedback on the accuracy of the formulation will be incorporated.

The formulation serves to educate clients about the diagnostic labels given to their particular clusters of symptoms, theories about aetiology and the efficacy of treatments to be offered. Once presented and agreed upon, the final part of discussing the initial formulation involves establishing an appropriate therapy contract that specifies therapy targets, number of sessions and frequency of therapy reviews. It is important at this stage to discuss with clients the importance of their role as active partners in the therapeutic process and that their input and effort is essential to the success of therapy.

The following case example illustrates how the information gathered through an assessment over a number of sessions is used to develop a formulation and therapy plan through collaboration between the client and the therapist.

Case example

Cassandra was referred as a 15-year-old secondary school student who was living with both parents and her younger brother. Her mother initiated the referral due to concerns about Cassandra's 'depression and anxiety' during the past two years. A comprehensive assessment interview took place over several sessions and revealed the following.

Cassandra had experienced depressive and anxiety symptoms over the past year with an exacerbation over the two months prior to the assessment. Cassandra described herself as 'generally unhappy, tearful at times, unable to enjoy things and having poor appetite and sleep'. She also described panic attacks occurring occasionally over the past year but escalating to twice daily for the two months prior to assessment. These were described as being of 10–20 minutes' duration and characterised by nausea, restlessness, a sense of wanting to escape, increased heart rate and sweating. Cassandra could not identify any clear precipitant to these anxiety attacks and reported experiencing them at school, home and elsewhere. The attacks spontaneously abated. Cassandra found that distraction could help to reduce severity and duration.

Cassandra reported that she had a history of poor social relationships, having had few friends at school, and that she experienced bullying from middle primary school onwards. She described experiencing separation anxiety when she commenced school and again at the transition to secondary school. Cassandra described herself as generally anxious when away from home. There was also a history of family relationship difficulties; Cassandra's mother had a history of frequent depressive episodes since before Cassandra was born, and she probably had post-natal depression following the birth of both children. Cassandra's father was described as 'absent a lot and a strict disciplinarian, unsympathetic to Cassandra's troubles'. Currently Cassandra had few friends, reported that other people did not like her and that she 'couldn't stand' most people. She reported that she rarely goes out. Cassandra also reported a history of academic difficulties whereby she struggled to pass each year level.

Cassandra expressed a number of unusual ideas during the course of the assessment. She reported that she believed that she could see auras around people and that she could at times foresee their future and gain knowledge of their character from this. She reported that she had believed this for as long as she could remember. She believed that she also had the ability to 'read people's feelings', i.e. can pick up their 'vibes'. This meant that she could tell that people (usually) reacted negatively to her and did not like her. Cassandra reported that she occasionally picked up positive feeling from people but this was becoming rarer. She usually felt more anxious when she had detected negative feelings. This primarily occurred with people that she knew but also sometimes with strangers. These experiences of detecting negative feelings in others had been present since she commenced secondary school but had increased in frequency over the past year.

Cassandra also believed that she had some capacity to read other people's thoughts and intentions at times. She gave examples of being able to correctly predict what people would do, e.g. 'knows which way person will turn when reaches corner'. This had been present for the past year, occurring several times each month. Cassandra also believed that her mother could read her thoughts. She had thought this off and on since she was very young but had become more convinced in the past few months. Currently, Cassandra thought that there was an 80% chance that her mother could usually read her mind.

The final unusual idea concerned a presence in her house. She described feeling a 'presence' every day for the past 11 months. She did not find this distressing; in fact, Cassandra was comforted by this presence, which could not be seen or heard but was 'sensed'. Cassandra reported that she thought that she could summon the presence whenever she wanted.

Formulation

A formulation was developed collaboratively with Cassandra after several assessment sessions that included introduction of the stress–vulnerability model of the development of psychosis. Cassandra was asked whether she could identify any features of her history that might suggest a personal vulnerability to psychosis. Cassandra identified her mother's history of depression as possibly indicating some genetic predisposition to mental illness. She also noted that she has always been an anxious person, suggesting a general vulnerability to psychological difficulties.

The therapist agreed with Cassandra's preliminary formulation and added that negative social experiences and the absence of consistent, supportive parenting are likely to have led her to expect further negative interactions with others, and to be anxious about this happening. Negative experiences in her early life have led to Cassandra having very low self-esteem, further contributing to her expectation of negative outcomes, leading to the development of anxiety and depression. As she has moved into adolescence, unusual ideas about social relationships and interactions have developed, taking her closer to the psychosis threshold. These ideas can be understood in the context of her history of poor social relationships and perhaps a desire to be closer to her mother and to experience positive interpersonal contact. This could explain her idea that her mother can read her mind and her sense of a benevolent presence in her home.

The therapist checked that these explanations were plausible for Cassandra and on getting her approval then moved to explain how the problems would be addressed in therapy. There would need to be a range of strategies to deal with Cassandra's anxiety, depression and low self-esteem, to challenge her unusual ideas and to build personal resilience and supportive social relationships. More specifically, behavioural tests would be devised to test the unusual ideas, anxiety management techniques would be practised to deal with panic, pleasurable activities that included a social component would be investigated and careful monitoring of successes and appropriate mastery activities would begin to address Cassandra's low self-esteem. It was agreed that Cassandra and the therapist would meet weekly for 20 weeks and then review progress to date. Cassandra indicated that she wanted to work on her panic attacks first.

KEY FEATURES OF CASE FORMULATION FOR UHR

The case formulation for UHR clients has the following components:

- A description of the problems and difficulties with which the client is presenting. This will include the therapist's interpretation of problems as well as those described by the client him/herself.
- A description of the client's past history and how this may have influenced the current presenting issues as well as past functioning. This includes acknowledging the client's own understanding of links between his or her history and current symptoms and functioning.
- A description of the methods currently used by the client to 'cope' with the difficulties and changes he or she has faced, an articulation of the strengths that can be brought into play to deal with problems and a description of risk and protective factors evident.
- The stress–vulnerability model of psychosis is used as the framework for understanding. That is, to outline known and putative risk factors for psychosis that have been highlighted in the assessment process as well as existing protective factors.
- The client's explanation of the development of mental state and functioning changes identified as pre-psychotic. Generating a formulation is a collaborative process and the therapist's interpretation of the client's history must be palatable to the client and open to comment and criticism.
- The formulation that is presented to the client is considered to be a working hypothesis to be evaluated and reviewed throughout therapy.
- The presentation of the formulation obviously requires a 'collaborative, respectful and thoughtful' therapeutic relationship.
- The presentation of the formulation can serve to 'cement' the therapeutic alliance and is an emotionally powerful aspect of therapy.

ACKNOWLEDGEMENTS

The authors would like to thank Lisa Phillips, Steven Leicester, Kathryn Baker, Lisa O'Dwyer and Carol Hulbert for their assistance with this chapter.

REFERENCES

Addington, D., Addington, J. & Maticka-Tyndale, E. (1993). Assessing depression in schizophrenia: the Calgary Depression Scale. *British Journal of Psychiatry*, **163** (Suppl. 22), 39–44.

American Psychiatric Association (1994). *DSM-IV: Diagnostic and Statistical Manual of Mental Disorders* (4th edn). Washington, DC: Author.

Beck, A.T., Ward, C.H., Mendelson, M., Mock, J. & Erbaugh, J. (1961). An inventory for measuring depression. *Archives of General Psychiatry*, **4**, 561–571.

First, M.B., Spitzer, R.L., Gibbon, M. & Williams, J.B.W. (1996). *Structured Clinical Interview for DSM-IV Axis 1 Disorders – Patient Edition (SCID – I/P, Version 2.0)*. New York: NY State Psychiatric Institute.

Frank, A.F. & Gunderson, J.G. (1990). The role of the therapeutic alliance in the treatment of schizophrenia. *Archives of General Psychiatry*, **47**, 228–236.

French, P. & Morrison, A.P. (2004). *Early Detection and Cognitive Therapy for People at High Risk of Developing Psychosis*. Chichester, UK: Wiley.

Goerung, P.N., Stylianos, S.K. & Stavely, K. (1988). Exploring the helping relationship between the schizophrenic client and the rehabilitation therapist. *American Journal of Orthopsychiatry*, **58**, 271–280.

Gottesman, I.I. & Shields, J. (1972). *Schizophrenia and Genetics: A Twin Study Vantage Point.* New York: Academic Press.

Gross, G. (1989). The 'basic' symptoms of schizophrenia. *British Journal of Psychiatry*, **155** (Suppl. 7), 21–25.

Guy, W. (1976). *ECDEU Assessment Manual for Psychopharmacology.* Washington, DC: US Department of Health, Education, and Welfare.

Hamilton, M. (1959). The assessment of anxiety state by rating. *British Journal of Medical Psychology*, **32**, 50–55.

Hamilton, M. (1960). A rating scale for depression. *Journal of Neurology, Neurosurgery and Psychiatry*, **23**, 56–62.

McGorry, P.D., Yung, A.R., Phillips, L.J., Yuen, H.P., Francey, S., Cosgrave, E.M. et al. (2002). Randomized controlled trial of interventions designed to reduce the risk of progression to first-episode psychosis in a clinical sample with subthreshold symptoms. *Archives of General Psychiatry*, **59** (10), 921–928.

Meehl, P.E. (1962). Schizotaxia, schizotypy, schizophrenia. *American Psychology*, **17**, 827–838.

Meehl, P.E. (1989). Schizotaxia revisited. *Archives of General Psychiatry*, **46**, 935–944.

Morrison, A.P., French, P., Walford, L., Lewis, S.W., Kilcommons, A., Green, J. et al. (2004). Cognitive therapy for the prevention of psychosis in people at ultra-high risk: Randomised controlled trial. *British Journal of Psychiatry*, **185**, 291–297.

Richter, P., Werner, J., Heerlein, A., Kraus, A. & Sauer, H. (1998). On the validity of the Beck Depression Inventory. *Psychopathology*, **31** (3), 160–168.

Spring, B.J. & Zubin, J. (1977). Reaction time and attention in schizophrenia: A comment on K.H. Nuechterlein's critical evaluation of the data and theories. *Schizophrenia Bulletin*, **3**, 437–444.

Wing, J.K., Cooper, J.E. & Sartorius, N. (1974). *The Measurement and Classification of Psychiatric Symptoms.* London: Cambridge University Press.

Yung, A.R. & McGorry, P.D. (1996a). The initial prodrome in psychosis: Descriptive and qualitative aspects. *Australian and New Zealand Journal of Psychiatry*, **30**, 587–599.

Yung, A.R. & McGorry, P.D. (1996b). The prodromal phase of first-episode psychosis: Past and current conceptualizations. *Schizophrenia Bulletin*, **22** (2), 353–370.

Yung, A.R., Yuen, H.P., Phillips, L.J., Francey, S. & McGorry, P.D. (2003). Mapping the onset of psychosis: The comprehensive assessment of at risk mental states (CAARMS). *Schizophrenia Research*, **60** (1), 30–31.

CHAPTER 4

Engagement and the Therapeutic Alliance

Jean Addington and David Penn

The purpose of this chapter is to consider engagement and the therapeutic alliance with a population at high risk of developing psychosis. This population has a suspected heightened risk by virtue of their current mental state, although, of course, this is not inevitable. These individuals may have sub-clinical or attenuated positive symptoms and are thus considered to be at "ultra high risk" (UHR). According to Yung and McGorry (1996), since we are dealing with degrees of risk of onset of psychosis, this mental state thought to potentially represent a prodrome is best termed an "At Risk Mental State", or ARMS. This is a state that suggests high but not inevitable risk of developing psychosis in the near future.

Our focus in this chapter is the engagement and development of a therapeutic alliance with these young clients with an ARMS. In our use of the term "therapy" we are usually referring to cognitive-behavioral therapy (CBT); however, this does not exclude the relevance of these ideas about engagement and therapeutic alliance for those involved in case management or other variations of therapy with this population. A unique aspect of enhancing engagement in this population is the possibility that early engagement may be extremely beneficial should transition to psychosis occur. If a young person has already engaged with a therapist, program, or service and developed an alliance with an individual or program, this may improve adherence to a range of treatments for psychosis and hopefully minimize or prevent the possibility of admissions to hospital or compulsory treatments.

Several potential barriers to engaging young UHR clients in treatment have been identified (Addington, 2003; Schaffner & McGorry, 2001). These include social isolation that is commonly apparent in this population and the issue of the stigma attached to mental illness and treatment. Careful attention to engagement issues and the building of a positive therapeutic alliance will assist the therapist to overcome these barriers.

Working with People at High Risk of Developing Psychosis: A Treatment Handbook.
Edited by J. Addington, S.M. Francey and A.P. Morrison. © 2006 John Wiley & Sons, Ltd.

ENGAGEMENT

Principles of Engagement

By engaging with the client we want to clarify his or her concerns and provide an understanding of what will happen in the treatment. It has to be demonstrated that not only do we need to identify and understand his or her problems and/or target symptoms, but also that his or her problems and concerns are taken seriously. Facilitating an atmosphere of safety and trust as early as possible and offering a sense of hope encourages engagement and forms the basis for developing a good therapeutic alliance. This is important not only for establishing a basis for assessment and intervention but for developing a consensus about problems and goals for therapy. Moreover, it encourages regular contact with the client. Thus, when attempting to engage a UHR client into therapy we need to consider several issues that may arise and potential solutions.

Reluctance to Attend Therapy

These young people often present as anxious or even reluctant to actually meet a therapist. They may not have had any prior contact with a therapist or mental health professional. Alternatively, many of them may have seen several health or counseling professionals as they may have been seeking help for some time, often unsuccessfully (Addington, van Mastrigt, Hutchinson & Addington, 2002). Some of these experiences may have led to reluctance to engage in services. Therefore, therapists need to first anticipate and acknowledge the client's concerns and ambivalences, secondly attempt to minimize any uncertainty and ambiguity, and thirdly openly address and normalize these concerns.

The client may have some preconceived ideas about the approach being used. If, for example, the approach is CBT, then the therapist should be aware of the young person's ideas and beliefs about cognitive therapy. Although an ongoing component of the CBT model is socializing the client to the approach, defining and briefly elaborating the aims and rationale of CBT may be helpful in the early stages. In fact the collaborative nature of a cognitive behavioral approach can in itself enhance engagement and the development of a positive therapeutic alliance.

In the literature these UHR clients are often described as "help-seeking" to differentiate them from individuals in the community who may have attenuated symptoms but for whom the symptoms cause no concern. However, at times the "help-seeking" is initiated by significant others, such as family members, or the young person may have been referred from other services. This may make engagement difficult if the young person is not particularly willing to attend. In such cases extra work around engagement issues, as exemplified in the case example below, may be required prior to commencing the actual therapy sessions.

Case example

Stephen, who was 13 years old, was referred to our program by his aunt after he voiced concerns of possibly becoming "like his mother", who had been diagnosed as having paranoid schizophrenia. Though his mother did not currently live with him, he had witnessed her going through several psychotic episodes throughout his life. Due to his mother's illness, Stephen assumed caring responsibilities for his mother and younger sister in his father's absence, and thus Stephen presented as quite independent and distant in comparison to other teenagers his age.

Upon his first presentation it became apparent quite quickly that he was not pleased about having to come in for regular appointments. In fact it became known that his family had pressured him to attend in spite of his reluctance. Thus, it became necessary to work on engagement issues before structured therapy could effectively begin. An aunt had mentioned the boy's passion for hockey; this was used as a stepping stone into a conversation that allowed him to be distracted from his unhappiness and anger about being at the clinic.

Discussing his personal views and interests and allowing him to guide the conversation went a long way to remove some of the negative feelings that he had displaced onto the therapist. This also allowed him to develop an alliance with the therapist, as it indicated to him that they were not communicating on completely different levels and could have similar interests.

Following this conversation the client became more relaxed, allowing a dialogue to ensue regarding his concerns and reservations about being in therapy, which led him to be more open to the possibility of coming in for the next appointment.

Social Isolation

In retrospective reviews of the early course of psychosis it is clear that social decline or withdrawal may precede the development of psychotic symptoms in the onset of a first episode of psychosis (Häfner, Loffler, Maurer, Hambrecht & an der Heiden, 1999). Thus, in both retrospective and prospective descriptions of individuals who may be prodromal for schizophrenia or other psychotic disorders, there is evidence that many are functioning poorly—particularly with respect to social and role functioning. Deterioration in role functioning and self-care, and social withdrawal or isolation, are often reported amongst other symptoms.

One of the three criteria that were established for diagnosing this putatively prodromal group by Alison Yung and Patrick McGorry in Melbourne (the Melbourne Criteria; McGorry, Yung & Phillips, 2001; Yung, McGorry, McFarlane, Patton & Rakkar, 1996) and elaborated on by McGlashan (COPS criteria; McGlashan et al., 2003; Miller et al., 2002) includes a decline in functioning. The three criteria are a mix of recent onset functional decline plus genetic risk, or recent onset of sub-threshold or brief threshold psychotic symptoms. The latter two reflect very brief or attenuated psychotic symptoms. However, the genetic risk and recent deterioration group included individuals who have a first degree relative with psychosis plus a 30% reduction over the past year in an individual's Global Assessment of Functioning Scale (GAF; American Psychiatric Association, 1994). This putatively prodromal diagnostic group clearly presents with isolation, withdrawal, and a decline in social functioning.

One of the most often used measures to rate prodromal symptoms is the Scale of Prodromal Symptoms (SOPS; Addington, 2004; Miller et al., 2002). On this scale symptoms can be rated between 0–6, where a rating of 3–5 puts a symptom into the putatively prodromal range. In a recent trial, 78% of putatively prodromal subjects rated between 3–5 for social isolation and 77% for deterioration in role function on their baseline scores. This is in comparison to a 60% rating in this range for suspiciousness, 50% for perceptual abnormalities, and 48% for conceptual disorganization (Miller et al., 2003). Comparing the premorbid functioning of these individuals to those who have already presented with a first episode (Addington, van Mastrigt & Addington, 2003) at all developmental stages (childhood, early and late adolescence), this sample of putatively prodromal patients actually rate more poorly than the first episode subjects (Addington, Zipursky, Perkins, Woods & McGlashan, 2004).

In general, studies describing these putatively prodromal individuals report GAF scores in the range of 40–50 (Miller et al., 2003; Morrison et al., 2004), which are comparable to those individuals who present with a first episode and also to those with a more chronic course of schizophrenia.

This is one group of UHR individuals with whom it is often quite difficult to engage. Therapists should expect to see a reasonable proportion of referrals presenting as socially isolated. Initial sessions should be short and focused on finding common ground. Here it is extremely important for the therapist to display warmth and empathy.

Case example

James, aged 22, was referred after his mother, who feared that her son was losing contact with reality, had taken him to the emergency room of a local hospital. The mother was also concerned because her son was becoming increasingly socially isolated. He had long-standing social anxiety, but his recent paranoid ideation confounded the situation to the point where he dropped out of school, quit his job, and rarely left his room or spoke with anyone outside his immediate family.

During his interview at the clinic, James described feeling extremely uncomfortable when out in public. He felt as if everyone around him, even friends and family, took notice of him and was judging him negatively. He also thought that his body language and facial expressions were unusual, and feared that people might notice. Worried about the possibility that people might mean him physical harm, James thought he should be vigilant when out in public. James was quite distressed about these thoughts and, as a result, made the conscious decision to avoid social interaction whenever possible. In fact, when the young man had to go out in public with his family he would avoid social interaction altogether by facing in the opposite direction to others. Social anhedonia was pervasive. He did not miss seeing his friends, and had no desire to socialize with his peers as it gave him no pleasure. He preferred to spend his free time alone and maintained an emotional distance from others, including his family.

This young man's history of social anxiety and withdrawal compounded the impact of his emerging attenuated psychotic symptoms, making engagement very difficult. The focus of early sessions was on attempts to develop a level of trust and comfort with the therapist, wherein the therapist needed to be aware of issues of concern that arose for James in the context of merely coming into the clinic, attending sessions, and being with the therapist. The therapist had to be attentive to any signs of concern and in a reassuring way use guided discovery to help James understand his interpretation of the events and help him consider alternative explanations.

Impact of Symptoms

The therapist needs to remain aware of the potential of psychotic symptoms to interfere with engagement. Although such symptoms may be brief or attenuated they may interfere with communication, trust, and even impact on the client's cognitive processing. These symptoms may include unusual thought content, overvalued beliefs, ideas of reference, suspicious ideas, or perceptual abnormalities. Further, many of these young people may already be demonstrating mild cognitive impairments as there is evidence that the cognitive deficits that are observed in those with psychosis often are present long before the onset of the psychotic symptoms (Hawkins et al., 2004; Jones, Rodgers, Murray & Marmot, 1994). Some of the very early symptoms as described by Schultze-Lutter (Schultze-Lutter, 2004; Schultze-Lutter, Ruhrmann & Klosterkötter, in press) include mild cognitive disturbances such as problems with expressive or receptive speech, problems with abstract thinking, or inability to divide attention. All these symptoms can impact communication and have an effect on engagement. One strategy here is to ask for regular feedback to check that the client has understood the therapist and equally that the therapist has understood the client. Such a collaborative approach will enhance clients' feelings that their views have been acknowledged, that they are being listened to and understood, and that the therapist is actually interested in what they have to say.

Fear of "Going Crazy"

Recent research identifies 30–50% of these young people as having the potential to convert to a psychotic illness (Yung et al., 2003). Many will present with worries and fear of "going crazy", developing schizophrenia, or wondering if they already have schizophrenia. They may have a very close relative who has schizophrenia, such as a parent or sibling. For most this is the first time or the beginning of having strange experiences, altered perceptions, or attenuated symptoms. They wonder if they may be "becoming crazy" or about to lose control. Awareness and understanding of the impact of these symptoms, thoughts, and worries of the individual and significant others will help engagement.

Case example

Sarah, a young woman in her mid-20s, revealed to a family doctor that she was afraid she was going crazy. Her recent unusual perceptual experiences were causing her to doubt the reality of the world around her. She was afraid that she was "losing her mind and that she might be getting schizophrenia". She had looked her symptoms up on the Internet and was aware of the recent film, "A Beautiful Mind". It took several attempts to arrange for her to come for an appointment; finally she came when we were able to reassure her that our clinic was not based within a hospital, rather it was in an old Victorian house on one of the downtown streets in Toronto.

Our way of engaging Sarah was to reassure her that although experiencing unusual perceptual experiences may mean that an individual is considered at risk, this does not necessarily mean that they will go on to become psychotic. In fact, only a minority of individuals with such symptoms do. Our assessment helped her see that indeed she only had mild unusual perceptual experiences, and that experiencing such symptoms was not terribly unusual. Through the assessment process she learned more about the range of attenuated symptoms that can occur and the degree of her own unusual experiences. The setting of the clinic, as discussed below, aided her engagement as not only did the "white-coated" medical profession waiting to admit her to hospital not exist, but she learned that a hospital admission would be very inappropriate for her.

Therapy Setting

As suggested in the above case, the setting for the therapy needs careful consideration. The early intervention and detection movement has mainly originated from mental health programs that existed within general hospitals and psychiatric hospitals. However, these young people have concerns and problems but the majority do not have diagnosable mental health problems. Furthermore, attending appointments in clinics that are possibly named "Schizophrenia Program" can reinforce the notion that these early signs might indicate future severe mental illness. Offering therapy in non-institutional places is more amenable to these clients and will likely aid engagement and participation.

The Toronto PRIME clinic, which is dedicated to working with these UHR young people, is housed in an old Victorian house on a busy downtown street. The PACE clinic in Melbourne is in a modern shop front in a suburban shopping mall (McGorry, Yung & Phillips, 2001). The EDIE program in Manchester, although run administratively from offices in a psychiatric facility, made a tremendous effort to provide all appointments in GP's offices, health centers, youth centers, local community centers, or even in the client's own home (French & Morrison, 2004). French and Morrison (2004) did suggest that although it is preferable for sessions to take place at some type of service setting in order to avoid interruptions, this preference has to be balanced against whether or not the person will attend sessions at these locations. However, with any home visit, therapist safety should always be considered a priority.

Stigma

It is well known that individuals with a mental illness, particularly severe mental illnesses such as schizophrenia and bipolar disorder, are stigmatized by society (Corrigan & Penn, 1999). Such stigmatization is present in the community (Crisp, Gelder, Rix, Meltzer & Rowlands, 2000; Tsang, Tam, Chan & Cheung, 2003), and among mental health professionals (Ryan, Robinson & Hausmann, 2001) and mental health graduate students (Mukherjee, Fialho, Wijetunge, Checinski & Surgenor, 2002). The consequences of stigma are significant: they can impact on quality of life, self-esteem, health care, work, and housing opportunities (discussed in Corrigan, 2004; Penn et al., in press).

Concerns regarding stigma may have important implications for engaging and keeping UHR individuals in treatment for a number of reasons. First, most individuals learn about mental illness from the media (Wahl, 1995), which depicts individuals with mental illness as dangerous and scary (Angermeyer & Schulze, 2001; Nairn, Coverdale & Classen, 2001; Wahl, 2002). These portrayals act as a clear disincentive to an individual to self-identify as needing therapy or medical treatment. This effect has also been born out empirically, as greater concerns regarding stigma were associated with less utilization of services among individuals at risk of mental illness (Leaf, Bruce, Tischler & Holzer, 1987) and among adolescents with a mental illness (based on the results of Penn et al., in press). In fact, by seeking treatment, UHR individuals are not only making themselves vulnerable to public or societal stigma, but to "self-stigma" as well (Corrigan, 2004; Corrigan & Watson, 2002). Self-stigma occurs when one internalizes negative stereotypes, resulting in lower self-esteem and self-efficacy. Therefore, the process of initiating treatment for prodromal symptoms may set in motion a cascade of negative beliefs regarding how society views the newly identified client and how they feel about themselves.

A second implication of stigma for UHR individuals is that it may contribute to poor treatment adherence. For example, concerns about stigma are related to adherence to drug regimens for epilepsy (Buck, Baker, Chadwick & Jacoby, 1997) and HIV (Pugatch, Bennett & Patterson, 2002), and to treatment continuation among elderly individuals with depression (Sirey et al., 2001a, 2001b). This suggests that actually engaging a UHR individual may be a double-edged sword; treatment may reduce prodromal symptoms at the cost of increasing client awareness that he or she has a mental illness, which can lead to self-stigma and shame (Corrigan, 2004).

There is no single technique that reduces stigma and the consequent barriers to treatment seeking and adherence. However, a variety of strategies drawn from our previous work and that of Corrigan and colleagues (discussed in Corrigan, 2004; Corrigan & Penn, 1999; Couture & Penn, 2003; Penn et al., in press) deserve mention. At the societal level, it is critical that media depictions of mental illness are balanced. The media is, perhaps, the most powerful tool for providing "contact" between the public and individuals with mental illness, which is a critical aspect of any stigma reduction strategy. In addition, grass roots community efforts, such as speakers with mental illness, drama performances by troupes which may include individuals with mental illness, and field trips to mental health facilities (e.g., club houses) may demystify mental illness (Estroff, Penn & Toporek, in press). This might be especially effective when coupled with community education programs on the identification of UHR individuals in high school settings. Once a UHR individual is engaged in treatment, such services should ideally be offered in "neutral environments", that is, those that are not explicitly associated with a medical or psychiatric setting, especially one in which more chronically ill individuals are receiving treatment.

Finally, it needs to be reinforced that we are offering treatment not for a diagnosable mental health problem but rather that we are offering interventions for whatever the presenting problem may be and that such interventions may have an impact such that mental illness may be prevented.

Case example

Robert, a 21-year-old college student, came to our clinic after seeing an advertisement for a free evaluation and therapy in the local newspaper. Robert reported that he had been having "strange experiences" for over a year, but had been reluctant to seek treatment. After arguing with a roommate in the dormitory, Robert moved into his own apartment off-campus. At about the same time, his girlfriend broke up with him. It was at that time that he started hearing odd sounds in his apartment. He wondered if they were coming from his neighbors (which he originally suspected), but noticed that they also occurred when they were out of town. Due to the low frequency, he ignored the noises at first. However, during his final exams they got worse and his grades began to drop.

He considered going to the counseling center, but was dissuaded when he considered what that would mean: that he was a "crazy person". He recalled watching horror movies during his freshman year that depicted "mental patients" killing people randomly. He did not want to be thought of as one of those people. Moreover, his father used to make derogatory comments about a cousin in therapy and how she was an embarrassment to the family. Thus, he didn't want to be ostracized. Unfortunately, the sounds did not go away the next semester and his grades continued to suffer. Rather than let this go on, he decided to confide in his best friend, deciding that it was worth the risk to disclose to someone and maybe get help. Much to Robert's relief, his friend was supportive and, in fact, had seen the advertisement for the clinic, which he gave to Robert.

Other Considerations for Engagement

These UHR individuals are usually adolescents or young adults. There may be differences between the therapist and client that can be attributed to age, gender, culture, or lifestyle. This needs to be acknowledged in discussions and attempts made to find some common ground. Accommodating to some of the needs of these young people may help. For example, since early morning appointments are most likely not a priority and if school and work are issues, then offering later appointments may be helpful and contribute to enhancing engagement. Issues that may fall in the realm of case management may arise. If case management is available, then this is an excellent advantage for some clients. However, it may not be available and it may be necessary to offer some extra help with some of the practical problems and even some crisis situations as they arise. Helping with many of these issues may lead to developing greater trust and willingness to participate in CBT.

THERAPEUTIC ALLIANCE

The therapeutic alliance refers to the quality of the working relationship between the client and the therapist. It is the central, core component of the process of psychotherapy and change. Originally, in psychodynamic therapy the alliance was believed to be the positive transference from patient to therapist, but later the concept developed into a more conscious and active collaboration between therapist and client, as in Rogerian client-centered therapy (Ackerman & Hilsenroth, 2003). An extensive review of psychotherapy in general (Lamber, 1992) suggests that up to 30% of outcome variance can be attributable to therapist variables, i.e., the therapeutic alliance. Current conceptualizations of the therapeutic alliance are based on the work of Bordin (1979), who defines the alliance as composed of the following three elements: tasks, bonds, and goals. Tasks are the within therapy behaviors that form the basis of the specific intervention; bonds refer to the mutual trust and personal attachments within the therapeutic relationship; and goals are the mutually agreed upon focus for treatment.

Therapeutic Alliance in CBT

Since one of the goals of CBT is to engage clients in a process of "collaborative empiricism", the early work on CBT implied that the therapeutic relationship was a given in the process of therapy. It was seen as something that was routinely and easily established, forming the background to the actual work of the therapy during which the therapist demonstrated warmth, respect, genuineness, and confidence in the process (Newman, 1998). However, as the range of patient populations for whom CBT is considered effective has expanded, the conceptualization of the therapeutic relationship in CBT has widened. CBT is now used to address a wider range of psychopathology and related problems, and the clients themselves are often more challenging because they may present with more chronic interpersonal difficulties. Newman (1998) suggested that the client–therapist relationship may be seen as a source of information about how the client sees and operates in relationships. As such, the therapeutic relationship can serve as the basis for modifying client beliefs about relationships.

There is increasing evidence of the important role for the therapeutic alliance in work with those with psychotic illness (Gehrs & Goering, 1994; Neale & Rosenheck, 1995; Svensson & Hansson, 1999). Bentall and colleagues (2003) examined the therapeutic alliance in CBT for psychosis suggesting that patient but not therapist ratings of the alliance predicted outcome. Thus, although potentially challenging, consideration of the therapeutic alliance within a CBT approach with putatively prodromal clients, many of whom have difficulties with interpersonal relationships, is a vital component of the treatment process.

Limited Sessions

CBT is usually a short-term, goal-oriented therapy. If a client has issues with basic trust it can be difficult to educate and socialize a client to the CBT model, conduct and complete the therapy, and hopefully make some significant changes in a relatively short period of time. For many young people considered to be at high risk of psychosis, placing trust in others can be difficult, as seen in some of the case examples above. Thus, a longer period of time to engage may be required before clients can relate or collaborate well enough to address their presenting problems. Consistency in the therapeutic relationship is essential, as the client needs to learn over time that the therapist will neither judge nor harm him or her. Since work with this UHR group is relatively new, the therapy may be limited to a specific number of sessions or be part of a clinical trial where sessions are limited. While limiting sessions may be unavoidable, one must be mindful that it is a potential barrier to engagement for the individual who needs a longer-term attachment and/or time to establish trust. Newman (1998) suggests that on the one hand therapists should be very much aware of time as it is "precious", but at the same time they should take care not to rush the client too much and attempt to expedite the accomplishment of goals. If the number of sessions is fixed at the outset, then the therapist needs to be honest and direct with the client at the beginning of therapy with respect to the number of sessions available.

One expectation of therapy is that it will have a significant impact on a client's life that endures beyond the completion of therapy despite the short-term nature of the treatment. It is hoped that a positive therapeutic relationship will assist the client to learn and remember the work of the therapy, i.e., the efforts made to change dysfunctional behaviors and acquire new skills. This means the therapist needs to convey positive regard and hope that the learning will be remembered within the context of a positive therapeutic relationship.

If, as a therapist, you demonstrate concern for the limited time by working hard between sessions and make your own contribution, this can foster the development of trust. Since homework is a specific component of CBT, the therapist should also do his or her homework. This can be accomplished in several ways. First, by taking and reviewing notes, the therapist can demonstrate that he or she remembers important details from session to session. In addition, the therapist can take responsibility to provide some learning materials. Another option is to comment: "I have been thinking of some of the things you said in the last session, and I really was aware of this . . ."

Finally, Newman (1998) presents an interesting concept of simple versus accurate empathy that may enhance the alliance. First, in terms of establishing an alliance the therapist can demonstrate "simple" empathy by listening, reflecting, and offering kindness and concern. However it may be more valuable to offer "accurate" empathy, which Newman defines as a mixture of data and therapist intuition. Rather than comment, "that must have been very difficult for you," about a given situation, it may help more to hypothesize why a situation must have been difficult for the person, such as, "that must have been very difficult for you to stand by and let happen, but it makes sense in terms of some of the perceptions you have been experiencing . . ."

Ruptures in the Therapeutic Alliance

When something goes wrong within the alliance it is referred to as a "rupture". Ruptures in the alliance are an expected part of treatment that can be resolved and may be valuable in offering opportunities for change and deepening the alliance (Safran & Muran, 2000). Therapists need to question why the rupture is occurring. Ruptures can be related to the relational bond or to disagreements about the therapy. There may even be multiple ruptures. There are ways to either avoid ruptures or to resolve them. Safran and Muran recommend that to resolve ruptures the therapist must acknowledge and disclose his or her contribution to the rupture.

There are some obvious pitfalls. The therapist needs to know the extent of the client's ability to participate in terms of the symptoms or deficits as have been discussed above. The therapist must ensure that they are not asking too much of the client. Bombarding clients with too much activity is to be avoided, especially considering both the attenuated symptoms and symptoms of anhedonia and isolation with which these UHR individuals may be concerned. Equally, care should be taken to ensure that clients do not feel rushed into tasks, activities, or homework before they are ready. Avoiding a power struggle around who may be right and wrong is recommended. Therapists make hypotheses, and as such they should emphasize that these are indeed **hypotheses** that need to be tested collaboratively with the client through the course of therapy.

SUMMARY

Our knowledge about engagement and developing a therapeutic alliance with this population is limited. From the few studies published to date, it seems that engagement in clinical trials offering medication is far more difficult than engagement in psychological interventions (Addington & Addington, 2005; Morrison et al., 2004). In this chapter we have reviewed the importance of engagement and the therapeutic alliance to the success of therapy with young people at UHR of psychosis. We have presented some of the special issues that may impede the engagement of these young individuals. These issues relate to the fear and stigma associated with mental illness, and the person's experiences and expectations of psychological therapy. It has been emphasized that these issues need to be continually addressed if these young people are to be successfully engaged in psychological interventions that are aimed at improving their functioning and reducing the chance of developing a psychotic illness (Morrison et al., 2004).

REFERENCES

Ackerman, S.J. & Hilsenroth, M.J. (2003). A review of therapist characteristics and techniques positively impacting the therapeutic alliance. *Clinical Psychology Review*, **23**, 1–33.

Addington, J. (2003). The prodromal stage of psychotic illness: observation, detection or intervention? *Journal of Psychiatry and Neuroscience*, **28**, 93–97.

Addington, J. (2004). The diagnosis and assessment of individuals prodromal for schizophrenic psychosis. *CNS Spectrum*, **9**, 588–594.

Addington, J. & Addington, D. (2005). Clinical trials in the prodromal stage of schizophrenia psychosis: who consents? [Letter to the editor]. *American Journal of Psychiatry*, **162**, 1387.

Addington, J., van Mastrigt, S. & Addington, D. (2003). Patterns of premorbid functioning in first episode psychosis: initial presentation. *Schizophrenia Research*, **62**, 23–30.

Addington, J., van Mastrigt, S., Hutchinson, J. & Addington, D. (2002). Pathways to care: help seeking behavior in first episode psychosis. *Acta Psychiatrica Scandinavica*, **106**, 358–364.

Addington, J., Zipursky, R.B., Perkins, D.O., Woods, S.W. & McGlashan, T.H. (2004). Decline in social functioning for those with an "at risk mental state". *Schizophrenia Research*, **70**, 37.

American Psychiatric Association. (1994). *DSM-IV: Diagnostic and Statistical Manual of Mental Disorders* (4th edn). Washington, DC: Author.

Angermeyer, M.C. & Schulze, B. (2001). Reinforcing stereotypes: How the focus on forensic cases in news reporting may influence public attitudes towards the mentally ill. *International Journal of Law and Psychiatry*, **24**, 469–486.

Bentall, R.P., Lewis, S.W., Tarrier, N., Haddock, G., Drake, R.E. & Day, J. (2003). Relationships matter: The impact of the therapeutic alliance on outcome in schizophrenia. *Schizophrenia Research*, **61**, 319.

Bordin, E.S. (1979). The generalizability of the psychoanalystic concept of the working alliance. *Psychotherapy: Theory, Research, and Practice*, **16**, 252–260.

Buck, D., Baker, G.A., Chadwick, D.W. & Jacoby, A. (1997). Factors influencing compliance with antiepileptic drug regimes. *Seizure*, **6**, 87–93.

Corrigan, P.W. (2004). How stigma interferes with mental health care. *American Psychologist*, **59**, 614–625.

Corrigan, P.W. & Penn, D.L. (1999). Lessons from social psychology on discrediting psychiatric stigma. *American Psychologist*, **54**, 765–776.

Corrigan, P.W. & Watson, A.C. (2002). The paradox of self-stigma and mental illness. *Clinical Psychology Science and Practice*, **9**, 35–53.

Couture, S. & Penn, D.L. (2003). Contact and the stigma of mental illness: A review of the literature. *Journal of Mental Health*, **12**, 291–305.

Crisp, A.H., Gelder, M.G., Rix, S., Meltzer, H.I. & Rowlands, O.J. (2000). Stigmatisation of people with mental illnesses. *British Journal of Psychiatry*, **177**, 4–7.

Estroff, S.E., Penn, D.L. & Toporek, J.R. (in press). From stigma to discrimination: An analysis of community efforts to reduce the negative consequences of having a psychiatric disorder and label. *Schizophrenia Bulletin*.

French, P. & Morrison, A.P. (2004). *Early Detection and Cognitive Therapy for People at High Risk of Developing Psychosis*. Chichester, UK: Wiley.

Gehrs, M. & Goering, P. (1994). The relationship between the working alliance and rehabilitation outcomes of schizophrenia. *Psychosocial Rehabilitation Journal*, **18**, 45–53.

Häfner, H., Loffler, W., Maurer, K., Hambrecht, M. & an der Heiden, W. (1999). Depression, negative symptoms, social stagnation and social decline in the early course of schizophrenia. *Acta Psychiatrica Scandinavica*, **100**, 105–18.

Hawkins, K.A., Addington, J., Keefe, R.S., Christensen, B., Perkins, D.O., Zipursky, R. et al. (2004). Neuropsychological status of subjects at high risk for a first episode of psychosis. *Schizophrenia Research*, **67**, 115–122.

Jones, P., Rodgers, B., Murray, R. & Marmot, M. (1994). Child development risk factors for adult schizophrenia in the British 1946 birth cohort. *Lancet*, **344**, 1398–1402.

Lamber, M. (1992). Psychotherapy outcome research: Implications for integrative and eclectic therapies. In J.G.M. Norcross (Ed.), *Handbook of Psychotherapy Integration*. New York: Basic Books.

Leaf, P.J., Bruce, M.L., Tischler, G.L. & Holzer, C.E. (1987). The relationship between demographic factors and attitudes toward mental health services. *Journal of Community Psychology*, **15**, 275–284.

McGlashan, T.H., Zipursky, R.B., Perkins, D.O., Addington, J., Miller, T.J., Woods, S.W. et al. (2003). A randomized double blind clinical trial of olanzapine vs. placebo in patients at risk for being prodromally symptomatic for psychosis. I: Study rationale and design. *Schizophrenia Research*, **61**, 7–18.

McGorry, P.D., Yung, A. & Phillips, L. (2001). The close-in or ultra high risk model: a safe and effective strategy for research and clinical intervention in prepsychotic mental disorder. *Schizophrenia Bulletin*, **29**, 771–790.

Miller, T.J., McGlashan, T.H., Rosen, J.L., Somjee, L., Markovitch, P., Stein, K. et al. (2002). Prospective diagnosis of the prodrome for schizophrenia: preliminary evidence of interrater reliability and predictive validity using the structured interview for prodromal states (SIPS). *American Journal of Psychiatry*, **159**, 863–865.

Miller, T.J., Zipursky, R.B., Perkins, D.O., Addington, J., Woods, S.W., Hawkins, K.A. et al. (2003). A randomized double blind clinical trial of olanzapine vs. placebo in patients at risk for being prodromally symptomatic for psychosis. II: Recruitment and baseline characteristics of the "prodromal" sample. *Schizophrenia Research*, **61**, 19–30.

Morrison, A.P., French, P., Walford, L., Lewis, S.W., Kilcommons, A., Green, J. et al. (2004). Cognitive therapy for the prevention of psychosis in people at ultra-high risk: Randomised controlled trial. *British Journal of Psychiatry*, **185**, 291–297.

Mukherjee, R., Fialho, A., Wijetunge, A., Checinski, K. & Surgenor, T. (2002). The stigmatization of psychiatric illness: The attitudes of medical students and doctors in a London teaching hospital. *Psychiatric Bulletin*, **26**, 178–181.

Nairn, R., Coverdale, J. & Claasen, D. (2001). From source material to news story in New Zealand print media: A prospective study of the stigmatizing processes depicting mental illness. *Australian and New Zealand Journal of Psychiatry*, **35**, 654–659.

Neale, M.S. & Rosenheck, R.A. (1995). Therapeutic alliance and outcome in a VA intensive case management program. *Psychiatric Services*, **30**, 719–721.

Newman, C.F. (1998). The therapeutic relationship and alliance in short-term cognitive therapy. In J.D. Safran & J.C. Muran (Eds), *The Therapeutic Alliance in Brief Psychotherapy* (pp. 95–122). Washington, DC: American Psychological Association.

Penn, D.L., Judge, A., Jamieson, P., Garczynski, J., Hennessy, M. & Romer, D. (in press). Stigma. In M. Seligman (Ed.), *Treatments for Adolescents That Work*. London: Oxford Press.

Pugatch, D., Bennett, L. & Patterson, D. (2002). HIV medication adherence in adolescents: a qualitative study. *Journal of HIV/AIDS Prevention and Education for Adolescents and Children*, **5**, 9–29.

Ryan, C.S., Robinson, D.R. & Hausmann, L.R. (2001). Stereotyping among providers and consumers of public mental health services: The role of perceived group variability. *Behavior Modification*, **25**, 406–442.

Safran, J.D. & Muran, J.C. (2000). Resolving therapeutic alliance ruptures. *Journal of Consulting and Clinical Psychology*, **64**, 233–243.

Schaffner, K.F. & McGorry, P.D. (2001). Preventing severe mental illnesses – new prospects and ethical challenges. *Schizophrenia Research*, **51**, 3–15.

Schultze-Lutter, F. (2004). Prediction of psychosis is necessary and possible. In C. McDonald, K. Schultz, R. Murray & P. Wright (Eds), *Schizophrenia: Challenging the Orthodox* (pp. 81–90). New York: Taylor and Francis.

Schultze-Lutter, F., Ruhrmann, S. & Klosterkötter, J. (in press). Can schizophrenia be predicted phenomenologically? In J.O. Johannessen, B. Martindale & J. Cullberg (Eds), *Evolving Psychosis. Different Stages, Different Treatments*. Brunner-Routledge, UK.

Sirey, J., Bruce, M.L., Alexopoulos, G.S., Perlick, D.A., Freidman, S.J. & Meyers, B.S. (2001a). Stigma as a barrier to recovery: Perceived stigma and patient rated severity of illness as predictors of antidepressant drug adherence. *Psychiatric Services*, **52**, 1615–1620.

Sirey, J.A., Bruce, M.L., Alexopoulos, G.S., Perlick, D.A., Friedman, S.J. & Meyers, B.S. (2001b). Stigma as a barrier to recovery: perceived stigma and patient-rated severity of illness as predictors of antidepressant drug adherence. *Psychiatric Services*, **52**, 1615–1620.

Svensson, B. & Hansson, L. (1999). The therapeutic alliance in cognitive therapy for schizophrenic and other long-term mentally ill patients: Development and relationship to outcome in an in-patient treatment programme. *Acta Psychiatrica Scandinavica*, **99**, 281–287.

Tsang, H.W., Tam, P.K., Chan, F. & Cheung, W.M. (2003). Sources of burdens on families of individuals with mental illness. *International Journal of Rehabilitation Research*, **26**, 123–130.

Wahl, O.F. (1995). *Media Madness: Public Images of Mental Illness*. New Brunswick, NJ: Rutgers University Press.

Wahl, O.F. (2002). Children's view of mental illness: A review of the literature. *Psychiatric Rehabilitation Skills*, **6**, 134–158.

Yung, A.R. & McGorry, P.D. (1996). The prodromal phase of first-episode psychosis: past and current conceptualizations. *Schizophrenia Bulletin*, **22**, 353–370.

Yung, A.R., McGorry, P.D., McFarlane, C.A., Patton, G.C. & Rakkar, A. (1996). Monitoring and care of young people at incipient risk of psychosis. *Schizophrenia Bulletin*, **22**, 283–303.

Yung, A.R., Phillips, L.J., Yuen, H.P., Francey, S.M., McFarlane, C.A., Hallgren, M. et al. (2003). Psychosis prediction: 12-month follow-up of a high-risk ("prodromal") group. *Schizophrenia Research*, **60**, 21–32.

CHAPTER 5

Assessing and Managing Stress

Lisa Phillips

Stress is commonly implicated in the onset and maintenance of psychotic disorders such as schizophrenia. The stress–vulnerability model, developed by Zubin and Spring (1977), suggests that the experience of stress is essential to the onset of acute psychosis. According to the model, an endogenous, organic diathesis or vulnerability interacts with internal or external stressors in the development of psychotic disorders. Zubin and Spring (1977) stated, 'each of us is endowed with a degree of vulnerability that, under suitable circumstances, will express itself in an episode of schizophrenic illness' (p. 109). The stress–vulnerability model of psychosis has a high degree of 'face validity': it makes intuitive sense that stressful experiences that are not well managed and result in distress and anxiety might induce the expression of psychotic symptoms in individuals with a pre-existing heightened vulnerability. The model also provides a possible explanation for some of the otherwise unexplained aspects of psychosis, such as the episodic nature of the illness. Importantly, the stress–vulnerability model opens possibilities for preventive intervention and treatment of symptoms, particularly through psychological strategies that enhance stress management and coping. This contrasts with the Kraepelinian view of psychosis causing progressive functional and intellectual deterioration with no possible return to premorbid levels and the accompanying nihilistic view of treatment.

In this chapter, research investigating the relationship between stress, coping and onset of psychosis is reviewed. It will be argued that although research investigating this relationship is plagued by poor methodology, and research with individuals at ultra high risk (UHR) of psychosis is only now beginning, there is a role for addressing the experience of stress and coping when providing treatment for the UHR group.

THE RELATIONSHIP BETWEEN STRESS AND ESTABLISHED PSYCHOTIC DISORDERS

The experience of stress by individuals with established psychotic disorders has been investigated for many years. By far the most common way of measuring stress in relation to psychosis is the 'life events' approach. The life events approach to quantifying stress relies

Working with People at High Risk of Developing Psychosis: A Treatment Handbook.
Edited by J. Addington, S.M. Francey and A.P. Morrison. © 2006 John Wiley & Sons, Ltd.

on the assumption that events such as the death of a loved one, moving house, illness of a pet, and so forth, are associated with a period of adaptation, and, often, even if the event is ultimately a positive one, a degree of distress.

Life events could impact on the development of psychotic disorders in at least two ways. First, stressful events might be necessary but not sufficient on their own to result in an episode of illness (Day et al., 1987). The second possibility is that life events 'trigger' the onset of a psychosis. According to this model, the psychosis would have occurred in any event but the experience of sufficient life stressors brings the onset of the disorder forward in time (Day et al., 1987). In this case, stress associated with the event is neither a necessary nor sufficient cause of illness.

Retrospective Studies

Most of the studies of the experience of life events by individuals with an established psychotic disorder have been retrospective, in which the experience of events over a specified period of time is explored. The results of these studies have been mixed. Some studies have found an increase in the number of life events experienced prior to the onset of an acute psychotic episode (Bebbington et al., 1993; Brown & Birley, 1968; Canton & Fraccon, 1985; Chaven & Kulhara, 1988; Day et al., 1987; Jacobs & Myers, 1976; Mazure, Quinlan & Bowers, 1997; Michaux, Gansereit, McCabe & Kurland, 1967; Schwartz & Myers, 1977); however, others have not (Chung, Langeluddecke & Tennant, 1986; Gruen & Baron, 1984; Malzacher, Merz & Ebonther, 1981; Ventura, Nuechterlein & Subotnik, 2000). These studies suggest that there is 'reasonably sound' evidence that stressful events precipitate the onset or relapse of a schizophrenia spectrum illness and that such events tend to cluster in the period of time immediately preceding the onset of a psychotic episode. It does not appear that stressful events are sufficient to cause an episode on their own but probably contribute to and possibly coincide with other factors to produce the conditions necessary for episode onset.

Studies that have compared the rate of life events experienced by individuals with psychotic disorders with individuals with another psychiatric diagnosis have also had mixed results. Chung et al. (1986) found no difference in the level of chronic stress between patients with schizophrenia, schizophreniform disorder or hypomania in the six months prior to episode onset or compared to a healthy comparison group. Individuals with schizophrenia report experiencing more life events than individuals with depression (Beck & Worthen, 1972; Clancy, Crowe, Winokur & Morrison, 1973; Dang, Shyam & Kumar, 1998; Jacobs, Prusoff & Paykel, 1974), but it is possible that this difference is a reflection of the reporting style of people who are depressed. Beck and Worthen (1972) suggested that the difference between depressive disorders and schizophrenia highlights the 'private nature of the symbolic processes' (p. 128) of many individuals with schizophrenia. In other words, simply assessing the frequency of stressful events experienced by individuals with schizophrenia is not sufficient to fully understand the relationship with the course of the disorder. The meaning given to events and the individual's appraisal of them may be of crucial importance.

Retrospective studies can be conducted more quickly than prospective or longitudinal studies and are the most common method of evaluating the potential relationship between stressful life events and the onset and course of psychotic disorders. However, there are some shortcomings to this approach, many of which are common to retrospective research in general. The central limitation is the reliance on participants' memory of events. This is relevant for patient groups as well as non-patient participants. Similarly, effort to obtain meaning needs to be considered. Participants might have attributed causality or otherwise unintentionally bias their response in an attempt to understand what has happened to them. This phenomenon is referred to as the telescoping effect, is endemic to retrospective research and is associated with effort after meaning phenomenon: patients tend to recall events as having occurred much closer to onset than is actually true in an attempt to find reasons to explain the onset of their illness (Day et al., 1987).

In addition, there are unique problems associated with the course and nature of psychotic disorders. First, the mental state of patients, particularly those interviewed shortly after hospital admission or contact with psychiatric services when one imagines their symptoms are most florid, is of concern to the validity of results. Being acutely unwell at the time of interview could obviously impact on the responses given. The impact of psychosis on memory and cognitive functioning is well documented (Heinrichs & Zakzanis, 1998) but not well controlled in the studies described above.

Differences in duration of illness among participants with psychotic disorders in these studies might also have had some bearing on results. Many studies failed to clearly indicate whether participants were experiencing a first or later episode of illness. Those studies that compared the life events of first onset patients with relapsing patients have indicated that first episode or early episode patients report a higher number of stressful events and in some cases more 'severe' events in the period of time preceding onset of their most recent episode than participants who have experienced multiple episodes (Canton & Fraccon, 1985; Castine, Meador-Woodruff & Dalack, 1998).

The relationship between frequency of stressful events and duration of illness might be critical to the understanding of the relationship between stress and psychosis. In bipolar disorder it has been shown that a kindling effect exists: higher levels of distress or stress precede the onset of a first manic episode than subsequent episodes (Ambelas, 1987; Dunner, Patrick & Fiee, 1979; Swann et al., 1990). A similar relationship might exist with schizophrenic illnesses (Castine et al., 1998), suggesting that it might be important to assess first episode patients separately from relapsing patients.

Prospective Studies

A number of prospective studies have investigated the relationship between the experience of stressful events and **relapse** of illness. As indicated above, an increase in the number of life events experienced immediately preceding a relapse has been reported in some studies (Canton & Fraccon, 1985; Castine et al., 1998; Pallanti, Quercioli & Pazzagli, 1997; Ventura, Nuechterlein, Lukoff & Hardesty, 1989), but not others (Hardesty, Falloon and Shirin 1985; Hirsch et al., 1996). Studies by McEvoy, Howe and Hogarty (1984), Bartkó, Mayláth & Herczeg, (1987), Ventura, Nuechterlein, Hardesty and Gitlin, (1992), Leff, Hirsch, Gaind, Rhode and Stevens (1973) have indicated that relapse psychotic episodes are more likely to be preceded by an increase in the frequency of stressful life events by individuals who were taking antipsychotic medication than individuals who are not. This suggests that neuroleptic medication 'protects' individuals with a psychotic disorder against everyday stress but additional stressors in the form of one or more life events might result in relapse. In other words, patients taking antipsychotic medication might need to experience higher levels of stress to suffer a relapse. It is noted that Day et al. (1987) stated that conclusions about the 'protective' nature of antipsychotic medication are purely speculative and a study by Hirsch, Cramer and Bowen (1992) found no significant relationship between compliance with antipsychotic medication, exposure to life events and risk of relapse. While the exact nature of the impact antipsychotic medication makes on the relationship between life events and psychosis is unknown, studies should at least make some note of medication use by participants. Unfortunately this has rarely been the case to date.

Only a small number of prospective studies of the potential relationship between stressful life events and psychotic episodes have been conducted. By and large, the criticisms made of the retrospective studies about defining the onset of a psychotic episode and shortcomings in the control groups can also be levelled at these prospective studies. Clearly more studies with a longitudinal design are required.

Life Event Studies – Conclusions and Problems

The relationship between life events and psychosis is not fully understood. For every study that has shown an association between the experience of life events and the onset of a psychotic episode, another has suggested otherwise. A number of methodological problems common to these studies have been outlined: (a) retrospective design, (b) inadequate subject numbers prohibiting generalisation of results, (c) the examination of events over a long time course which may mask the possibility that stressors might impact on symptoms over a much shorter period of time (three to six weeks, for example, compared to a year); and (d) demographic and other differences between control and subject groups influencing the number and type of stressful events that are reported (Hirsch, et al., 1992).

Other criticisms include the enrolment in studies of only individuals for whom the onset of the psychotic episode that is being evaluated can be clearly dated and the focus only on individuals with schizophrenia. This limits the generalisability of results. Additionally, most studies have focused exclusively on independent life events. A number of studies illustrating that a higher level of dependent events is associated with episode onset suggest that the impact of those events should not be totally ignored (Brown & Birley, 1968; Dohrenwend, 1974; Fontana, Marcus, Noel & Rakusin, 1972; Leff et al., 1973; Michaux et al., 1967). Finally, most studies have focused on the relationship between stressful life events and the experience of positive psychotic symptoms (usually as markers of psychotic episode onset). Some reviewers have suggested that non-specific symptoms associated with psychosis, such as depression and sleep disturbance, may be more influenced by stressors than first rank symptoms (Hardesty et al., 1985; Norman & Malla, 1991), although Fenton and McGlashan (1994) suggested the opposite.

Other Types of Stress

Norman and Malla (1993) suggested that individuals with schizophrenia are more likely to be adversely affected by chronic difficulties and stressors experienced in comparatively normal circumstances than by more unusual major life changes and challenges. They demonstrated that the level of distress reported by individuals with schizophrenia was significantly correlated with the number of minor stressors experienced, but not with the number of life events (Norman & Malla, 1991). Beck and Worthen (1972) reported that individuals with schizophrenia are likely to attribute symptom exacerbation to stressors of 'low severity'.

Norman and Malla have conducted a number of studies investigating the role of minor stressors in the course of schizophrenia. In the first study they reported that over the course of a year individuals with schizophrenia who experienced a relapse reported more major and minor stressful events than non-relapsing patients (Malla, Cortese, Shaw & Ginsberg, 1990). No significant differences were found between the groups when major and minor events were considered separately but small subject numbers might have influenced this result. In a second study, they evaluated the longitudinal relationship between symptomatology and daily stressors or hassles (Norman & Malla, 1994). The experience of hassles was an independent predictor of depression, somatic concerns, anxiety and positive psychotic symptoms (particularly reality distortion) over and above the influence of prior level of symptoms. Finally, they reported that hassles and distress were more consistent correlates of symptoms than life events, which were significantly correlated only with positive psychotic symptoms and anxiety (Malla & Norman, 1992).

A novel approach to assess the potential relationship between daily life stress and level of reactivity for individuals with psychosis has been employed by Myin-Germeys, van Os, Schwartz, Stone and Delespaul (2001). In this *in vivo* study, 42 patients with a psychotic disorder, 47 of their first-degree relatives and 49 control subjects recorded their activities, thoughts, mood and appraisals of the current situation at 10 time points over six consecutive days. Positive and negative aspects of mood were rated as well as four different stress variables: event-related stress, activity-related stress, thought-related stress and social stress. No differences were found between relatives or controls on any of the four stress measures. The patient group scored significantly higher than the control group on the event-related stress measure and higher on the social stress measure than both other groups. The patient group also reported significantly higher levels of both negative and positive mood than both other groups who did not differ from one another. The four stress variables were all significantly associated with mood: an increase in subjective stress was associated with an increase in negative affect and a decrease in positive affect in all groups. Different patterns of stress reactions were noted, however. The patients with psychosis recorded more intense emotional reactions to stress than the control subjects. Their family members responded to stress with a decrease in positive mood that was similar to that of the patient group but an increase in negative mood that was intermediary to the patient and control groups.

Myin-Germeys and colleagues concluded that daily life stress and mood is related in a dose-response fashion with level of genetic or familial risk of psychosis. They stated that stress reactivity could be viewed as a vulnerability marker for psychosis but as the study was cross-sectional, this possibility has not been evaluated. They also conceded that the differences seen in stress reactivity between the groups could be associated with different environmental and social circumstances. For example, many studies have shown that patients with psychosis report lower levels of social support than others. Furthermore, a lack of social support has been associated with increased emotional reactivity towards daily stressors. Alternatively, patients with psychotic disorders are more sensitive to environmental stress and therefore would be more likely to report higher levels of stress in a given situation.

Studies of expressed emotion (EE) have indicated that individuals with schizophrenia who are discharged from hospital to a high EE environment have a higher risk of relapse than those who live in a low EE environment (Bachman et al., 2002). If living within a high EE environment is regarded as an environmental stressor, EE fits well within the stress–vulnerability model of schizophrenia and psychosis (Gleeson, Jackson, Stavely &

Burnett, 1999). Complex models have been developed to explain the interaction between the individual and the level of EE in their environment in more detail (Nuechterlein, 1987; Nuechterlein et al., 1994).

In quasi-experimental studies all participants are exposed to the same stressful event. The earliest example of such a study indicated a six-fold increase in hospitalisation rates for schizophrenia among US soldiers during the first year of military service compared to the second year (Steinberg & Durrell, 1968). Increased hospital admission rates during the first year were not due to a pre-existing illness and prodromal symptoms did not influence the decision to join the army. Although it was recognised that the men who developed schizophrenia might have developed the disorder even if they had not joined up, the authors of the study concluded that: emotional stress associated with the necessity of making a social adaptation was effective in inducing schizophrenic symptoms (p. 1102). In other words they concluded that the stress associated with joining the army and commencing army training was not sufficient to **trigger** a psychotic episode.

Other quasi-experimental studies have indicated that stress associated with combat can precipitate the onset of psychosis (Paster, 1948; Wagner, 1946). Tennant (1985), however, noted that the onset of psychosis following exposure to warfare is quite rare and such episodes are brief. Migration is another situation that provides an opportunity to assess the relationship between stress and schizophrenia although results from such studies have been mixed (Tennant, 1985). The main difficulty with these studies is that it is possible that individuals who are predisposed to develop schizophrenia or are in the prodromal phase are more likely to migrate.

CONCLUSION

Despite over 40 years of research, the relationship between the experience of stress and the onset and course of psychotic disorders remains unclear. Although some studies have demonstrated an apparent association between the experience of stressful events and the onset of a psychotic episode or increase in psychotic symptomatology, others have failed to demonstrate this association.

Most importantly, investigations of the relationship between stress and psychosis have not taken into consideration the individuals' appraisal of stressors. Appraisal is a pivotal process in determining the impact of stressful experiences on an individual (Folkman, Lazarus, Dunkel-Schetter, DeLongis & Gruen, 1986). Norman and Malla (1993, p. 168) stated the meaning of some events to a patient, and therefore the level of stress engendered by them, is likely to be lost on anyone who is not familiar to his/her circumstances. Zubin and Spring (1977) agreed: 'It is doubtful that all response systems will be identically affected by any stressful event' (p. 111). Research investigating the potential relationship between stress and psychotic disorders has not yet examined the experience of stressors in this broader way.

COPING AND ESTABLISHED PSYCHOTIC DISORDERS

Although the experience of stressful events is highlighted in the stress–vulnerability model of schizophrenia, the reaction and response to stressors might also be important in determining the onset and course of illness. Wiedl and Schottner (1991) stated that the degree of effective coping with stressors might significantly affect processes that contribute to the illness course. Successful coping might be integral to the processes of 'integration' that is important in recovery from psychotic illness (McGlashan, Levy & Carpenter, 1975). Studies of coping strategies utilised by individuals with psychotic disorders have focused either on coping with symptoms or coping with other stressors such as life events and hassles.

Coping with Psychotic Symptoms

Individuals with established psychotic disorders utilise a range of task- and emotion-focused strategies to cope with symptoms (Boschi et al., 2000; Breier & Strauss, 1983; Bulnes, Valdes, Aragon & Fernandez, 1997; Carr, 1988; Cohen & Berk, 1985; Dittmann & Schlutter, 1990; Farhall & Gehrke, 1997; Kumar, Thara & Rajkumar, 1989; Lee, Lieh-Mak, Yu & Spinks, 1993; McNally & Goldberg, 1997; Rudnick, 2001; Thurm & Häfner, 1987; Yanos, 2001). The effectiveness of the strategies used by patients to cope with psychotic symptoms has not really been assessed. Tarrier (1987) reported that people with schizophrenia perceived that almost 25% of the strategies they employed to cope with their symptoms were ineffective and Takai, Uematsu, Kaiya, Inoue and Ueki (1990) suggested that individuals with more severe symptoms were more likely to report that they were unable to find a satisfactory way of coping with them. Tarrier (1987) reported that patients who coped best with their symptoms used multiple coping strategies, whilst Falloon and Talbot (1981) reported that individuals who relied on a limited number of strategies were more confident in their efficacy.

Lee and colleagues (1993) attempted to assess the relationship between strategies used to cope with symptoms and clinical outcome. Positive social functioning was associated with cognitive coping strategies, stress reduction, efforts at self-improvement and hospital admission; good quality of life was associated with positive work performance, stress reduction and self-improvement; and symptom improvement was associated with psychotropic medication and self-improvement. The authors suggest that these results indicate that successful outcome depends on a range of coping strategies and treatment approaches being available.

Kanas and Barr (1984) hypothesised that patients learn successful coping techniques over time through trial and error. Thurm and Häfner (1987) found that the longer an individual had been unwell, the more strategies they used to cope with symptoms, but 'paradoxically' the more relapses experienced, the fewer strategies were used. It is not known whether employing fewer coping strategies leads to more relapses or whether more relapses lead to a feeling of helplessness and discouragement. Other studies that have compared coping strategies with different durations of illness have had mixed results. Whilst Wiedl and Schottner (1991) reported that people with schizophrenia with fewer hospital admissions were more likely to use problem-focused coping, Takai et al. (1990) found that people who had spent less time in hospital were more likely to use emotion-focused coping. Cohen and Berk (1985), however, failed to find an association at all between the type of coping strategies used and the likelihood of having been hospitalised in the previous 18 months. Takai et al. (1990) reported that individuals with a later onset of illness utilised more coping strategies, but Falloon and Talbot (1981) failed to find a difference between the type of coping used by people with an early versus late onset of illness or between those with recent versus prolonged illness.

In summary, the investigations described above have revealed that a wide range of strategies is employed by individuals with psychotic disorders to cope with their symptoms. Most studies indicated that individuals had a number of strategies they implemented at different times, depending on the type of symptoms they were experiencing (Böker, Brenner & Wurgler, 1989) and the level of distress associated with them (Aldwin & Revenson, 1987; Nayani & David, 1996; Vitaliano, Maiuro, Russo & Becker, 1987), although the focus in these studies is only on positive and negative symptoms. Importantly, these studies indicate that patients with psychosis do not see themselves as 'passive victims' of their illness but believe that they can influence its course. Unfortunately most studies have been cross-sectional with small sample sizes.

General Coping

It is not surprising that Wiedl (1992) reported that the causes of distress for patients with psychotic disorders extend beyond their symptoms to aspects of personal and interpersonal functioning. What is surprising is that there has been limited research addressing how individuals with psychotic disorders cope with more generalised stressors, particularly in light of the large body of research reviewed earlier that has investigated those sources of distress and anxiety. Little is known about the way people with a psychotic illness cope with ambient tensions, daily hassles and stressful life events and how coping with these might influence the onset or course of illness.

Those studies that have been conducted have revealed that individuals with psychotic disorders utilise a range of strategies to cope with general stressors compared to healthy comparison or other diagnostic groups. Brenner, Böker, Muller, Spichtig and Wurgler (1987) reported that people with schizophrenia were **more** likely to use problem-focused coping strategies than a clinical comparison group of people with a 'neurotic' illness and a healthy control group, yet van den Bosch, van Asma, Rambouts and Louwerens (1992) reported that patients were significantly **less** likely to use problem solving and more likely to report depressive reaction to stress than healthy controls. Additionally, they reported that patients with schizophrenia were more likely to report using avoidance than the healthy comparison group.

Jansen, Gispen-de Wied and Kahn (1999) assessed the coping styles in different situations of patients with schizophrenia and healthy comparison subjects. Globally, the patient group reported using significantly less active coping techniques and sought social support less than the comparison group but employed avoidance and passive coping more. When presented with a fictional non-social situation (being stuck in traffic), the patient group reported that they would use significantly more confrontational coping, seeking social support and accepting responsibility, whilst in a fictional social situation (an argument with a friend) they said they would use more distancing, escape/avoidance and planful problem solving than the comparison group.

Two studies have specifically investigated the general coping strategies used by individuals with recent onset psychotic disorders. Ventura et al. (2000) reported that a control group was more likely to report using cognitively- and behaviourally oriented coping strategies than a first episode psychosis group but there was no difference in the tendency to use avoidance coping techniques. High levels of self-efficacy and the experience of stressors rated as distressing were associated with the use of active problem-focused coping techniques by the patient group.

MacDonald, Pica, McDonald, Hayes and Baglioni (1998) reported that young people with a recent onset psychotic disorder perceived that they coped less well with stressors than age- and gender-matched healthy controls. Those patients who reported symptom related distress coped by internalising, seeking social support and distraction. Those experiencing stress associated with social relationships reported using problem-solving, seeking social support and internalising. Finally the patients experiencing stress associated with everyday functioning reported using internalising and seeking social support. This study demonstrated that coping strategies vary depending on the type of stressor experienced.

No studies have investigated whether the general coping strategies used by individuals with psychotic disorders change over time as the illness progresses, even though it has been shown that strategies used to cope with symptoms change with illness duration. Thus, the only conclusion that can be drawn from the few studies assessing coping strategies of individuals with psychotic disorders is that individuals generally have a range of coping strategies that they employ depending on the type of stressor that is experienced. Whether the type of strategy changes over time as illness progresses and with recovery is yet to be determined. These studies have focused on the coping strategies of individuals with schizophrenia: research focusing on strategies used by individuals with other psychotic disorders is yet to take place. Prospective studies are also required – none have been conducted to date.

CONCLUSION

It is premature to make any firm conclusions about coping strategies used by individuals with psychotic disorders to cope with either general stressors or with the symptoms of their illness. Although it has consistently been reported that individuals with psychotic disorders utilise different coping strategies – particularly more emotion-focused coping – than healthy comparison groups, little is known about differences in strategies used by individuals with schizophrenia compared to individuals with other psychotic disorders or whether a relationship exists between coping style and the onset, course and likelihood of recovery from a psychotic disorder.

STRESS AND COPING BY YOUNG PEOPLE AT HEIGHTENED RISK OF PSYCHOSIS

Although the relationship between the experience of stress, coping and the onset of acute psychosis has now been investigated for many years, there is no compelling evidence of such an association. Further, it is unknown whether (a) the potential relationship between stress and psychosis is a simple linear one and the quality and meaning of stressful experiences are unimportant, (b) the probability of experiencing psychotic symptoms increases as more undesirable or threatening events are experienced or (c) particular types of stressful events need to be experienced to promote the development of psychotic symptoms. To fully investigate the relationship between the experience of stress and the onset of psychotic disorders, longitudinal studies need to be undertaken with UHR cohorts. In this section, the few published studies in this area will be reviewed and preliminary results will be presented from an ongoing study.

Previously Published Research

Only one study has been published that has investigated the degree of stress experienced by UHR subjects. Miller et al. (2001) reported that the number of life events experienced prior to recruitment to the Edinburgh High Risk Project was associated with the level of psychotic symptoms reported at baseline in both the UHR and comparison groups and there were no differences between the groups in the number of events experienced. The experience of 'intermediate' or 'minor' stressors was not associated with symptom levels. Although psychotic symptoms were associated with the experience of life stressors it is not possible to make any conclusions about direction of the association because symptom onset dates were not recorded. The independence of stressful events from symptoms was also not recorded. The finding that only major stressors influenced the experience of psychotic symptoms suggests that seriously upsetting events are required to trigger psychotic symptoms and that the aggregation of several smaller events did not appear to be sufficient. This possibility has not yet been further investigated. Similarly, the association between the experience of stress and the development of a psychotic disorder in the UHR group has not yet been reported. Hopefully research exploring this association is forthcoming.

No studies have assessed strategies used by individuals at heightened risk of psychosis in coping with their symptoms and changed functioning. Lewin et al. (2001) in Newcastle, Australia, compared the strategies used to cope with general stressors by 'at risk' (experiencing sub-threshold psychotic symptoms or had a first- or second-degree relative with a psychotic disorder), first episode psychosis and established schizophrenia groups. In this cross-sectional study, the 'at risk' group used less adaptive coping and had fewer social supports than those participants with either first episode or established schizophrenia. There was an increase in adaptive coping and level of support seeking as the 'level of schizophrenia' increased across the groups (i.e. from at risk to first episode to established schizophrenia). This suggests that the strategies used to cope with general stressors change as psychotic disorders progress. Only a prospective study can assess this possibility fully. To date there have been no published reports on the role coping might play in the onset of psychosis in an UHR group.

One study was found that attempted to assess the contributions of stress, coping and social support by individuals thought to be at heightened risk for developing schizophrenia. In this study, Schuldberg, Karwacki and Burns (1996) divided a cohort of 'non-clinical' undergraduate psychology students into three groups according to responses to the 'psychosis-proneness' scales developed by Chapman and colleagues (Chapman & Chapman, 1980; Chapman, Chapman, Kwapil, Eckblad & Zinser, 1994). The Per-Mag group reported experiencing sub-threshold perceptual abnormalities and/or magical thinking. The anhedonic group reported an inability to perceive pleasure thought to be indicative of sub-clinical negative symptoms. There was also a comparison group who did not score highly on any of the psychosis-proneness scales.

The anhedonic individuals experienced a greater number of hassles in the month prior to answering the questionnaire than the other groups. Per-Mag individuals were more likely than control subjects to rate stressful academic events as ones they could change but anhedonic subjects were less likely than control subjects to perceive academic events in this light. These differences were not significant, however. Thus there were only minor differences in the stressful experiences of the three groups. Strategies used to cope with everyday experiences were compared between the groups. Per-Mag subjects reported using 'accepting responsibility' for events and using 'escape-avoidance' more than the anhedonia or control groups. The anhedonia group reported using positive reappraisal more than the other groups.

Although this study is commended for attempting to extend the boundaries of previous research, it too is beset with many shortcomings. First, all participants were drawn from a university population. This has obvious implications on the ability to extend results of this study to the wider population. Second, the method through which the UHR (psychosis prone) individuals are identified is problematic. Only the Per-Mag scale has been associated with transition to psychosis over a 10-year period (Chapman et al., 1994) and it could be argued that the Chapman scales assess aspects of personality rather than psychosis-proneness. The rate of transition to psychosis in the cohort is not reported in any case. Therefore the results of this study may, in fact, not have any bearing on any relationship between stress and psychosis. In conclusion, previous work that has attempted to assess the experience of stress and coping by individuals at high risk of developing psychosis have indicated that the UHR individuals possibly experience higher levels of stressors than comparison groups and utilise different coping strategies.

Personal Assessment and Crisis Evaluation (PACE) Clinic Study

A study based at the PACE Clinic in Melbourne, Australia, has attempted to provide more information about the experiences of stress and coping by young people at heightened risk of psychosis. The study has a longitudinal design but only preliminary cross-sectional results can be reported so far.

The experiences of stress and coping over a 12-month period of young people who met PACE Clinic intake criteria (Phillips et al., 2002; Yung, Phillips & McGorry, 2004) were compared with the experiences of a healthy comparison group. Demographic characteristics of the two groups are shown in Table 5.1.

The PACE group were significantly younger than the comparison group, were less likely to be married or in a *de facto* relationship and had spent fewer years in formal education. In line with the age difference between the groups, more members of the PACE group were enrolled in secondary education at the time of entry into the study whilst more members of the comparison group had either completed or were currently enrolled in some form of tertiary education. Members of the PACE group were more likely to be living with family (in most cases their parents) at the time of entry into the study than the comparison group. A high percentage of the comparison group was living in a residential college for tertiary students (38%). The majority of members of both groups were born in Australia, as were their parents. To further characterise the groups, levels of psychopathology according to the Brief Psychiatric Rating Scale (BPRS: Overall & Gorham, 1962), Scale for the Assessment of Negative Symptoms (SANS: Andreasen, 1982) and Global Assessment of Functioning (GAF: APA, 1994) at intake are shown in Table 5.2. The PACE group had significantly higher levels of general psychopathology (BPRS – total score), positive psychotic symptoms (BPRS – psychotic subscale), negative psychotic symptoms (SANS score) and significantly lower levels of global functioning (GAF) than the comparison group.

A range of measures of stress and coping were administered to both groups. Although only baseline comparisons can be reported at present, eventually longitudinal comparisons will be performed. The relationship between the stress and coping measures and onset of

Table 5.1 Descriptive information for the PACE and healthy comparison groups

Variable	PACE (n = 141)	Comparison (n = 32)	χ^2	p-value
% male	45.39	43.75	0.028	0.866
% never married	96.45	87.50	4.240	0.039
Occupation (%)			40.03	0.000
secondary student	47.90	0.00		
tertiary student	16.90	59.38		
unemployed	21.10	21.88		
homemaker	2.10	0.00		
unskilled	4.20	0.00		
skilled manual/clerical	5.60	15.63		
admin/minor professional	2.10	3.13		
% born in Australia	81.56	81.25	0.002	0.967
% mother born in Australia	68.79	68.75	0.000	0.996
% father born in Australia	57.45	46.25	0.015	0.902
Living arrangements (%)			82.461	0.000
living with partner/parents/siblings	83.69	9.38		
living with friends	9.93	50.00		
living alone	4.26	3.13		
other	2.13	37.50		

Variable	X	SD	X	SD	t	P-value
Age (years)	18.72	3.16	21.47	3.10	−4.460	0.000
Education (years completed)	12.29	1.99	14.91	1.12	−7.156	0.000

psychosis in the PACE participants who developed acute levels of psychotic symptoms will also be reported at a later stage.

The number of life events experienced by each study participant in the month preceding assessment was recorded using the Life Event Interview Schedule (LEIS: Ventura, unpublished). This is a semi-structured interview that assesses the occurrence of major and minor

Table 5.2 Psychopathology at intake for the PACE and comparison groups

	PACE		Comparison			
	x	sd	x	sd	t	p-value
BPRS	25.92	10.55	2.13	2.30	12.668	0.000
BPRS-psychotic subscale	5.87	3.10	0.28	0.89	10.102	0.000
SANS	31.08	16.04	1.03	1.71	10.558	0.000
GAF	56.45	8.90	81.06	4.08	−15.260	0.000

Note: BPRS psychotic subscale = sum of scores for Suspiciousness, Unusual Thought Content, Hallucinations and Conceptual Disorganisation items.

Table 5.3   LEIS scores for the PACE and comparison groups

	PACE		Comparison			
	x	sd	x	sd	t	p-value
Number of events reported	3.25	1.79	3.63	1.50	−1.09	0.279
Familiarity of events	4.62	2.13	4.47	1.83	0.34	0.734
Degree of control over events	3.29	2.08	4.02	1.95	−1.77	0.079
Degree of advance notice of events	3.26	1.82	4.58	2.30	−3.38	0.001
Amount of time spent thinking about events	4.89	2.12	4.99	1.28	−0.25	0.804
Change in routine due to events	4.39	2.24	4.38	1.21	0.05	0.964
Desirability of events	3.35	1.83	4.04	1.57	−1.93	0.056
Success coping with events	4.93	1.95	6.14	1.44	−3.23	0.002
How upset events made them feel	3.62	1.80	4.62	1.47	−2.87	0.005

life events associated with a wide range of aspects of human functioning: school, family, employment relationships and home, for example. The scale also assesses the individual's appraisal of the relevance of the event to his or her life and provides some indication of coping with the event. Each of the LEIS subscales is measured on a nine-point Likert scale. Results of the LEIS are shown in Table 5.3. The number of events reported by the PACE group did not differ from the number reported by the comparison group. However, there were significant differences between the groups in their perception of the events they experienced. There were no differences between the groups in the degree of familiarity of the events they experienced, the amount of time they spent thinking about the events or the degree of change in routine the events caused. The PACE group reported having significantly less advance notice of events occurring and perceived that they coped with events less well than the comparison group. Further, they experienced events that were less desirable than those experienced by the comparison group and were significantly more upset by events than the comparison group were.

The experience of minor stressful events or 'hassles' was assessed using the Hassles Scale (Kanner, Coyne, Scharfer & Lazarus, 1981). Although the PACE and comparison groups reported experiencing comparable numbers of hassles in the month prior to interview, the PACE group indicated higher levels of distress associated with the hassles they experienced – both associated with individual hassles and cumulatively (Table 5.4).

The level of distress experienced by the two groups was assessed using the Perceived Stress Scale (PSS: Cohen, Kamarck & Mermelstein, 1983). In accordance with the results

Table 5.4   Hassles Scale scores for the PACE and comparison groups

	PACE		Comparison			
	x	sd	x	sd	t	p-value
Number of hassles reported	41.93	22.11	38.16	17.61	0.89	0.374
Cumulated distress associated with hassles	73.64	40.35	53.50	28.55	2.65	0.009
Distress associated with individual hassles	1.77	0.41	1.36	0.23	5.39	0.000

Table 5.5 PSS scores for the PACE and comparison groups

| | PACE | | Comparison | | | |
	x	sd	x	sd	t	p-value
Global level of distress	32.78	8.51	22.06	7.47	6.47	0.000
General distress	17.56	5.47	10.78	4.65	6.41	0.000
Perceived ability to cope	8.48	3.32	5.78	2.41	4.29	0.000

reported above, the PACE group reported significantly higher levels of general distress than the comparison group (Table 5.5). The PSS divides general distress into General distress and Perceived ability to cope. The PACE group reported significantly higher scores on these two factors.

Finally, the Coping Inventory for Stressful Situations (CISS: Endler & Parker, 1990) was used to assess the types of coping strategies the PACE and comparison groups reported using in response to stressful events (Table 5.6). The CISS has three scales: Task-focused coping, Emotion-focused coping and Avoidance. Avoidance is further divided into Distraction and Social diversion. Whilst the PACE group was more likely to utilise emotion-focused coping strategies, the comparison group was more likely to utilise task-focused strategies. There was a significant difference between the groups in the use of avoidance strategies, with the PACE group more likely to utilise avoidance overall. It appears that this difference was due to the comparison group being more likely to utilise social diversion than the PACE group (there was no difference between the groups in the use of distraction).

This comparison of stress and coping between a group of young people at high risk of developing a psychosis and a healthy comparison group did not indicate significant differences between the groups in the level of stressful events they experienced. It did indicate that the members of the groups perceive those stressors differently and respond to them differently. In particular, the PACE group reported feeling more distressed and less able to cope with stressors than the comparison group. The PACE group were also more likely to respond to stressors emotionally whilst the comparison group were more likely to utilise task-oriented coping strategies.

As indicated earlier, the aim of this study is to determine if stress and coping contribute to the onset of acute psychosis in the UHR cohort. These preliminary results provide some insight into the difficulties experienced by young people who are possibly experiencing the early onset phase of a psychotic disorder.

Table 5.6 CISS scores for the PACE and comparison groups

| | PACE | | Comparison | | | |
	x	sd	x	sd	t	p-value
Task-focused coping	41.38	13.50	52.69	11.26	−4.34	0.000
Emotion-focused coping	50.93	12.15	31.38	9.33	8.44	0.000
Avoidance	42.04	10.80	46.16	7.88	−2.01	0.046
Distraction	20.47	6.28	19.09	5.01	1.15	0.254
Social diversion	14.41	4.97	18.25	3.56	−4.09	0.000

STRESS MANAGEMENT IN THE UHR GROUP

Although the results of the PACE study do not yet provide any information about how stress and coping might contribute to the onset of psychosis, they do indicate that young people attending the PACE Clinic are experiencing more difficulties responding to stressors that they might experience compared to healthy young people. It is likely that the level of distress experienced by the PACE group influences the level of psychiatric symptomatology they experience.

Stress management has been an integral component of the psychological treatment that has been developed at the PACE Clinic for young people who are identified as being at heightened risk of developing psychosis. The treatment provided at PACE is primarily cognitive-behavioural in orientation following the success demonstrated with this approach in the treatment of people with both first episode and established psychotic disorders (Drury, Birchwood, Cochrane & MacMillan, 1996; Kuipers et al., 1997; Lewis et al., 2001; Sensky et al., 2000). The underlying goal of the specific psychological treatment offered at the PACE Clinic to young people identified as being at UHR of psychosis is to strengthen the individual's coping resources, thereby reducing their vulnerability to developing further, or more severe, symptoms. This may ultimately avert the onset of an acute psychotic episode. It is thought that the elements of the treatment provided at PACE can be applied in other clinics where this client group is seen.

The stress–vulnerability model of psychosis is the backbone of the psychological treatment provided at PACE. Therefore, strategies for managing stress and the individual's coping response are a core component of the treatment. This implies that the implementation of appropriate coping strategies may ameliorate the influence of vulnerability (Böker et al., 1989). As indicated earlier, further research is required to support this assumption.

The full psychological intervention developed at the PACE Clinic has been described in detail elsewhere (Phillips & Francey, 2004). With respect to managing stress and enhancing coping, the treatment has two foci. The first is the provision of case management. This is the provision of practical assistance to deal with issues that can alleviate distress such as finding housing, arranging social security payments, enrolling in school, applying for employment and so forth. This level of assistance has been found to be essential when working with PACE clients due to their high level of need in these practical areas. It has also been found that neglecting difficulties in more fundamental aspects of daily living may impact on the efficacy of the other components of therapy that are provided to clients, in addition to raising the level of distress they experience.

The psychological treatment provided at PACE also includes more traditional stress management techniques, including relaxation training, education about stress and coping, and more specific cognitive strategies (Bernstein & Borkovec, 1973; Clark, 1989; Clark, Salkovskis & Chalkley, 1985; Liberman, King, De Risi & McCann,1975; Ost, 1987). These strategies educate the client to recognise and monitor their own stress levels, to develop an understanding of precipitants to distress, to recognise associated physiological and behavioural correlates of stress and to develop appropriate strategies for coping with stressful events. Strategies include:

• Psychoeducation about the nature of stress and anxiety. The physical, behavioural and cognitive signs of stress are discussed with the client in detail, drawing upon their personal experiences. The concepts of healthy or adaptive stress compared to unhealthy levels of stress are discussed.

- Stress monitoring. The client is encouraged to monitor levels of stress and distress including recording triggering events or situations as well as consequences or responses. This can assist in the identification of helpful and non-helpful situations and responses.
- Stress management techniques such as relaxation, meditation, exercise, distraction are introduced.
- Maladaptive coping techniques are identified, for example excessive substance use and/or excessive social withdrawal. Psychoeducation is provided, aimed at reducing health damaging behaviours and promoting more adaptive responses to stress.
- Cognitions associated with subjective feelings of stress or heightened anxiety are identified through monitoring.
- Cognitive restructuring is introduced, which counters dysfunctional thoughts (e.g. negative self-talk, irrational ideas) with more positive coping statements (Meichenbaum, 1975), positive reframing and challenging (Beck, Emery & Greenberg, 1985; Beck, Rush, Shaw & Emery, 1979).
- Goal setting and time management are introduced.
- Assertiveness training is provided.
- Problem-solving strategies are discussed.

The psychological treatment provided at the PACE Clinic has not yet been evaluated on its own. An early study found that the psychological treatment in conjunction with low-dose antipsychotic medication was successful in delaying the onset of psychosis in an UHR cohort (McGorry et al., 2002). A study that is currently underway at PACE aims to tease apart the relative impacts of the psychological and pharmacological therapies. It is thought that the inclusion of stress management techniques in the therapy helps to make it more relevant for clients because it has a link to 'real-life'.

CONCLUSION

The experience of stress is commonly thought to play a role in the onset of psychotic disorders. Although a causative or contributory role of stress and coping in the development of psychosis has not yet been clearly demonstrated in research studies, a range of studies has indicated that the level of stress experienced by individuals with established psychotic disorders and their coping responses differ from individuals without a psychotic disorder. More recent research has indicated that young people who are thought to be at heightened risk of developing psychosis do not experience heightened levels of stress compared to others but interpret those stressors differently and cope with them differently than young people who are not experiencing psychological difficulties. This is the rationale for making stress management the centrepiece of the psychological treatment that is provided at the PACE Clinic for the high-risk cohort.

ACKNOWLEDGEMENTS

The author gratefully acknowledges the valued assistance and contributions of the clients and other staff of the PACE Clinic in the development of this chapter. Thanks also to the sponsors and supporters of the PACE Clinic – particularly the National Health and Medical Research Council, Stanley Foundation and Janssen-Cilag Pharmaceuticals.

REFERENCES

Aldwin, C.M. & Revenson T.A. (1987). Does coping help? A reexamination of the relation between coping and mental health. *Journal of Personality and Social Psychology*, **53**, 337–348.

Ambelas, A. (1987). Life events and mania: a special relationship? *British Journal of Psychiatry*, **135**, 15–21.

American Psychiatric Association (1994). *Diagnostic and Statistical Manual of Mental Disorders*. Washington, DC: Author.

Andreasen, N. (1982). Negative symptoms in schizophrenia: definition and reality. *Archives of General Psychiatry*, **39**, 784–788.

Bachman, S., Bottmer, C., Jacob, S., Kronmüller, K., Backenstrass, M., Mundt, C. et al. (2002). Expressed emotion in relatives of first-episode and chronic patient with schizophrenia and major depressive disorder: a comparison. *Psychiatry Research*, **112**, 239–250.

Bartkó, G., Mayláth, E. & Herczeg, I. (1987). Comparative study of schizophrenic patients relapsed on and off medication. *Psychiatry Research*, **22**, 221–227.

Bebbington, P., Wilkins, S., Jones, P., Foerster, A., Murray, R., Toone, B. et al. (1993). Life events and psychosis: Initial results from the Camberwell Collaborative Psychosis Study. *British Journal of Psychiatry*, **162**, 72–79.

Beck, A.T., Emery, G. & Greenberg, R. (1985). *Anxiety Disorders and Phobias: A Cognitive Perspective*. New York: Basic Books.

Beck, A.T., Rush, A.J., Shaw, B.F. & Emery, G. (1979). *Cognitive Therapy of Depression*. New York: Guilford Press.

Beck, J. & Worthen, K. (1972). Precipitating stress, crisis theory and hopitalisation in schizophrenia and depression. *Archives of General Psychiatry*, **26**, 123–129.

Bernstein, D.A. & Borkovec, T.D. (1973). *Progressive Relaxation Training: A Manual for the Health Professionals*. Champaign, IL: Research Press.

Böker, W., Brenner, H.D. & Wuergler, S. (1989). Vulnerability-linked deficiencies, psychopathology and coping behaviour of schizophrenics and their relatives. *British Journal of Psychiatry*, **155** (Suppl. 5), 128–135.

Boschi, S., Adams, R.E., Bromet, E.J., Lavelle, J.E., Everett, E. & Galambos, N. (2000). Coping with psychotic symptoms in the early phases of schizophrenia. *American Journal of Orthopsychiatry*, **70**, 242–252.

Breier, A. & Strauss, J.S. (1983). Self-control in psychotic disorders. *Archives of General Psychiatry*, **40**, 1141–1145.

Brenner, H.D., Böker, W., Muller, J., Spichtig, L. & Wurgler, S. (1987). On autoprotective efforts of schizophrenics, neurotics and controls. *Acta Psychiatrica Scandinavica*, **75**, 405–414.

Brown, G. & Birley, J. (1968). Crises and life changes and the onset of schizophrenia. *Journal of Health and Social Behaviour*, **9**, 203–214.

Bulnes, N.J., Valdes, A.J., Aragon, M.L.V. & Fernandez, M.N.L. (1997). Psychopathological verbal expression of self-perceived stress in three groups of psychotic patients. *Psychopathology*, **30**, 39–48.

Canton, G. & Fraccon, I.G. (1985). Life events and schizophrenia: a replication. *Acta Psychiatrica Scandinavica*, **71**, 211–216.

Carr, V. (1988). Patients' techniques for coping with schizophrenia: an exploratory study. *British Journal of Medical Psychology*, **61**, 339–352.

Castine, M.R., Meador-Woodruff, J.H. & Dalack, G.W. (1998). The role of life events in onset and recurrent episodes of schizophrenia and schizoaffective disorder. *Journal of Psychiatric Research*, **32**, 283–288.

Chapman, L.J. & Chapman, J.P. (1980). Scales for rating psychotic and psychotic-like experiences as continua. *Schizophrenia Bulletin*, **6**, 476–489.

Chapman, L.J., Chapman, J.P., Kwapil, T.R., Eckblad, M.E. & Zinser, M.C. (1994). Putatively psychosis-prone subjects ten years later. *Journal of Abnormal Psychology*, **103**, 171–183.

Chaven, B.S. & Kulhara, P. (1988). A clinical study of reactive psychosis. *Acta Psychiatrica Scandinavica*, **78**, 712–715.

Chung, R.K., Langeluddecke, P. & Tennant, C. (1986). Threatening life events in the onset of schizophrenia, schizophreniform psychosis and hypomania. *British Journal of Psychiatry*, **148**, 680–685.

Clancy, J., Crowe, R., Winokur, G. & Morrison, J. (1973). The Iowa 500: Precipitating factors in schizophrenia and primary affective disorder. *Comprehensive Psychiatry*, **14**, 197–202.

Clark, D.M. (1989). Anxiety states: Panic and generalized anxiety. In K. Hawton, P.M. Salkovskis, J. Krik & D.M. Clark (Eds), *Cognitive Behaviour Therapy for Psychiatric Problems: A Practical Guide* (pp. 52–96). Oxford: Oxford University Press.

Clark, D.M., Salkovskis, P.M. & Chalkley, A.J. (1985). Respiratory control as a treatment for panic attacks. *Journal of Behaviour Therapy and Experimental Psychology*, **16**, 23–30.

Cohen, C.I. & Berk, L.A. (1985). Personal coping styles of schizophrenic outpatients. *Hospital and Community Psychiatry*, **36**, 407–410.

Cohen, S., Kamarck, T. & Mermelstein, R. (1983). A global measure of perceived stress. *Journal of Health and Social Behaviour*, **24**, 385–396.

Dang, R., Shyam, R. & Kumar, P. (1998). A comparative study of life events in unipolar depression and schizophrenia. *Journal of Personality and Clinical Studies*, **14**, 27–30.

Day, R., Nielsen, J.A., Korten, A., Ernberg, G., Dube, K.C., Gebhart, J. et al. (1987). Stressful life events preceding the acute onset of schizophrenia: A cross-national study from the World Health Organisation. *Culture, Medicine and Psychiatry*, **11**, 123–205.

Dittmann, J. & Schlutter, R. (1990). Disease consciousness and coping strategies of patients with schizophrenic psychosis. *Acta Psychiatrica Scandinavica*, **82**, 318–322.

Dohrenwend, B.P. (1974). Problems in defining and sampling the relevant population of stressful life events. In B.P. Dohrenwend & B.S. Dohrenwend (Eds), *Stressful Life Events: Their Nature and Effects* (pp. 1–15). New York: Raven Press.

Drury, V., Birchwood, M., Cochrane, R. & MacMillan, F. (1996). Cognitive therapy and recovery from acute psychosis: a controlled trial. I: Impact on psychotic symptoms. *British Journal of Psychiatry*, **169**, 593–601.

Dunner, D.L., Patrick, V. & Fiee, R.R. (1979). Life events at the onset of bipolar affective disorder. *American Journal of Psychiatry*, **136**, 1194–1198.

Endler, N.S. & Parker, J.D.A. (1990). *Coping Inventory for Stressful Situations (CISS): Manual.* Ontario: Multi-health Systems.

Falloon, I.R.H. & Talbot, R.E. (1981). Persistent auditory hallucinations: coping mechanisms and implications for management. *Psychological Medicine*, **11**, 329–339.

Farhall, J. & Gehrke, M. (1997). Coping with hallucinations: exploring stress and coping framework. *British Journal of Clinical Psychology*, **36**, 259–261.

Fenton, W.S. & McGlashan, T.H. (1994). Antecedents, symptom progression and long-term outcome of the deficit syndrome in schizophrenia. *American Journal of Psychiatry*, **151**, 351–356.

Folkman, S., Lazarus, R.S., Dunkel-Schetter, C., DeLongis, A. & Gruen, R.J. (1986). Dynamics of a stressful encounter: cognitive appraisal, coping and encounter outcomes. *Journal of Personality and Social Psychology*, **50**, 992–1003.

Fontana, A.F., Marcus, J.L., Noel, B. & Rakusin, J.M. (1972). Prehospitalisation coping styles of psychiatric patients: The goal directedness of life events. *Journal of Nervous and Mental Disease*, **155**, 311–331.

Gleeson, J., Jackson, H.J., Stavely, H. & Burnett, P. (1999). Family intervention in early psychosis. In P.D. McGorry & H.J. Jackson (Eds.), *Recognition and Management of Early Psychosis* (pp. 376–406). Cambridge: Cambridge University Press.

Gruen, R. & Baron, M. (1984). Stressful life events and schizophrenia: Relation to illness onset and family history. *Neuropsychobiology*, **12**, 206–208.

Hardesty, J., Falloon, I.R.H. & Shirin, K. (1985). The impact of life events, stress and coping on the morbidity of schizophrenia. In I.R.H. Falloon (Ed.), *Family Management of Schizophrenia* (pp. 137–152). Baltimore: Johns Hopkins University Press.

Heinrichs, R.W. & Zakzanis, K.K. (1998). Neurocognitive deficit in schizophrenia: a quantitative review of the evidence. *Neuropsychology*, **12**, 426–445.

Hirsch, S., Bowen, J., Emmani, J., Cramer, P., Jolley, A., Haw, C. et al. (1996). A one year prospective study of the effects of life events and medication in the aetiology of schizophrenic relapse. *British Journal of Psychiatry*, **168**, 49–56.

Hirsch, S., Cramer, P. & Bowen, J. (1992). The triggering hypothesis of the role of life events in schizophrenia. *British Journal of Psychiatry*, **161**, 84–87.

Jacobs, S. & Myers, J. (1976). Recent life events and acute schizophrenic psychosis: A controlled study. *Journal of Nervous and Mental Disease*, **162**, 75–87.

Jacobs, S.C., Prusoff, B.A. & Paykel, E.S. (1974). Recent life events in schizophrenia and depression. *Psychological Medicine*, **4**, 444–453.

Jansen, L.M.C., Gispen-de Wied, C.C. & Kahn, R.S. (1999, April). *Coping with Stress in Schizophrenia*. Paper presented at the VIIth International Congress on Schizophrenia Research, Santa Fe, NM.

Kanas, N. & Barr, M.A. (1984). Self-control of psychotic productions in schizophrenics. *Archives of General Psychiatry*, **41**, 919–920.

Kanner, A.D., Coyne, J.C., Scharfer, C. & Lazarus, R. (1981). Comparison of two modes of stress measurement: Daily hassles and uplifts vs major life events. *Journal of Behavioural Medicine*, **4**, 1–39.

Kuipers, E., Garety, P., Fowler, D.F., Dunn, G., Bebbington, P., Freeman, D. et al. (1997). London–East Anglia randomised controlled trial of cognitive-behavioural therapy for psychosis. *British Journal of Psychiatry*, **171**, 319–327.

Kumar, S., Thara, R. & Rajkumar, S. (1989). Coping with symptoms of relapse in schizophrenia. *European Archives of Psychiatry and Neurological Science*, **239**, 231–215.

Lee, P.W.H., Lieh-Mak, F., Yu, K.K. & Spinks, J.A. (1993). Coping strategies of schizophrenic patients and their relationship to outcome. *British Journal of Psychiatry*, **163**, 177–182.

Leff, J.P., Hirsch, S.R., Gaind, R., Rhode, P.D. & Stevens, B.C. (1973). Life events and maintenance therapy in schizophrenic relapse. *British Journal of Psychiatry*, **123**, 659–680.

Lewin, T.J., Carr, V.J., Halpin, S., Barnard, R.E., Beckmann, J., Walton, J.M., et al. (2001, April/May). *Coping with Psychosis: Demographic and Dispositional Correlates*. Paper presented at the VIIIth International Congress on Schizophrenia Research, Whistler, BC.

Lewis, S.W., Tarrier, N., Haddock, G., Bentall, R., Kinderman, P., Kingdon, D. et al. (2001). A randomised controlled trial of cognitive behavior therapy in early schizophrenia. *Schizophrenia Research*, **49** (Suppl.), 263.

Liberman, R.P., King, I., De Risi, W.J. & McCann, M. (1975). *Personal Effectiveness*. Champaign, IL: Research Press.

MacDonald, E., Pica, S., McDonald, S., Hayes, R.L. & Baglioni, A.J. (1998). Stress and coping in early psychosis: Role of symptoms, self-efficacy and social support in coping with stress. *British Journal of Psychiatry*, **172** (Suppl. 33), 122–127.

Malla, A.K., Cortese, L., Shaw, T.S. & Ginsberg, B. (1990). Life events and relapse in schizophrenia: a one year prospective study. *Social Psychiatry and Psychiatric Epidemiology*, **25**, 221–224.

Malla, A.K. & Norman, R.M.G. (1992). Relationship of life events and daily stressors to symptomatology in schizophrenia. *Journal of Nervous and Mental Disease*, **180**, 664–667.

Malzacher, M., Merz, J. & Ebonther, D. (1981). Einscheidende lebensereignisse im vorfeld akuter schizophrener episoden. *Archiv für Psychiatrie und Nervenkrankheiten*, **230**, 227–242.

Mazure, C.M., Quinlan, D.M. & Bowers, M.B. (1997). Recent life stressors and biological markers in newly admitted psychotic patients. *Biological Psychiatry*, **41**, 865–870.

McEvoy, J.P., Howe, A.C. & Hogarty, G.E. (1984). Differences in the nature of relapse and subsequent inpatient course between medication-compliant and noncompliant schizophrenic patients. *Journal of Nervous and Mental Disease*, **172**, 412–416.

McGlashan, T.H., Levy, S.T. & Carpenter, W.T. (1975). Integration and sealing over: clinically distinct recovery styles from schizophrenia. *Archives of General Psychiatry*, **32**, 1269–1272.

McGorry, P.D., Yung, A.R., Phillips, L.J., Yuen, H.P., Francey, S., Cosgrave, E.M. et al. (2002). A randomized controlled trial of interventions designed to reduce the risk of progression to first episode psychosis in a clinical sample with subthreshold symptoms. *Archives of General Psychiatry*, **59**, 921–928.

McNally, S.E. & Goldberg, J.O. (1997). Natural cognitive coping strategies in schizophrenia. *British Journal of Medical Psychology*, **70**, 159–167.

Meichenbaum, D.H. (1975). Self-instructional methods. In F.H. Kanfer & A.P. Goldstein (Eds), *Helping People Change: A Textbook of Methods* (pp. 357–391). New York: Pergamon.

Michaux, W.W., Gansereit, K.H., McCabe, O.L. & Kurland, A.A. (1967). Psychopathology and measurement of environmental stress. *Community Mental Health Journal*, **3**, 358–372.

Miller, P., Lawrie, S.M., Hodges, A., Clafferty, R., Cosway, R. & Johnstone, E.C. (2001). Genetic liability, illicit drug use, life stress and psychotic symptoms: preliminary findings from the Edinburgh study of people at high risk for schizophrenia. *Social Psychiatry and Psychiatric Epidemiology*, **36**, 338–342.

Myin-Germeys, I., van Os, J., Schwartz, J.E., Stone, A.A. & Delespaul, P.A. (2001). Emotional reactivity to daily life stress in psychosis. *Archives of General Psychiatry*, **58**, 1137–1144.

Nayani, T.H. & David, A.S. (1996). The auditory hallucination: a phenomenological survey. *Psychological Medicine*, **26**, 177–189.

Norman, R.M.G. & Malla, A.K. (1991). Subjective stress in schizophrenic patients. *Social Psychiatry and Psychiatric Epidemiology*. **26**, 212–216.

Norman, R.M.G. & Malla, A.K. (1993). Stressful life events and schizophrenia. I: a review of the research. *British Journal of Psychiatry*, **162**, 161–166.

Norman, R.M.G. & Malla, A.K. (1994). A prospective study of daily stressors and symptomatology in schizophrenic patients. *Social Psychiatry and Psychiatric Epidemiology*, **29**, 244–249.

Nuechterlein, K.H. (1987). Vulnerability models: state of the art. In H. Häfner, W. Gattaz & W. Jangerik (Eds), *Searches for the Cause of Schizophrenia* (pp. 8–22). Berlin: Springer-Verlag.

Nuechterlein, K.H., Dawson, M.E., Ventura, J., Gitlin, M., Subotnik, K.L., Snyder, K.S. et al. (1994). The vulnerability/stress model of schizophrenic relapse: A longitudinal study. *Acta Psychiatrica Scandinavica*, **89** (Suppl. 382), 58–64.

Ost, L.G. (1987). Applied relaxation: Description of a coping technique and review of controlled studies. *Behaviour Research and Therapy*, **25**, 397–410.

Overall, J.E. & Gorham, D.R. (1962). The Brief Psychiatric Rating Scale. *Psychological Reports*, **10**, 799–812.

Pallanti, S., Quercioli, L. & Pazzagli, A. (1997). Relapse in young paranoid schizophrenic patients: A prospective study of stressful life events, P300 measures and coping. *American Journal of Psychiatry*, **154**, 792–798.

Paster, S.J. (1948). Psychotic reactions among soldiers of World War II. *Journal of Nervous and Mental Disease*, **108**, 54–66.

Phillips, L.J. & Francey, S.M. (2004). Changing PACE: Psychological interventions in the pre-psychotic phase. In P.D. McGorry & J. Gleeson (Eds), *Psychological Interventions in Early Psychosis: A Practical Treatment Handbook* (pp. 23–40). Chichester, UK: Wiley.

Phillips, L.J., Leicester, S.B., O'Dwyer, L.E., Francey, S.M., Koutsogiannis, J., Abdel-Baki, A. et al. (2002). The PACE Clinic: identification and management of young people at 'ultra' high risk of psychosis. *Journal of Psychiatric Practice*, **8**, 255–269.

Rudnick, A. (2001). The impact of coping on the relation between symptoms and quality of life in schizophrenia. *Psychiatry*, **64**, 304–308.

Schuldberg, D., Karwacki, S.B. & Burns, G.L. (1996). Stress, coping and social support in hypothetically psychosis-prone subjects. *Psychological Reports*, **78**, 1267–1283.

Schwartz, C.C. & Myers, J.K. (1977). Life events and schizophrenia. II: Impact of life events on symptom configuration. *Archives of General Psychiatry*, **34**, 1242–1245.

Sensky, T., Turkington, D., Kingdon, D., Scott, J.L., Scott, J., Siddle, R. et al. (2000). A randomised controlled trial of cognitive-behavioural therapy for persistent symptoms in schizophrenia resistant to medication. *Archives of General Psychiatry*, **57**, 165–72.

Steinberg, H. & Durrell, J. (1968). A stressful social situation as a precipitant of schizophrenic symptoms: An epidemiological study. *British Journal of Psychiatry*, **114**, 1097–1105.

Swann, A.C., Sekunda, S.K., Stokes, P.E., Croughan, J., Davis, J.M., Koslow, S.H. et al. (1990). Stress, depression and mania: Relationship between perceived role of stressful life events and clinical and biochemical characteristics. *Acta Psychiatrica Scandinavica*, **81**, 389–397.

Takai, A., Uematsu, M., Kaiya, H., Inoue, M. & Ueki, H. (1990). Coping styles to basic disorders among schizophrenics. *Acta Psychiatrica Scandinavica*, **82**, 289–294.

Tarrier, N. (1987). An investigation of residual psychotic symptoms in discharged schizophrenic patients. *British Journal of Clinical Psychology*, **26**, 141–143.

Tennant, C.C. (1985). Stress and schizophrenia: a review. *Integrated Psychiatry*, **3**, 248–261.

Thurm, I. & Häfner, H. (1987). Perceived vulnerability, relapse risk and coping in schizophrenia: an exploratory study. *European Archives of Psychiatry and Neurological Science*, **237**, 46–53.

Van den Bosch, R.J., van Asma, M.J.O., Rambouts, R. & Louwerens, J.W. (1992). Coping style and cognitive dysfunction in schizophrenic patients. *British Journal of Psychiatry*, **161**, 123–128.

Ventura, J., Nuechterlein, K.H., Hardesty, J.P. & Gitlin, M. (1992). Life events and schizophrenic relapse after withdrawal of medication. *British Journal of Psychiatry*, **161**, 615–620.

Ventura, J., Nuechterlein, K.H., Lukoff, D. & Hardesty, J.P. (1989). A prospective study of stressful life events and schizophrenic relapse. *Journal of Abnormal Psychology*, **98**, 407–411.

Ventura, J., Nuechterlein, K.H. & Subotnik, K.L. (2000, April). *Cognitive Appraisal and Approaches to Coping with Interpersonal Stressors in the Early Course of Schizophrenia*. Paper presented at the IInd International Conference on Early Psychosis, New York.

Vitaliano, P.P., Maiuro, R.D., Russo, J. & Becker, J. (1987). Raw versus relative scores in the assessment of coping strategies. *Journal of Behavioural Medicine*, **10**, 1–18.

Wagner, P.S. (1946). Psychiatric activities during the Normandy offensive. June 20–August 20, 1944: An experience with 5,203 neuropsychiatric casualties. *Psychiatry*, **9**, 341–363.

Wiedl, K.H. (1992). Assessment of coping with schizophrenia: stressors, appraisals and coping behaviour. *British Journal of Psychiatry*, **161** (Suppl. 8), 114–122.

Wiedl, K.H. & Schottner, B. (1991). Coping with symptoms related to schizophrenia. *Schizophrenia Bulletin*, **17**, 525–538.

Yanos, P.T. (2001). Proactive coping among persons diagnosed with severe mental illness: an exploratory study. *Journal of Nervous and Mental Disease*, **182**, 121–123.

Yung, A.R., Phillips, L.J & McGorry, P.D. (2004). *Treating Schizophrenia in the Prodromal Phase*. London: Taylor and Francis.

Zubin, J. & Spring, B. (1977). Vulnerability: A new view of schizophrenia. *Journal of Abnormal Psychology*, **86**, 103–126.

CHAPTER 6

Treatment Targets in the Pre-psychotic Phase

Paul Patterson, Amanda Skeate and Max Birchwood

INTRODUCTION

Early intervention in first-episode psychosis is widely accepted as a positive development for client care and recovery, quickly becoming established as the standard approach in many parts of the world. Much less is known about the efficacy of interventions with those at ultra high risk (UHR) of developing psychosis, but the concept is proving to be equally appealing, generating many clinical and research programmes in recent years. In this chapter we describe some of the current theoretical issues relating to identification and treatment of individuals at UHR of developing psychosis, with a specific focus on the impact of co-morbidity. Practical aspects of working with co-morbid symptoms are then described through the experience of the Birmingham Early Detection & Intervention Team (ED:IT). If an acceptance of diagnostic uncertainty is a recommendation for working with first-episode clients, it becomes a requirement when working with clients at UHR of psychosis – it is here that difficulties surrounding symptom identification are compounded by the need to take developmental stage, family risk and co-morbid disorders into account. The Personal Assessment and Crisis Evaluation (PACE) Clinic in Melbourne, Australia, has developed the referral/inclusion criteria that are employed by most services working in this area and these are the UHR categories referred to and described later in the chapter and in more detail in Chapter 2.

YOUNG PEOPLE AND EMOTIONAL DISTRESS

First, episode psychosis peaks in the late teens and early twenties (Jablensky & Cole, 1997) at a uniquely vulnerable stage. We know that the prodromal period of early symptoms begins on average 1–5 years prior to the first episode (Häfner, 2000; Yung, Phillips, Yuen & McGorry, 2004) when a young person is facing an array of psychosocial developmental tasks. Identity formation, autonomy from family, increased importance of peer and intimate friendships, educational and vocational pressures combine with rapid biological development to leave

Working with People at High Risk of Developing Psychosis: A Treatment Handbook.
Edited by J. Addington, S.M. Francey and A.P. Morrison. © 2006 John Wiley & Sons, Ltd.

the young person open to many potential sources of injury to their psychological health and self-esteem (Aggleton, Hurry & Warwick, 2000; Harrop & Trower, 2003). Given the wide prevalence of emotional distress in the general population of young people (Pearce, 2000), and the high levels of emotional dysfunction found in young people with psychosis (Birchwood, Iqbal, Chadwick & Trower, 2000), it would be surprising if young people at UHR of developing psychosis were not to display an equal range of affective distress.

Edwards and McGorry (2002) describe the difficulty in categorising the variety of mental health problems faced by young people in this age group, which is compounded by the developmental age and tasks required of this period. These factors, combined with the lack of an agreed aetiological understanding of the prodromal period and the fact that psychotic symptoms are commonly experienced by healthy young people (Verdoux et al., 1998), present primary care and mental health services with a huge challenge to identify individuals as being at high risk of psychosis. This has implications for both educational strategies for the promotion of early detection, and for defining the appropriate treatment targets for therapeutic interventions aimed at reducing the transition to psychosis. This must necessarily involve recognising both the extent of co-morbidity within this group and whether the methods of identifying disorders currently employed are assisting or impeding recovery.

CO-MORBIDITY

The clinical relevance of co-morbidity (where an individual has symptoms that meet more than one diagnostic category) to mental health has been well established in several large-scale studies (Bijl & Ravelli, 2000; Kessler et al., 1994). Co-morbidity has been associated with greater functional disability, longer illness duration, more severe symptoms and rapid onset (Andrade, Eaton & Chilcoat, 1994; Bijl & Ravelli, 2000; de Graaf, Bijl, Ten Have, Beekman & Vollebergh, 2004; Kessler et al., 1994; Kessler & Frank, 1997; Roy-Byrne et al., 2000; Vollrath & Angst, 1989). Co-morbidity is a common finding in general adult population surveys using structured diagnostic interviews, with 14% of an American sample reporting three or more lifetime co-morbid disorders for which less then 50% had received any specialist mental health treatment (Kessler et al., 1994). Depression, anxiety disorders and alcohol abuse have been reported as common co-morbid disorders in the general population in the Netherlands Mental Health Survey and Incidence Study (Bijl, Ravelli & van Zessen, 1998).

Co-morbidity is also clearly relevant to mental disorders in young people. Examining a large sample of young people aged 14–24 years in a general population, Wittchen, Nelson and Lachner (1998) found that lifetime depressive disorders (16.8%), anxiety disorders (14.4%) and substance disorders (lifetime 17.7%; 12-month 11.4%) were all common. Co-morbidity was substantial and significantly related to greater reductions in work productivity and increased rates of help-seeking from professionals. Anxiety in young people may present in a wide range of associated conditions, from generalised anxiety disorder and phobias to panic disorder and post-traumatic stress disorder (PTSD; Anderson, Williams, McGee & Silva, 1987). PTSD itself is often associated with traumatic or abusive experiences in childhood and is a common correlate of serious mental disorders (Allen, 2001). 'Shame' and 'guilt' are other emotional states showing strong associations with psychopathology in young people (Gilbert, Allan, Ball & Bradshaw, 1996). The prevalence of depressive states in young people has been estimated at between 2 and 6%, depending on criteria employed with some evidence that both depression and suicide in young people has been increasing in recent decades (Poznanski & Mokros, 1994). In the UK, suicide is the second most common cause of death in young people aged 15–24 (Office of Population Census and Surveys, 1990) with an increase in rates for young men since the 1970s. Finally, it is well established that later adolescence is also associated with more frequent appearance of a first psychotic illness, with 51% of new cases of schizophrenia falling within the 15–25 year age group and 82.5% in the 15–35 age range (Jablensky & Cole, 1997; Sartorius et al., 1986).

Although it is rare for psychotic symptoms to be experienced independently from a range of co-morbid affective disorders, when psychosis is suspected the focus of assessment is usually on positive symptoms. Especially for a client in the early stage of psychosis, this may mean that other symptoms that are distressing and burdensome are overlooked. When working with young people who display attenuated psychotic symptoms, the extent of the disability linked to co-morbidity is obvious and high levels of distress are commonly reported. Often the attribution for distress is not the presence of psychotic symptomatology *per se*, but rather the restrictions and vulnerabilities associated with affective disorders where extreme states of anxiety and hypervigilance, disturbances of sleep and appetite and substance use may have contributed to the emotional vulnerability. The PACE group confirm the most common co-morbid problems experienced by those at UHR of developing psychosis as being social anxiety, generalised anxiety, panic disorder, obsessive-compulsive symptoms, post-traumatic symptoms and substance use (Yung & McGorry, 1996; Yung et al., 2003). A focus on the aetiology and treatment of these symptoms would therefore seem to be warranted. In the following section we examine the impact of classification systems on identification (and therefore on treatment) of co-morbidity in clients at UHR of developing psychosis.

THE INFLUENCE OF CLASSIFICATORY SYSTEMS ON ASSESSMENT AND TREATMENT

At the turn of the century, the Kraepelinian approach to classification of mental disease assessment was based on classifying large numbers of case histories of asylum patients according to cause, symptomatology, course and final stage, thus producing a system of classification and distinction between the affective and non-affective psychoses that has retained influence to the present day. Jaspers described how psychiatrists should assess symptoms (particularly of psychosis) by their form rather than by their content, which has in turn influenced psychiatric practice. A powerful legacy of these historical developments has been to encourage a hierarchical attitude to disorders when assessing clients. Thus the psychoses have generally been treated as 'true medical diseases' having distinct organic causes whereas neurotic disorders were assumed to be psychogenic in origin, with treatment strategies often influenced accordingly.

The consequences of such 'trumping rules' (Foulds & Bedford, 1975; Freeman & Garety, 2003), encouraged by the DSM-IV requirement to list a 'principal diagnosis' (American Psychiatric Association, 1994), can bias clinicians towards treating psychotic symptoms to the exclusion of other disorders. Maj (2005) describes how psychiatric co-morbidity may also be missed due to the rule in DSM-III that the same symptom could not appear in more than one disorder. This can serve to actually under-represent the level of psychiatric co-morbidity between disorders.

The clinical utility of diagnosing individuals with psychotic disorders has also been drawn into question as alternative approaches based on the identification of individual symptoms have developed. These approaches seem to allow a clearer focus for therapeutic intervention (e.g., Costello, 1993) and are reinforced by findings that a dimensional structure of psychosis may best represent the heterogeneity of symptoms allowing a more naturalistic basis for planning therapeutic interventions. There are practical pitfalls of a narrow focus in psychiatric assessment:

> ...diagnostic categories are mutually exclusive and assign patients to one sole group, thereby losing important psychopathological (and clinically relevant) information. Thus, if true allowance is made for 'co-morbidity' by assessing several symptom dimensions along a continuum of psychosis, more data may be available for making informed treatment decisions and prognostic statements. (van Os et al., 1999, p. 603).

Edwards and McGorry (2002) also stress the relative insensitivity of current diagnostic classificatory systems to account for the wide range of problems associated with 'at-risk' mental health states and suggest that a dimensional and qualitative approach to assessment may be a more appropriate method to allow accurate translation of symptomatology into clinical intervention strategies.

RISK FACTORS RELATED TO UHR RESEARCH

At present there is a relatively small evidence base in the nascent field of UHR research emphasising the role of emotional dysfunction. However, recent research has identified an increasing number of psychosocial risk factors related to psychotic symptom development. Some of this work has suggested a common aetiology for psychotic symptoms and affective co-morbid disorders and warrants continued high-level attention to further clarify the best focus of clinical interventions as our understanding of continuum models of psychotic experience grows.

Childhood Trauma

Schneiderian symptoms have been shown to be highly correlated with childhood trauma and other dissociative symptom clusters in both clinical samples (Fink & Golinkoff, 1990; Ross et al., 1990) and in the general population (Ross & Joshi, 1992). Many individuals with dissociative disorders have previous diagnoses of schizophrenia (Allen, 2001) and have been prescribed antipsychotic medication, suggesting that some dissociative and psychotic symptoms may be difficult to differentiate. A history of childhood abuse in adult outpatients has been reported to be a strong predictor of suicidality (Read, Perry, Moskowitz & Connolly, 2001). Childhood sexual abuse in the general population is also related to schizotypy, some symptoms of which are 10 times more common in adults who were maltreated as children (Berenbaum, 1999; Startup, 1999). New lines of research have established the role of trauma as a risk factor for many mental health disorders, including psychosis (Bebbington et al., 2004; Janssen et al., 2004; Read, Agar, Argyle & Aderhold, 2003). Although the evidence is currently being accumulated, it does seem important that a traumagenesis focus of aetiology in psychosis may clarify some of the apparent heterogeneity of co-morbid symptoms.

PTSD

Although evidence is increasingly linking traumatic life events to subsequent relapse and emergence of florid symptoms in clinical samples (e.g. Bebbington et al., 1993), few studies have assessed the prevalence of PTSD in individuals with psychosis. Mueser and colleagues (1998) found that 43% of a sample with severe mental illness (n = 275) had co-morbid PTSD, predicted by numbers of traumas experienced and childhood sexual abuse, yet in only 2% of cases had a formal diagnosis been made. Links between PTSD symptoms and co-morbid major depressive disorder have been established (Zimmerman & Mattia, 1999). Romme and Escher (2000) describe how, for individuals experiencing auditory hallucinations ('voice-hearers'), the emotional processes recognised as important to recovery from trauma are extremely relevant. They and others suggest that many psychotic 'voice hearing' experiences are linked to earlier experiences of trauma and demonstrate that personal accounts of recovery often include emotional explanations of the experience useful in giving meaning to their experiences (May, 2004; Romme & Escher, 1989). May (2004) cites a further benefit of clients employing 'traumagenesis' explanations of symptom development where these are appropriate, giving the psychotic process a functional role.

> Rather than just being an affliction, psychological processes such as splitting off from experience and dissociation can be seen as adaptive strategies that have enabled the person to survive adversity... For many this is a more coherent and enabling narrative than the bio-medical narrative about psychosis. (May, 2004, p. 253).

Anxiety and Biology

Freeman and Garety (2003) suggest that raised levels of emotional dysfunction preceding and accompanying psychosis indicates an aetiological role for emotion in the development of delusions and hallucinations. Evidence is accumulating that many psychotic symptoms appear to be on a continuum through normal and clinical populations (Claridge, Clark & Davis, 1997; Johns & van Os, 2001; Verdoux & van Os, 2002) with schizotypal signs present in non-clinical populations (McGorry et al., 1995). Delusions and hallucinations are experienced by large numbers of individuals without psychosis in both normal and clinical populations (Poulton et al., 2000; van Os, Hanssen, Bijl & Ravelli, 2000; Verdoux et al., 1998). Furthermore, an increase in arousal and anxiety has been associated with the occurrence of positive symptoms of schizophrenia (Delespaul, deVries & van Os, 2002; Freeman, Garety & Kuipers, 2001), and conversely patients with anxiety and mood disorders have been found to have elevated scores on positive psychosis items (Hanssen et al., 2003). In addition, affective symptoms are prevalent in schizophrenia (Taylor, 1992; van Os et al., 1999) and it has been suggested that there may even be aetiological continuity and overlap between affective disorder and schizophrenia with only quantitative differences in effect sizes (van Os et al., 1999). Elevated levels of anxiety and depression have been linked to positive psychotic symptom scores that are intermediate to those of non-patients and psychosis cases (van Os et al., 1999). This accumulation of evidence supports a focus on co-morbid anxiety in clients at UHR and as such could be a primary focus for preventative interventions.

Developmental Processes

Much of the psychotic 'experience' as well as the associated co-morbid symptoms may be induced from the developmental stage young people are in when experiencing attenuated positive symptoms. Egocentricism and grandiosity are normal attributes of adolescence, and failed or foiled attempts to negotiate developmental tasks such as independence from parents and forming attachments to peer groups can lead to isolation. This in turn can lead to egocentric interpretations of the motivations of others (immature theory of mind skills) and compromised psychological development:

> People seem to be stuck in the middle of the uncomfortable turbulent experiences of adolescence such as loneliness, grandiosity, depression and delusion-like fantasy, yet unlike most adolescents they do not emerge from them ... the self-same teenage 'troubles' now deteriorate into the emergence of psychotic symptoms (Harrop & Trower, 2003, p. 49).

Within the cognitive framework, traumatic histories and developmental anomalies may influence the cognitive schemas that govern the processing of self and social information. Such schemas have been observed to be active in the emotional response to psychosis in the way in which the person hearing voices appraises their interpersonal significance (i.e. their power and omnipotence; Birchwood, Meaden, Trower, Gilbert & Plaistow, 2000), and also in the distress and persistence of voices in young adolescents (Escher, Romme, Buiks, Delespaul & van Os, 2002). Persecutory delusions may be protective against low self-esteem, establishing a clear link between emotional disturbance and psychotic symptoms (Bentall, Kinderman & Kaney, 1994; Lyon, Kaney & Bentall, 1994). More optimistically, Andrews and Brown (1995) suggest that positive life events in late adolescence can help to restore a disturbed developmental trajectory to within normal limits.

The Role of Depression

Depression is a serious problem for individuals diagnosed with psychosis and presents a challenge for mental health professionals. It is not clear whether depression is intrinsic to psychotic disorder or can be viewed as separate and distinct. In one study it was reported that depressive pathology occurred prior to the onset of positive symptoms, with no significant relationship between the onset of depression and the current level of psychosis (Green, Nuechterlein, Ventura & Mintz, 1990). Further work demonstrated that in clients with psychosis, those who were also depressed have been found to have a significantly longer duration of acute psychotic phase of illness, better pre-morbid adjustment and an excess of stressful life events (Chintalapudi, Kulhara & Avasthi, 1993). Depression may be viewed as a psychological response (demoralisation) to an apparently uncontrollable life event (the psychosis) and its disabling consequences (Birchwood, Mason, Macmillan & Healy, 1993). It may be that a consideration of issues related to control are necessary in any description of factors that may contribute to vulnerability to psychosis, as well as depression and expectations of how to deal with significant alterations in available roles and goals (Champion & Power, 1995). In UHR clients depression should always be seen as a major target for therapeutic intervention.

SUMMARISING THE ASSOCIATION OF PSYCHOTIC SYMPTOMS AND EMOTIONAL DYSFUNCTION

Birchwood (2003) has suggested several ways in which emotional dysfunction can develop in parallel with psychotic symptoms, thus causing uncertainty for a therapeutic focus. Emotional disorders can be intrinsic to psychosis (e.g. depression), or develop as psychological reactions to the impact of psychotic symptoms. In the UHR field, it is perhaps the association of emotional disorders with developmental traumas that are most prominent. Birth cohort and retrospective studies reveal that first-episode psychosis is often preceded by social difficulty and emotional disorder as well as by sub-threshold 'psychotic' experience stretching back into early adolescence (Poulton et al., 2000). These childhood antecedents interact in a social environment and there is now considerable evidence that social factors may influence morbidity and outcome of psychosis. Examples include urban living, particularly deprivation, membership of marginalised social groups, the impact of migration and the (favourable) correlates of 'developing-nation' status (Harrison, Gunnell, Glazebrook, Page & Kwiecinski, 2001). Further evidence emphasising the importance of emotional dysfunction in the aetiology of psychotic symptoms is currently unfolding and as the association of both psychotic symptoms and emotional dysfunction with developmental difficulty becomes established, a clearer understanding of the pathogenesis of 'at-risk' states may also become apparent, with implications for treatment strategies. This suggests the need for a clinical service that has an emphasis on treating the full range of co-morbid symptoms to give the best possibilities for prevention of transition to psychosis.

THE BIRMINGHAM EARLY DETECTION & INTERVENTION TEAM – ED:IT

The Early Detection & Intervention Team (ED:IT) was created in January 2002 as part of the Birmingham Early Intervention Service to provide assessment, intervention and psychological treatments to young people identified as being at high risk of developing a psychotic illness. Early intervention services for psychosis are being set up throughout the UK and the service established in Birmingham included one of the first programmes for UHR clients. Based in an inner-city community setting, ED:IT employs a multi-disciplinary team of psychologists, nursing and vocational staff and receives referrals from both statutory sources such as community mental health teams and non-statutory services such as housing and drugs agencies across the city. The service operates an assertive outreach model, thought to be particularly useful for work with adolescents, visiting clients in suitable community settings or in their own homes. This has a dramatic impact on engagement and encourages the formation of a therapeutic alliance both with clients, and, where appropriate, family members. Such a mode of working is in marked contrast to many statutory services that operate a 'three strikes and you're out' approach to client appointments, discharging those who fail to attend, often with little in the way of follow-up.

ED:IT provides psychological therapies, principally cognitive-behavioural techniques, and conducts mental health promotion workshops aimed at reducing stigma and fear of mental health problems. Interventions are individually tailored to match clients' primary needs and include general case management to reduce stress related to housing, benefits or educational needs. All clients are offered cognitive-behavioural therapy (CBT) at the onset of treatment and general case management to foster engagement and reduce initial levels of stress. An extended assessment is carried out at baseline and at regular follow-up periods and clients are offered a service for up to 18 months. This is flexible and dependent on progress: earlier or later discharge can be mutually agreed. ED:IT does not advocate the use of neuroleptic medication with UHR clients, but may accept clients who have recently been prescribed neuroleptic medication.

Referral Criteria

The PACE 'at risk mental state' (ARMS) criteria (Yung & McGorry, 1996) are assessed using the Structured Interview for Prodromal States (SIPS: Miller et al., 2002) for three non-exclusive categories of UHR status defined by the following features:

- Attenuated positive symptoms of psychosis within the previous year.
- Brief limited intermittent psychotic symptoms (BLIPS) within the previous year – i.e. positive symptoms at a psychotic level but which have resolved within a week without intervention.
- Family history of psychosis plus reduction in functioning within the previous year.
- The Birmingham group also employ a fourth category based on the Bonn Scale of Basic Symptoms (BSABS: Klosterkötter, Hellmich, Steinmeyer & Schultze-Lutter, 2001) – subjectively experienced deficits in thought, language, perception, motor skills and energy.

In addition to these criteria there must be evidence of distress, dysfunction and help-seeking. The core age group is 16–30 years although consultation is provided to child and adolescent services with respect to 14- and 15-year-olds.

Co-morbid Distress in ED:IT Clients

In order to examine levels of distress and co-morbidity in ED:IT clients, the baseline assessments of an initial cohort were reviewed. This data is displayed in Table 6.1. Clearly, significant levels of affective distress were present in the initial ED:IT cohort. For these clients (n = 41, mean age 19.3), mean scores on the Beck Depression Inventory Scale (BDI: Beck, Steer, Ball & Ranieri, 1996) indicated the presence of major depression. The BDI question on suicidal ideation (Q9) presented clear evidence of the severity of emotional distress in this sample, with over 65% of clients endorsing suicidal ideation during the previous week. Similarly on the Positive and Negative Syndrome Scale (PANSS: Kay, Fiszbein & Opler, 1987) mean scores indicated the presence of moderately high levels of positive and negative symptoms as well as high levels of general psychopathology including anxiety. These scores were just below average for schizophrenia samples according to the scale norms (Kay, Opler & Fiszbein, 2000). Levels of dissociation as measured by the Dissociative Experiences Scale (DES: Bernstein & Putnam, 1986; Carlson et al., 1993) were found to be similar to that of a schizophrenia sample (Putnam et al., 1996). Total

Table 6.1 Distress markers in ED:IT clients at referral

	Male (range)	Female (range)	Total (SD)
N	26	15	41
Age	20.2 (16–32)	17.5 (16–26)	19.3 (3.5)
PANSS+	15.2 (8–27)	14.7 (7–21)	15.0 (4.5)
PANSS–	13.5 (7–24)	13.1 (8–32)	13.4 (5.2)
PANSS Gen	36.2 (17–49)	34.9 (21–54)	35.7 (9.0)
Anxiety (PANSS)	3.7 (1–5)	3.4 (2–5)	3.6 (1.1)
GAF	47.9 (27–70)	47.7 (28–64)	47.8 (11.7)
BDI	26.7 (7–50)	23.0 (4–38)	25.4 (10.2)

• PANSS – Positive and Negative Syndrome Scale (Kay, Fiszbein & Opler, 1987)
• GAF – Global Assessment of Functioning (from Structured Clinical Interview for DSM, Spitzer, Williams, Gibbon & First, 1992)
• BDI – Beck Depression Inventory (Beck et al., 1996)

mean score for schizotypal thinking in the ED:IT group was also very high when compared to general population norms and norms for English undergraduates (Hall & Habbits, 1996; Raine, 1991). It is, perhaps, worth reflecting that despite the relatively high levels of psychopathology and distress evident from these figures, these young people would not normally have any specialised treatment service available to them. This is discussed further in the conclusion.

Interventions developed at ED:IT

It was clear from the levels of psychopathology observed in the initial cohort of UHR clients into ED:IT (see Table 6.1) that interventions aimed at alleviating emotional distress were warranted. Treatment acceptance was very high and case management was seen as an often useful engagement tool as well as being a vital support for clients. Individually tailored CBT forms the core of the treatment offered by ED:IT with the focus being on the emotional distress of these young people thought to be at risk of developing psychosis. Other treatment components available include psychoeducation, supportive counselling, family work, and group-based interventions. Table 6.2 displays the percentage of the initial ED:IT cohort that participated in the different types of intervention available.

Table 6.2 Intervention uptake for ED:IT clients (n = 41)

Intervention type	Uptake n = 41
Case management	100%
Individual therapy – CBT	86.7%
Group therapy – CBT	24.4%
Family support/intervention	35.5%
Neuroleptic medication*	6.7%

* Provided by external agency

Psychoeducation and support is offered to family members with the approval of the client. In many cases, family conflicts and other interpersonal difficulties have been regarded as 'part of the problem' by clients, and therefore family work has always been considered within the context of the therapeutic alliance with the client. Additionally, a series of group interventions has been developed to work directly on issues related to social anxiety which were prominent in the cohort. This was in response to client questions such as 'Am I the only one who has these (anxiety) symptoms?' and involved a range of components including psychoeducation on the biological and cognitive nature of anxiety, problem solving, positive reinforcement and planned behavioural experiment strategies over a fixed number of sessions. The following case example illustrates the application of both individual and group-based therapy in the treatment of distressing social anxiety in a young person presumed to be at UHR of psychosis by virtue of having both a family history of psychosis and the experience of attenuated positive psychotic symptoms.

Case example

Sally, a 19-year-old unemployed woman who lived with her parents, was referred to the specialist service for young people at high risk of developing psychosis after receiving generic psychiatric services for approximately 18 months. Her primary diagnosis of social anxiety with depression had been treated unsuccessfully with a combination of drug therapy and support. At intake assessment, it was apparent that previous over-concern that other people perceived her negatively had worsened and Sally often experienced strong feelings of being in danger from others. However, there was no evidence of systematised persecutory beliefs. In addition, she was terrified by increasingly frequent perceptual and cognitive abnormalities (e.g. non-specific auditory hallucinations and having the 'sensation' of thought insertion). She feared that she would develop schizophrenia as her mother had done as a young adult. Nevertheless, there was no evidence that Sally met criteria for a first episode of psychosis, although she was at UHR due to attenuated psychotic symptoms and having a first-degree relative with a psychotic illness combined with her own recent deterioration in functioning.

In drawing up a problem and goal list, Sally prioritised a desire to reduce her distress in social situations, and overcome her fear of being negatively evaluated by others (e.g. social anxiety). It was evident that the prospect of leaving her house resulted in anticipatory anxiety with concurrent distressing physical symptoms, which resulted in avoidance of most social situations (i.e. safety behaviour). Together the therapist and Sally developed a collaborative formulation. This process highlighted that Sally's fear of peoples' negative judgements was caused by actual traumatic experiences such as the family being ostracised by neighbours and being bullied at school. Sally developed the rule that in order to be 'safe from others', she was required to appear 'perfect'; however, anxiety reactions such as blushing prevented her from achieving this and contributed to a maintenance cycle.

The intervention focused on supporting Sally to break the cycle of avoidance and modify her beliefs about the judgements of other people. It was also critical for the therapist to carry out psychoeducation about anxiety and psychosis, to allow for the re-attribution of blame and a more accurate understanding of these problems. Attending a group designed to build up social confidence, which employed principles of normalisation, behavioural experiments and cognitive challenges, allowed Sally to address some of her difficulties whilst interacting with peers. Sally's improvement was protracted due to her entrenched beliefs about herself and others, but she did begin to leave the house more regularly. Moreover, increased insight into the root of her difficulties did reduce unrealistic feelings of being in danger from others, and as levels of depression and anxiety improved, other attenuated psychotic symptoms also reduced significantly and ceased to be a source of distress.

What Clients Want

Individuals in the UHR state are experiencing distress and help-seeking, i.e. they want treatment. Often the presenting problems of greatest concern to the client are not the psychotic symptoms *per se*, but other emotional difficulties. Social anxiety, depression and suicidal ideation, the effects of earlier trauma and subjective distress are all common reasons for young people to seek help from services. The first intake of n = 41 to ED:IT were primarily seeking help for distress other than psychotic symptoms, despite it usually being the presence of attenuated positive symptoms which mark them out as being 'at UHR' of psychosis. All ED:IT clients who requested individual CBT created a problem list, which became the focus for treatment prioritisation. As can be seen in the problem lists generated by clients (Table 6.3), they are clearly requesting assistance for issues related to depression, anxiety and the experience of trauma.

An examination of the high take-up rates for individual therapy, group therapy and case management (see Table 6.2) suggest that to respond appropriately to clients' needs requires a flexible approach and consideration of a range of intervention strategies (Phillips & Francey, 2004). Cognitive behavioural techniques are one of the key interventions available to services but the focus for such techniques may need to be directed at the distressing symptoms most responsive to amelioration. We have previously argued (Birchwood, 2003) that CBT is a therapy to reduce emotional dysfunction and distress and that its application to delusional beliefs is something of an anomaly. CBT in early psychosis will fail to resolve distress and emotional dysfunction unless it moves away from the positive symptoms *per se* and focuses on the different psychological pathways to emotional dysfunction. Equally, patient services have much to gain from a cross-fertilisation of approaches between child and adult mental health services in the development of services for young people at UHR of developing psychosis.

The results of a study recently conducted in Manchester, UK, supports this position. Morrison et al. (2004) reported results for their randomised controlled trial of cognitive therapy in an ultra-high risk cohort showing a reduction in transition to psychosis over a 12-month follow-up period. They employed a problem-oriented, time-limited and educational intervention of up to 26 sessions over a six-month period focused on a priority list agreed between therapist and patient. A process of de-catastrophising fears based on inappropriate appraisals was employed for psychotic symptomatology. Various models were utilised to work on emotional dysfunction (e.g. Wells & Matthews, 1994). An example of the client

---

Table 6.3 Common themes for problem lists

- Loneliness or isolation
- Social anxiety
- Lack of confidence or low self-esteem
- Feeling 'different'
- Concerns about 'going mad' (due to symptoms)
- Previous trauma
- Accommodation being unsuitable or unsafe
- Vocational or educational issues

collaborating with a therapist to determine his own therapeutic needs can be seen in the case example below:

Case example

Jamie is a 16-year-old student from an African-Caribbean background. A housing worker, trained in recognising when a young person may be at high risk of developing psychosis, referred him directly to the specialist youth service for this client group. At intake assessment, Jamie openly described sub-threshold auditory hallucinations, paranoia and ideas of reference. However, Jamie was most distressed by his unremitting low mood and concurrent suicidal ideation. Symptoms of depressed mood included sleep and appetite disturbance, feeling hopeless and poor motivation. Utilising a structured interview and scoring classification of prodromal symptoms (Miller et al., 2002) he met criteria for an at-risk phase of psychosis with attenuated psychotic symptoms.

Following assessment, Jamie agreed to meet for cognitive-behavioural therapy and with the therapist drew up a problem list and goals according to the protocol described by French and Morrison (2003). Jamie identified that his primary goal was to reduce his distress related to his depression. Together Jamie and the therapist developed a formulation focusing on this problem.

Jamie had moved to the housing project to escape an emotionally abusive, highly critical parent. Initially, he had perceived this transition as positive, but had struggled to cope successfully with the demands of living independently. Examining core beliefs and dysfunctional assumptions revealed that Jamie had extremely high expectations of himself and disliked accepting help from others (e.g. 'I must be perfect'; 'If I can't do things myself it means I am weak and vulnerable'). Accumulating symptoms of impaired sleep and poor motivation resulted in a maintenance cycle of increasing inability to function and subsequent hopelessness about the future. The onset of quasi-psychotic experiences was interpreted catastrophically as further evidence that his future was ruined ('Now I'm going mad and will never achieve anything').

The process of developing a shared formulation enabled Jamie to reinterpret his current symptoms as the consequence of extremely difficult life circumstances rather than a personal failure, resulting in increased hope for attaining goals in the future. Identifying the source of his ambivalence towards receiving assistance allowed Jamie to challenge the validity of his assumption and to be more willing to accept help. Further therapeutic sessions supported Jamie in gradually increasing his activity level, modifying his perfectionist standards and to discuss his confused beliefs about his relationship with his parent. Jamie's attenuated psychotic symptoms subsided quickly after he began therapy, and with support he resumed his studies.

What Clients Get

It is salutary to remember that the majority of clients with sub-threshold symptoms of psychosis would not have access to a specialist service in the UK at the present time. Despite the opportunity for delaying or even preventing the onset of psychosis in those at UHR, and the intuitive appeal of such services to clinicians, many clients are reliant on primary care outpatient appointments or non-statutory counselling and support agencies, which may not be able to offer ongoing support and monitoring over the extended periods of time required to delay or prevent transition to psychosis. Biological models of treatment for psychosis are generally seen as primary in the UK and often psychological treatments are regarded as exotic 'add-ons' rather than core interventions, as can be surmised from the experience of implementing psychological approaches to family intervention in psychosis (Fadden & Birchwood, 2002). The sheer level of distress encountered by ED:IT staff from young clients who would not normally be getting such a service does seem to justify further investment in service development and the provision of psychological treatments for this group.

Mental Health Promotion Strategies

Early in ED:IT's development it became clear that a high proportion of clients treated in mental health primary care services had already made the transition to psychosis in the months and sometimes years prior to our assessment, without this being recognised by services. A series of workshops aimed at professional colleagues was therefore developed, themed on identifying early signs of psychosis. These have proven very useful in encouraging accurate referrals and reducing the duration of untreated psychosis in some clients. This experience revealed that services often find it difficult to accurately apply diagnostic criteria in clinical settings and highlighted the necessity for specialist services such as ED:IT to provide consistent assessments of current and past risk of psychosis. Without such an approach, the danger of missing or misclassifying attenuated psychotic symptoms remains high within generic primary care settings. A related programme of educational interventions for general practitioners in Birmingham is currently being evaluated (the 'REDIRECT' project), whilst an ongoing programme of mental health workshops for any staff working with young people continues to be popular.

CONCLUSION

It can be seen that large numbers of young people who would not normally be offered a specialised service are currently in emotional distress and at high risk of increasing psychopathology without appropriate intervention. Depression, anxiety disorders, PTSD, dissociative disorders and other expressions of emotional distress are often subsumed under the impact of a psychotic presentation, yet are clearly linked to negative outcomes including suicide (Birchwood et al., 2000). It would therefore seem both clinically and theoretically important to re-evaluate diagnostic approaches to client assessment with an understanding that, aetiologically and symptomatically, many of the presentations of distress may be interrelated. For both epidemiological and clinical reasons, co-morbidity holds valuable information that needs to be understood.

Therapeutic interventions may similarly be targeted to focus on the core symptoms of emotional distress such as anxiety and mood disorders (where CBT can be employed to its strengths) rather than a primary focus on positive psychotic symptoms. This would seem to be warranted from the clinical research literature as a potential component in a preventative strategy for working with UHR clients. Further exploration of the aetiology of anxiety and its biological correlates in clients may prove to be a valuable strategy for UHR research in the future. Overall, much of the evidence base would seem to require an urgent re-evaluation of current assessment and diagnostic approaches to ensure that the effectiveness of clinical interventions are optimised, and to allow the real possibility of applying preventative treatments to a young, vulnerable and highly distressed group of clients.

At a time when they are facing a range of developmental challenges, many young people are experiencing disabling levels of emotional dysfunction, which may contribute to both formation of psychotic symptomatology and to transition to psychosis if left untreated. A more subtle investigation into the complexity of the factors influencing adolescent development and pathology that does not exclusively focus on psychotic categorisation would seem to hold the potential for the greatest relief of distress and negative outcomes. Targeting more resources at this stage may lead to better outcomes for a large proportion of young people who may otherwise be facing the insidious onset of a career as a psychiatric patient. Much research and evaluation remains to be carried out in this new and developing field, but initial reports and the possibility of developing preventative approaches to psychosis suggest that it is an area likely to generate much enthusiasm for the foreseeable future.

REFERENCES

Aggleton, P., Hurry, J. & Warwick, I. (Eds) (2000). *Young People and Mental Health*. Chichester, UK: Wiley.

Allen, J.G. (2001). *Traumatic Relationships and Serious Mental Disorders*. Chichester, UK: Wiley.

American Psychiatric Association (1994). *DSM-IV: Diagnostic and Statistical Manual of Mental Disorders* (4th edn). Washington, DC: Author.

Anderson, J.C., Williams, S., McGee, R. & Silva, P.A. (1987). DSM-III disorders in preadolescent children. Prevalence in a large sample from the general population. *Archives of General Psychiatry*, **44**, 69–76.

Andrade, L., Eaton, W.W. & Chilcoat, H. (1994). Lifetime comorbidity of panic attacks and major depression in a population-based study. Symptom profiles. *British Journal of Psychiatry*, **165**, 363–369.

Andrews, B. & Brown, G.W. (1995). Stability and change in low self-esteem: The role of psychosocial factors. *Psychological Medicine*, **25**, 23–31.

Bebbington, P., Wilkins, S., Jones, P., Foerster, A., Murray, R., Toone, B., et al. (1993). Life events and psychosis. Initial results from the Camberwell Collaborative Psychosis Study. *British Journal of Psychiatry*, **162**, 72–79.

Bebbington, P.E., Bhugra, D., Brugha, T., Farrell, M., Lewis, G., Meltzer, H., et al. (2004). Psychosis, victimisation and childhood disadvantage: Evidence from the second British National Survey of Psychiatric Morbidity. *British Journal of Psychiatry*, **185**, 220–226.

Beck, A.T., Steer, R.A., Ball, R. & Ranieri, W. (1996). Comparison of Beck Depression Inventories -IA and -II in psychiatric outpatients. *Journal of Personality Assessment*, **67**, 588–597.

Bentall, R.P., Kinderman, P. & Kaney, S. (1994). The self, attributional processes and abnormal beliefs: towards a model of persecutory delusions. *Behaviour Research and Therapy*, **32**, 331–341.

Berenbaum, H. (1999). Peculiarity and reported childhood maltreatment. *Psychiatry*, **62**, 21–35.

Bernstein, E.M. & Putnam, F.W. (1986). Development, reliability, and validity of a dissociation scale. *Journal of Nervous and Mental Disease*, **174**, 727–735.

Bijl, R.V. & Ravelli, A. (2000). Current and residual functional disability associated with psychopathology: Findings from the Netherlands Mental Health Survey and Incidence Study (NEMESIS). *Psychological Medicine*, **30**, 657–668.

Bijl, R.V., Ravelli, A. & van Zessen, G. (1998). Prevalence of psychiatric disorder in the general population: Results of the Netherlands Mental Health Survey and Incidence Study (NEMESIS). *Social Psychiatry and Psychiatric Epidemiology*, **33**, 587–595.

Birchwood, M. (2003). Pathways to emotional dysfunction in first-episode psychosis. *British Journal of Psychiatry*, **182**, 373–375.

Birchwood, M., Iqbal, Z., Chadwick, P. & Trower, P. (2000). Cognitive approach to depression and suicidal thinking in psychosis. 1. Ontogeny of post-psychotic depression. *British Journal of Psychiatry*, **177**, 516–521.

Birchwood, M., Mason, R., Macmillan, F. & Healy, J. (1993). Depression, demoralization and control over psychotic illness: A comparison of depressed and non-depressed patients with a chronic psychosis. *Psychological Medicine*, **23**, 387–395.

Birchwood, M., Meaden, A., Trower, P., Gilbert, P. & Plaistow, J. (2000). The power and omnipotence of voices: Subordination and entrapment by voices and significant others. *Psychological Medicine*, **30**, 337–344.

Carlson, E.B., Putnam, F.W., Ross, C.A., Torem, M., Coons, P.M., Dill, D. et al. (1993). Validity of the Dissociative Experiences Scale in screening for multiple personality disorder: A multicenter study. *American Journal of Psychiatry*, **150**, 1030–1036.

Champion, L.A. & Power, M.J. (1995). Social and cognitive approaches to depression: towards a new synthesis. *British Journal of Clinical Psychology*, **34** (Pt. 4), 485–503.

Chintalapudi, M., Kulhara, P. & Avasthi, A. (1993). Post-psychotic depression in schizophrenia. *European Archives of Psychiatry and Clinical Neuroscience*, **243**, 103–108.

Claridge, G., Clark, K. & Davis, C. (1997). Nightmares, dreams and schizotypy. *British Journal of Clinical Psychology*, **36** (Pt. 3), 377–386.

Costello, C.G. (Ed.) (1993). *Symptoms of Schizophrenia*. Chichester, UK: Wiley.

de Graaf, R., Bijl, R.V., Ten Have, M., Beekman, A.T.F. & Vollebergh, W.A.M. (2004). Rapid onset of comorbidity of common mental disorders: Findings from the Netherlands Mental Health Survey and Incidence Study (NEMESIS). *Acta Psychiatrica Scandinavica*, **109**, 55–63.

Delespaul, P., deVries, M. & van Os, J. (2002). Determinants of occurrence and recovery from hallucinations in daily life. *Social Psychiatry and Psychiatric Epidemiology*, **37**, 97–104.

Edwards, J. & McGorry, P.D. (2002). *A Guide to Establishing Early Psychosis Services*. London: Martin Dunitz.

Escher, S., Romme, M., Buiks, A., Delespaul, P. & van Os, J. (2002). Formation of delusional ideation in adolescents hearing voices: a prospective study. *American Journal of Medical Genetics*, **114**, 913–920.

Fadden, G. & Birchwood, M. (2002). British models for expanding family psychoeducation in routine practice. In H.P. Lefley & D.L. Johnson (Eds), *Family Interventions in Mental Illness*. Westport, CT: Praeger.

Fink, D. & Golinkoff, M. (1990). Multiple personality disorder, borderline personality disorder, and schizophrenia: a comparative study of clinical features. *Dissociation*, **3**, 127–134.

Foulds, G.A. & Bedford, A. (1975). Hierarchy of classes of personal illness. *Psychological Medicine*, **5**, 181–192.

Freeman, D. & Garety, P.A. (2003). Connecting neurosis and psychosis: The direct influence of emotion on delusions and hallucinations. *Behaviour Research and Therapy*, **41**, 923–947.

Freeman, D., Garety, P.A. & Kuipers, E. (2001). Persecutory delusions: Developing the understanding of belief maintenance and emotional distress. *Psychological Medicine*, **31**, 1293–1306.

French, P. & Morrison, A.P. (2003). *Early Detection and Cognitive Therapy for People at High Risk of Developing Psychosis*. Chichester, UK: Wiley.

Gilbert, P., Allan, S., Ball, L. & Bradshaw, Z. (1996). Overconfidence and personal evaluations of social rank. *British Journal of Medical Psychology*, **69** (Pt. 1), 59–68.

Green, M.F., Nuechterlein, K.H., Ventura, J. & Mintz, J. (1990). The temporal relationship between depressive and psychotic symptoms in recent-onset schizophrenia. *American Journal of Psychiatry*, **147**, 179–182.

Häfner, H. (2000). Onset and early course as determinants of the further course of schizophrenia. *Acta Psychiatrica Scandinavica*, Suppl. 44–48.

Hall, G. & Habbits, P. (1996). Shadowing on the basis of contextual information in individuals with schizotypal personality. *British Journal of Clinical Psychology*, **35**, 595–604.

Hanssen, M., Peeters, F., Krabbendam, L., Radstake, S., Verdoux, H. & van Os, J. (2003). How psychotic are individuals with non-psychotic disorders? *Social Psychiatry and Psychiatric Epidemiology*, **38**, 149–154.

Harrison, G., Gunnell, D., Glazebrook, C., Page, K. & Kwiecinski, R. (2001). Association between schizophrenia and social inequality at birth: Case-control study. *British Journal of Psychiatry*, **179**, 346–350.

Harrop, C. & Trower, P. (2003). *Why does Schizophrenia Develop at Late Adolescence? A Cognitive-developmental Approach to Psychosis*. Chichester, UK: Wiley.

Jablensky, A. & Cole, S.W. (1997). Is the earlier age at onset of schizophrenia in males a confounded finding? Results from a cross-cultural investigation. *British Journal of Psychiatry*, **170**, 234–240.

Janssen, I., Krabbendam, L., Bak, M., Hanssen, W., Vollebergh, R., de Graaf, R. et al. (2004). Childhood abuse as a risk factor for psychotic experiences. *Acta Psychiatrica Scandinavica*, **109**, 38–45.

Johns, L.C. & van Os, J. (2001). The continuity of psychotic experiences in the general population. *Clinical Psychology Review*, **21**, 1125–1141.

Kay, S.R., Fiszbein, A. & Opler, L.A. (1987). The positive and negative syndrome scale (PANSS) for schizophrenia. *Schizophrenia Bulletin*, **13**, 261–276.

Kay, S.R., Opler, L.A. & Fiszbein, A. (2000). *Positive and Negative Syndrome Scale (PANSS) User's Manual*. Multi-health Systems, Toronto.

Kessler, R.C. & Frank, R.G. (1997). The impact of psychiatric disorders on work loss days. *Psychological Medicine*, **27**, 861–873.

Kessler, R.C., McGonagle, K.A., Zhao, S., Nelson, C.B., Hughes, M., Eshleman, S. et al. (1994). Lifetime and 12-month prevalence of DSM-III-R psychiatric disorders in the United States. Results from the National Comorbidity Survey. *Archives of General Psychiatry*, **51**, 8–19.

Klosterkötter, J., Hellmich, M., Steinmeyer, E.M. & Schultze-Lutter, F. (2001). Diagnosing schizophrenia in the initial prodromal phase. *Archives of General Psychiatry*, **58**, 158–164.

Lyon, H.M., Kaney, S. & Bentall, R.P. (1994). The defensive function of persecutory delusions. Evidence from attribution tasks. *British Journal of Psychiatry*, **164**, 637–646.

Maj, M. (2005). 'Psychiatric comorbidity': An artifact of current diagnostic systems? *British Journal of Psychiatry*, **186**, 182–184.

May, R. (2004). 'Making sense of psychotic experience and working towards recovery.' In J.F.M. Gleeson & P.D. McGorry (Eds), *Psychological Intervention in Early Psychosis: A Treatment Handbook*. Chichester, UK: Wiley.

McGorry, P.D., McFarlane, C., Patton, G.C., Bell, R., Hibbert, M.E., Jackson, H.J. et al. (1995). The prevalence of prodromal features of schizophrenia in adolescence: A preliminary survey. *Acta Psychiatrica Scandinavica*, **92**, 241–249.

Miller, T.J., McGlashan, T.H., Rosen, J.L., Somjee, L., Markovich, P.J., Stein, K. et al. (2002). Prospective diagnosis of the initial prodrome for schizophrenia based on the Structured Interview for Prodromal Syndromes: preliminary evidence of interrater reliability and predictive validity. *American Journal of Psychiatry*, **159**, 863–865.

Morrison, A.P., French, P., Walford, L., Lewis, S.W., Kilcommons, A., Green, J. et al. (2004). Cognitive therapy for the prevention of psychosis in people at ultra-high risk: Randomised controlled trial. *British Journal of Psychiatry*, **185**, 291–297.

Mueser, K.T., Goodman, L.B., Trumbetta, S.L., Rosenberg, S.D., Osher, F.C., Vidaver, R. et al. (1998). Trauma and post traumatic stress disorder in severe mental illness. *Journal of Consulting and Clinical Psychology*, **66**, 493–499.

Office of Population Census and Surveys (1990). *Mortality Statistics. Causes: England and Wales*. London: HMSO.

Pearce, J. (2000). Emotional disorders in young people. In P. Aggleton, J. Hurry & I. Warwick (Eds), *Young People and Mental Health* (Chapt. 3). Chichester, UK: Wiley.

Phillips, L.J. & Francey, S.M. (2004). 'Changing PACE: psychological intervention in the prepsychotic phase.' In J.F.M. Gleeson & P.D. McGorry (Eds), *Psychological Intervention in Early Psychosis: A Treatment Handbook*. Chichester, UK: Wiley.

Poulton, R., Caspi, A., Moffitt, T.E., Cannon, M., Murray, R. & Harrington, H. (2000). Children's self-reported psychotic symptoms and adult schizophreniform disorder: A 15-year longitudinal study. *Archives of General Psychiatry*, **57**, 1053–1058.

Poznanski, E.O. & Mokros, H.B. (1994). Phenomenology and epidemiology of mood disorders in children and adolescents. In W.M. Reynolds & H.F. Johnston (Eds), *Handbook of Depression in Children and Adolescents* (pp. 3–17). New York: Plenum Press.

Putnam, F.W., Carlson, E.B., Ross, C.A., Anderson, G., Clark, P., Torem, M. et al. (1996). Patterns of dissociation in clinical and nonclinical samples. *Journal of Nervous and Mental Disease*, **184**, 673–679.

Raine, A. (1991). The SPQ: A scale for the assessment of schizotypal personality based on DSM-III-R criteria. *Schizophrenia Bulletin*, **17**, 555–564.

Read, J., Agar, K., Argyle, N. & Aderhold, V. (2003). Sexual and physical abuse during childhood and adulthood as predictors of hallucinations, delusions and thought disorder. *Psychology and Psychotherapy*, **76**, 1–22.

Read, J., Perry, B.D., Moskowitz, A. & Connolly, J. (2001). The contribution of early traumatic events to schizophrenia in some patients: a traumagenic neurodevelopmental model. *Psychiatry*, **64**, 319–345.

Romme, M.A.J. & Escher, S. (1989). *Hearing Voices*. London: Mind Publications.

Romme, M.A.J. & Escher, S. (2000). *Making Sense of Voices: The Mental Health Professional's Guide to Working with Voice Hearers*. London: Mind Publications.

Ross, C.A. & Joshi, S. (1992). Paranormal experiences in the general population. *Journal of Nervous and Mental Disease*, **180**, 357–361.

Ross, C.A., Miller, S.D., Reagor, P., Bjornson, L., Fraser, G.A. & Anderson, G. (1990). Structured interview data on 102 cases of multiple personality disorder from four centers. *American Journal of Psychiatry*, **147**, 596–601.

Roy-Byrne, P.P., Stang, P., Wittchen, H.U., Ustun, B., Walters, E.E. & Kessler, R.C. (2000). Lifetime panic-depression comorbidity in the National Comorbidity Survey. Association with symptoms, impairment, course and help-seeking. *British Journal of Psychiatry*, **176**, 229–235.

Sartorius, N., Jablensky, A., Korten, A., Ernberg, G., Anker, M., Cooper, J.E. et al. (1986). Early manifestations and first-contact incidence of schizophrenia in different cultures. A preliminary report on the initial evaluation phase of the WHO Collaborative Study on determinants of outcome of severe mental disorders. *Psychological Medicine*, **16**, 909–928.

Spitzer, R.L., Williams, J.B., Gibbon, M. & First, M.B. (1992). The Structured Clinical Interview for DSM-III-R (SCID). I: History, rationale, and description. *Archives of General Psychiatry*, **49**, 624–629.

Startup, M. (1999). Schizotypy, dissociative experiences and childhood abuse: Relationships among self-report measures. *British Journal of Clinical Psychology*, **38** (Pt. 4), 333–344.

Taylor, M.A. (1992). Are schizophrenia and affective disorder related? A selective literature review. *American Journal of Psychiatry*, **149**, 22–32.

Van Os, J., Gilvarry, C., Bale, R., Van Horn, E., Tattan, T. & White, I. (1999). A comparison of the utility of dimensional and categorical representations of psychosis. UK700 Group. *Psychological Medicine*, **29**, 595–606.

Van Os, J., Hanssen, M., Bijl, R.V. & Ravelli, A. (2000). Strauss (1969) revisited: A psychosis continuum in the general population? *Schizophrenia Research*, **45**, 11–20.

Verdoux, H. & van Os, J. (2002). Psychotic symptoms in non-clinical populations and the continuum of psychosis. *Schizophrenia Research*, **54**, 59–65.

Verdoux, H., van Os, J., Maurice-Tison, S., Gay, B., Salamon, R. & Bourgeois, M. (1998). Is early adulthood a critical developmental stage for psychosis proneness? A survey of delusional ideation in normal subjects. *Schizophrenia Research*, **29**, 247–254.

Vollrath, M. & Angst, J. (1989). Outcome of panic and depression in a seven-year follow-up: Results of the Zurich study. *Acta Psychiatrica Scandinavica*, **80**, 591–596.

Wells, A. & Matthews, G. (1994). *Attention and Emotion. A Clinical Perspective*. Hove, UK: Erlbaum.

Wittchen, H.U., Nelson, C.B. & Lachner, G. (1998). Prevalence of mental disorders and psychosocial impairments in adolescents and young adults. *Psychological Medicine*, **28**, 109–126.

Yung, A.R. & McGorry, P.D. (1996). The initial prodrome in psychosis: Descriptive and qualitative aspects. *Australian and New Zealand Journal of Psychiatry*, **30**, 587–599.

Yung, A.R., Phillips, L.J., Yuen, H.P., Francey, S.M., McFarlane, C.A. & Hallgren, M. (2003). Psychosis prediction: 12-month follow up of a high-risk ('prodromal') group. *Schizophrenia Research*, **60**, 21–32.

Yung, A.R., Phillips, L.J., Yuen, H.P. & McGorry, P.D. (2004). Risk factors for psychosis in an ultra high-risk group: Psychopathology and clinical features. *Schizophrenia Research*, **67**, 131–142.

Zimmerman, M. & Mattia, J.I. (1999). Psychiatric diagnosis in clinical practice: Is comorbidity being missed? *Comprehensive Psychiatry*, **40**, 182–191.

CHAPTER 7

Substance Use and the 'At Risk' Period

Steven Leicester

INTRODUCTION

The topic of substance use and psychosis appears to be one of, if not the most common lines of discussion that emerges from community education forums about young people thought to be at 'ultra' high risk (UHR) for psychosis. Often at these forums a commonly asked question is: 'Isn't what you're describing due to substance use?'

Like most questions relating to psychiatry and adolescence, a simple 'yes' or 'no' would be insufficient and potentially misleading. Many of the non-specific symptoms described by UHR clients such as paranoia, perceptual changes, behavioural changes and altered cognitive functioning are strikingly similar to the effects of intoxication from an array of substances. The overlap in symptoms between substance use and emerging psychotic phenomena creates a potential for diagnostic uncertainty and a lack of clarity in the causal relationship between substance use and psychosis. There is growing evidence to suggest that substance use has an adverse impact on the emergence and course of psychosis; however, the exact nuances of this relationship remain a source of considerable debate.

SUBSTANCE USE RATES

General Population

A number of large scale population studies have attempted to gauge rates of substance misuse within the general population, including the Epidemiological Catchment Area (ECA) study (Robins & Regier, 1991) and the National Comorbidity Study (NCS) (Kessler et al., 1994), both of which were conducted in the USA. These studies reported problematic alcohol misuse as amongst the most widely reported mental health disorders. The ECA study reported substance use disorders in 6% of its sample, whilst the NCS found that approximately one in four individuals reported a lifetime history of substance use disorders, with 11% meeting criteria for a substance use disorder in the previous 12 months. An

Working with People at High Risk of Developing Psychosis: A Treatment Handbook.
Edited by J. Addington, S.M. Francey and A.P. Morrison. © 2006 John Wiley & Sons, Ltd.

Australian study found similar trends in alcohol use with 6.5% reporting an alcohol disorder in the previous 12 months and approximately 2% reporting a substance use disorder in the previous 12 months (Teeson, Hall, Lynskey & Degenhardt, 2000). In the American and Australian studies cannabis was reported as the most widely used illicit substance. Furthermore, substance misuse appeared to be more prevalent in males. For example, ECA results indicated that 24% of males but only 5% of females reported a lifetime alcohol use disorder and the NCS reported similar trends.

These three studies all found that problematic substance use was most common during the adolescent to early adult years, a particularly pertinent detail given that this is the most common period of emerging psychotic phenomena. Smart and Ogbourne (2000) conducted a comprehensive multi-country review of alcohol and illicit substance use amongst students aged from 13 to 17. Whilst rates and characteristics of alcohol and substance use varied immensely among countries, alcohol was by far the most commonly used substance, and in all but two countries cannabis was the most frequently used illicit substance. Given the diversity of substance use rates among countries, caution should be taken when making assumptions of substance use characteristics among different populations.

Established Psychosis

Research amongst people with established psychotic disorders has revealed considerably higher rates of substance misuse than in the general population (Cantor-Graae, Nordstrom & McNeil, 2001; Degenhardt, Hall & Lynskey, 2003; McCreadie, 2002). Lifetime prevalence of substance use disorders has been reported as high as 59% in psychotic populations (Fowler, Carr, Carter & Lewin, 1998; Kendler, Gallagher, Abelson & Kessler, 1996). Caantor-Graae et al. (2001) conducted an extensive review of 47 studies investigating substance misuse within psychotic populations and found that lifetime prevalence of use disorders ranged from 40 to 60% in most Western samples.

Substance Misuse and Early Psychosis

During the past decade a number of studies have endeavoured to focus on characteristics of substance use specifically in early or first episode psychosis. This is particularly relevant for UHR research since it offers further insight into the development of substance use patterns and greater understanding of the relationship between emerging psychotic phenomena and substance use.

In an epidemiological study conducted in the USA, high rates of substance misuse were observed amongst 541 first admission psychosis patients, with alcohol and cannabis being the most commonly abused substances (Rabinowitz et al.,1998). Approximately 58% of males reported a lifetime substance use diagnosis, with 17% reporting current substance abuse, whilst 32% of females had a lifetime substance use diagnosis and 6% reported current abuse. A study conducted with 357 early psychosis patients in Canada found similar patterns to the US study, with approximately 40% meeting criteria for a substance use disorder (van Mastright, Addington & Addington, 2004). Cantwell and colleagues (1999) conducted a study with 168 first episode patients and also found high rates of substance misuse, with 37% meeting criteria for a substance use disorder. These studies consistently indicate that rates of substance misuse within first episode groups are similar to those observed for people with more established psychotic disorders. Further similarities to results from established psychosis studies include higher rates of substance misuse amongst males and alcohol and cannabis repeatedly reported as the most commonly misused substances. These findings suggest that for many people patterns of substance misuse may become established before the onset of psychosis, and remain through much of the course of illness. A number of studies examining the temporal relationship between substance use and psychosis have reported that substance use generally precedes the onset of psychosis by one to five years (Allebeck, Adamsson, Engstrom & Rydberg, 1993; Cleghorn et al.,1991; Hides, Lubman & Dawe, 2004; Linszen, Dingemans & Lenior, 1994).

SUBSTANCE USE AND THE COURSE OF PSYCHOSIS

A number of models have been put forward in an attempt to explain these high rates of comorbidity. The 'vulnerability model' suggests that substance misuse may precede the onset of illness and is considered as a precipitant or contributor towards the emergence of psychotic phenomena. Studies that have demonstrated a temporal relationship between substance use and increased risk of the development of psychosis support this hypothesis (Arsenault, Cannon, Witton & Murray, 2004; Smit, Bolier & Cuijpers, 2004). Further support for the 'vulnerability' model comes from studies which have demonstrated earlier age of onset, heightened rates of relapse, slower recovery and poorer functioning for substance users with psychosis compared to non-substance users (Addington & Addington, 1998; Kovasznay et al., 1997; Pencer & Addington, 2003; Sorbara, Lirand, Assens, Abalan & Verdoux, 2003).

The 'self-medication model' proposes that patients use substances as a means to alleviate distress associated with symptoms of psychosis. Authors such as Khantzian (1997) have proposed that a central feature of this model is that people select substances that offer them the most subjective relief from discomfort. However, a number of studies found no evidence to suggest that an increase in symptoms was related to an increase in substance use (Hamera, Schneider & Deviney, 1995; Verdoux, Gindre, Sorbora, Tournier & Swendsen, 2003a).

More recently a 'personality model' of high rates of substance use within psychotic populations has prompted considerable discussion (Blanchard, Brown, Horan & Sherwood, 2000; Hides et al., 2004). This model hypothesises that a number of enduring personality traits including neuroticism and impulsivity contribute to the lifetime risk of psychosis and substance misuse. Further research utilising longitudinal designs is required to explore the interaction of personality factors upon substance use and psychosis (Hides et al., 2004).

Existing models of comorbidity have begun to offer further insight into the relationship dynamics between substance use and psychosis. However, accurate clarification of the processes involved is yet to occur, suggesting that the interaction between psychosis and substance use is a highly complex matter, involving myriad variables, which may vary from person to person.

For more than a decade, evidence has been mounting to give further weight to the hypothesis that substance use influences the development and maintenance of psychosis (Boyle & Offord, 1991; Brook, Cohen & Brook, 1998; Kovasznay et al., 1997; Hall, 1998; Sorbara et al., 2003). Substance misuse as a precipitant for positive psychotic symptoms has been demonstrated in numerous studies with tetrahydrocannabinol (THC), lysergic acid diethylamide (LSD), amphetamine, cocaine, psilocybin and phencyclidine (Barondes, 1999; Griffiths, Cavanagh & Oates, 1972; Hall, 1998; Horowitz, 1969).

The apparent cross-over between numerous psychotic phenomena with poly-substance use highlights the difficulty in delineating substance use and emerging psychotic disorders. This difficulty is particularly relevant for assessing early psychosis or identifying UHR clients when an array of new clinical concerns and substance use may be occurring simultaneously, thus making accurate diagnosis during this critical period particularly challenging (Jackson, McGorry & Dudgeon, 1995). In a retrospective study of people with comorbid psychosis and substance misuse, approximately half were initially given a diagnosis of drug-induced psychosis, which may have extended their period of untreated psychosis (Addington & Addington, 1998). Linszen and Lenior (1999) propose that one needs to balance the risk of 'over-diagnosing' a psychotic disorder against missing a psychosis-related diagnosis and potentially delaying crucial treatment.

Numerous studies have demonstrated that substance use in general has a detrimental effect on the course of early psychosis. In a two-year follow-up study of early psychosis patients, the risk of readmission was three times as high for those with substance misuse and substance use was associated with increased duration of psychotic symptoms (Sorbara et al., 2003). Furthermore, earlier age of onset, greater persistence of positive symptoms, higher rates of antisocial behaviour and lowered overall functioning have all been demonstrated to occur at significantly higher levels for early psychosis patients with comorbid substance misuse (Addington & Addington, 1998; DeQuardo, Carpenter & Tandon, 1994; Kovasznay et al., 1997; Pencer & Addington, 2003; Sorbara et al., 2003).

However, in an extensive review of studies addressing relationships between substance misuse and early psychosis, Rabinowitz et al. (1998) found that there were very few consistent clinical differences between people with and without substance misuse. The authors suggest this may indicate there is limited evidence that substance misuse has a negative effect on early psychosis. This finding also highlights that the interactions between psychotic symptoms and substance misuse are extremely diverse and not easily captured through traditional research designs.

A Focus on Cannabis

Over the past decade there has been a growing push towards researching the role of cannabis use in the development and maintenance of psychiatric conditions. Cannabis has been reported as the most widely used illicit substance among young people in many Western societies (Kessler et al., 1994; Robins & Regier, 1991; Smart & Ogbourne, 2000; Teeson et al., 2000). Furthermore, cannabis use has been shown to contribute to a range of non-psychotic mental health problems. Bovasso (2001) conducted a long-term follow-up study over a 15-year period using 1 920 participants and observed that those with a baseline diagnosis of cannabis abuse were four times more likely to have depressive symptoms at follow-up. Teenage cannabis use was shown to have a relationship with increased risk of adolescent anxiety and depression (Patton et al., 2002). Cannabis use during adolescence has also been demonstrated to contribute to an array of psychosocial difficulties, including heightened risk of leaving school early, other illicit substance use and antisocial behaviour (Fergusson, Horwood & Swain-Campbell, 2002; Lynskey, Coffey, Degenhardt, Carlin & Patton, 2003; Macleod et al., 2004).

There is considerable epidemiological evidence for an association between cannabis and psychosis; however, there is limited consensus surrounding the reasons for this association (Hall, Degenhardt & Teeson, 2004). Biological evidence suggests that cannabis use may exacerbate psychotic phenomena, since cannabinoids such as THC have been shown to increase the release of dopamine which has been associated with the expression of psychotic symptoms (Adams & Martin, 1996; Hall, 1998). A number of studies provide evidence to suggest that cannabis use can produce exacerbation or recurrence of pre-existing positive psychotic symptoms (Arsenault et al., 2004; van Os et al., 2002). Cannabis use in individuals with established psychosis has been demonstrated to worsen symptomatology, adversely effect compliance to treatment, as well as increasing rates of suicidality, relapse and readmission (Bersani, Orlandi, Kotzalidis & Pancheri, 2002; Linszen et al., 1994). It is important to highlight that an association between cannabis use and positive psychotic symptoms, such as hallucinatory phenomena and paranoid ideation, has been observed within both clinical and non-clinical populations (Johns et al., 2004; van Os et al., 2002; Verdoux et al., 2003a). Such a relationship, regardless of whether symptoms are at threshold level for a psychotic disorder, could be considered adequate support for the argument that cannabis use is at the very least a risk factor in the development of psychosis.

The question of whether cannabis use can cause psychosis is particularly pertinent for UHR research, especially for those who present as meeting criteria for both UHR and cannabis misuse. Our current mindset is to assume that cannabis use adds to vulnerability for psychosis. Previous reviews of cross-sectional or clinical studies were often unable to delineate temporal relationships between cannabis use and psychosis and had difficulty controlling for selection bias and the influence of other substances (Degenhardt, 2003). However, in recent years results from five large longitudinal studies have been published from Sweden (Zammit, Allebeck, Andreason, Lundberg & Lewis, 2002), Israel (Weiser, Knobler, Noy & Kaplan, 2002), New Zealand (Arsenault et al., 2002; Fergusson, Horwood & Swain-Campbell, 2003) and the Netherlands (van Os et al., 2002). These studies have taken considerable steps towards more accurately observing temporal relationships between cannabis and psychosis as well as accounting for selection bias and other drug use in non-experimental designs. The results offer converging support for the hypothesis that cannabis use increases the risk for psychosis, particularly for 'vulnerable people' such as those with a history of psychosis. Furthermore, cannabis appears to play its own unique role in the development of psychotic disorders by doubling the risk of developing psychosis, even when factors such as other substance use, IQ, social integration and education level are taken into account (Arsenault et al., 2004; Smit et al., 2004).

'AT RISK' POPULATIONS

Studies of substance use rates and characteristics within high-risk populations remain quite limited and further research in this area is certainly needed. In a sample of 60 young people, 7% reported current substance use, with cannabis being the most prevalent (Miller et al., 2003). Phillips and colleagues (2002) were able to review substance use in a sample of 100 UHR clients and found that 18% met criteria for cannabis dependence within the previous 12 months, whilst other substance use was minimal. These reported rates, particularly from Phillips' study, suggest that substance misuse falls somewhere between the estimated use of the general population and those with established psychosis.

Identifying substance use within UHR populations is particularly difficult since the UHR individuals that do come to service attention are generally recognising they are experiencing difficulties and seeking support. Hutchison and Lee (2002) compared groups of first episode psychosis patients and found that those with substance abuse took considerably longer to access support following the onset of their psychotic symptoms. This suggests that substance use may lower the likelihood that UHR clients seek assistance and treatment and extend the duration of untreated psychosis, which has been shown to increase the risk of poorer treatment outcomes and greater long-term disability (Birchwood, 2000).

A number of studies have endeavoured to explore the role of substance use with individuals thought to be at increased risk of psychosis. Miller et al. (2001) conducted a study with young people deemed at high risk of psychosis due to genetic loading and a non-clinical control group. It was found that cannabis and other illicit drugs predicted the occurrence of psychotic symptoms within both groups. A dose–response effect was observed, in that higher rates of consumption correlated with higher likelihood of experiencing positive psychotic symptoms in both groups. Unfortunately, due to small numbers in the comparison group it was not possible to show whether the effect of substance use was more powerful for the 'at risk' individuals.

An Australian group at the Personal Assessment and Crisis Evaluation (PACE) Clinic looked at the role cannabis may have had on a group of young people identified as being at high risk of psychosis due to state and trait factors (Phillip et al., 2002). Results from this study suggested that cannabis use did not significantly contribute to the risk of transition to psychosis within a 12-month period. A major limitation of this study is the relatively short 12-month follow-up period. Henquet and colleagues (2005) expanded their follow-up period to four years in a prospective cohort study of 2 437 randomly selected young people from a regional population. The authors used the 'paranoid ideation' and 'psychoticism' scales of a symptom checklist (SCL-90-R; Derogatis, 1983) in order to identify those with a high predisposition to psychosis. They found that any cannabis use around the baseline period increased the risk of psychosis at follow-up in a dose–response fashion. Furthermore, the effect of cannabis use on the psychosis outcome was significantly stronger for those identified at baseline as having a high predisposition towards psychosis compared to those without a high predisposition.

A further study found that the effects of cannabis use were modified according to the individual's level of vulnerability to psychosis (Verdoux et al., 2003a). They assessed vulnerability to psychosis using the Community Assessment of Psychotic Experiences (CAPE; Stefanis et al., 2001; Verdoux, Sorbara, Gindre, Swendsen & van Os, 2003b). Individuals identified as having a high vulnerability to psychosis were more likely to report unusual perceptual experiences as well as feelings of thought influence and were less likely to experience pleasurable effects from cannabis when compared to those without a high predisposition for psychosis. This finding suggests that exposure to cannabis may promote psychotic experiences in people with an existing vulnerability.

Whilst the majority of these studies suggests that substance misuse is detrimental to people thought to be at high risk of psychosis, the results are tentative at best. All of these studies incorporated vastly different criteria for defining 'high risk' and varied their approaches to measuring substance use. Further research should ideally incorporate long-term follow-up designs with standardised assessments for defining vulnerability to psychosis.

PRINCIPLES OF TREATMENT

The following discussion will incorporate general principles pertaining to working with substance use within UHR groups. This discussion does not specify a specific treatment plan; rather, it outlines ideas that reflect current best practice within early psychosis and UHR services. Cognitive Behavioural Therapy (CBT) has been used within UHR populations at a number of services, with the overall aims of addressing presenting distressing conditions and reducing the risk of transition to psychosis (Bechdolf, Wagner & Hambrecht, 2002; French & Morrison, 2004; Phillips & Francey, 2004). We would currently advocate that CBT continues to form the foundations of psychological treatment and that further research continues in this area. Specific substance use interventions have yet to be evaluated for young people identified as being at high risk of psychosis. Therefore, as with many approaches and models in the UHR fields, we continue to incorporate treatment principles from the early psychosis field.

There have been few well-controlled trials addressing substance use for people with established psychosis (Degenhardt, 2003; Drake, Mercer-McFadden, Mueser, McHugo & Bond, 1998). The very nature of such research is fraught with difficulties, as the risks of withholding treatment for 'comparison groups' is great and research trials are often conducted in clinical environments where integrated and comprehensive treatment is already the standard. In an extensive review of integrated mental health and substance abuse treatments, Drake and colleagues (1998) found that the interventions displaying the most encouraging results differed from other interventions by incorporating an array of components including assertive outreach and motivational interviewing. Such programmes illustrated that comprehensive, integrated approaches aid in engaging and retaining patients, as well as helping to reduce substance use over time.

Further clarification of the relationships between substance misuse and psychotic disorders will aid in the development of specialised treatment interventions (Linszen & Lenior, 1999). Despite this, there is still a range of practically oriented approaches that can be adopted which are aimed towards enhancing engagement and reducing the risk of further mental illness. It is important to highlight that brief interventions can be very useful, and reviews have demonstrated that they are consistently more effective than no intervention – and often as effective as more extensive interventions in reducing problematic substance misuse such as alcohol abuse (Bien, Miller & Tonigan, 1993).

There is broad agreement that people presenting with substance use and other mental health concerns require integrated, specialised treatment approaches that focus on both psychiatric symptoms and substance use (Bellack & Gearon, 1998; Bradley & Toohey, 1998; Degenhardt, 2003; Drake et al., 1998). Such a model incorporates expert skills from mental health and substance use specialities, creating an integrated programme of assessment and treatment (Drake, Bartels, Teague, Noordsy & Clarke, 1993). This differs considerably from 'parallel treatment' (Ries, 1993), which posits traditional mental health treatment as always primary and linking other needs such as substance use treatment in an ad hoc and separated manner.

Generally speaking, a harm minimisation approach is widely adopted throughout substance use treatment with first episode psychosis populations (Hinton, Elkins, Edwards & Donovan, 2002). The driving concept is to work towards reducing the problems that derive from substance use as much as possible. Ideally this can be achieved through abstinence;

however, for many clients this is not feasible or realistic. Substance use should not be vilified and demands to reduce or cease substance use should be avoided in most cases. Focus can be placed on building and maintaining a collaborative therapeutic relationship and techniques that may threaten engagement such as demonising or taking a punitive approach towards a client's substance use should not be adopted. Rumbold and Hamilton (1998) highlight that clients are more likely to consider change in their substance use if they remain engaged within the therapeutic process.

Assessment – Moving Towards the Client's Explanatory Model

A number of authors highlight that poor assessment of dual diagnosis clients from both substance use and mental health services has contributed to high resource use and relatively poor treatment outcomes for dual-diagnosis patients (Bradley & Toohey, 1998; Rorstad & Checinski, 1996). As previously mentioned, there is considerable overlap in symptom presentation that can occur between substance misuse and psychotic phenomena (Jackson et al., 1995; Olin & Keating, 1998), which can lead to misdiagnosis and subsequent inappropriate treatment. There is a strong need for accurate and detailed assessment of psychiatric symptoms and substance use to be conducted for all UHR clients, and for regular reviews to occur throughout the treatment period. The emphasis of assessment should not only be for diagnostic certainty, but for a committed focus towards empathic engagement and development of a client-focused formulation.

A range of key features for assessment can be adopted from the early psychosis field (Hinton et al., 2002). These include:

- Assessment of substance use should obtain thorough histories, including substance use of family and peers, as well as detailed accounts of the context of such use, e.g. social environments, major events in the person's life. Consideration should be made to understanding the precipitants towards use, changing use patterns over time, perceived costs and benefits, as well as an evaluation of the individual's motivation to change (Phillips & Francey, 2004).
- Regular reviews of substance use should become a routine feature of clinical care. This reinforces the clinical importance of substance use within treatment and allows for heightened awareness, from both therapist and client, of any change in both substance taking and mental health.
- Personal impact and insight related to the substance use should be a focus of assessment and reviews. Insight is a fundamental factor involved in engagement and motivation towards change.
- It is important to keep the assessment and reviews of substance use within the context of mental health. Keep it as an integrated approach and try to avoid considering substance use in isolation from mental health and well-being.

Ideally a thorough and collaborative approach towards assessment should result in the development of the client's own explanatory model of both their substance use and mental health. Such a model can act as a central feature towards developing individualised and flexible treatment planning. A fundamental feature of intervention within the UHR stage is collaboration, where both the client and therapist work together in deciding the direction of treatment, and the client is genuinely acknowledged as the 'expert' of his or her own experience (Phillips & Francey, 2004). Furthermore, an accurate and individualised approach towards assessment will aid in clarifying the motivation, commitment and resources the client has towards change. Elkins, Hinton and Edwards (2004) highlight that if significant disparity occurs between the client's motivation towards change and the selected mode of treatment, rapport and engagement can be greatly threatened.

Psychoeducation

Psychoeducation is recognised as a core component of treatment within early psychosis (Edwards & McGorry, 2002) and forms a major foundation of treatment within UHR populations (Phillips & Francey, 2004). Psychoeducation should include, but not be limited to:

* Information about risk of psychosis, including factors which potentially increase risk such as stress and substance misuse.
* Information about concerns that brought clients to services.
* Treatment options and approaches.
* Specific information regarding drug and alcohol use.

Appropriate psychoeducation can provide an opportunity for accurate information dissemination as well as offering a level of responsibility with the client to make educated decisions in their treatment process (McGorry, 1995). It is important to highlight that psychoeducation should be provided throughout treatment and not be restricted to the initial introductory phase (Hinton et al., 2002; Phillips & Francey, 2004).

Ensuring that clients are encouraged to openly discuss their thoughts about psychoeducation material and incorporating their responses within formulations can maintain collaboration. Provision of information alone may not be sufficient to engage clients, therefore it is essential to explore and elicit clients' reactions and interpretations of the material provided (Edwards & McGorry, 2002). It is very important that psychoeducation material is tailored towards the individual client's needs, rather than presented as a generic education package (Phillips & Francey, 2004). It is the therapist's responsibility to attain an adequate collection of psychoeducation material. Ideally material should cover a range of mediums, including written, video and Internet sites, with a focus on making delivery of materials as interactive as possible.

Motivational Interviewing (MI)

MI can be incorporated within a CBT framework and has been demonstrated to be adaptable to integrated mental health settings (Baker & Hambridge, 2002; Drake et al., 1998). Barrowclough and colleagues (2001) compared 'routine care' which consisted of psychiatric management via case management of medication, monitoring and access to community programmes, with a programme of 'integrated treatment', which included routine care as well as MI, CBT and family intervention for people with comorbid schizophrenia and substance use disorders. Those participants receiving the integrated programme demonstrated greater improvement in general functioning, reduction in positive symptoms and increased days of substance abstinence over a 12-month period, compared to those receiving routine care. MI is an approach that focuses on consolidating an individual's commitment towards changing his or her substance use and was initially developed as an intervention for alcohol misuse (Miller, 1983). The 'trans-theoretical model' of behaviour change outlines that an individual may move through a series of stages in the process of changing his or her behaviour (DiClemente & Prochaska, 1998; DiClemente & Velasquez, 2002; Prochaska, DiClemente & Norcross, 1992). The stages of change include pre-contemplation, where the individual is not considering a step towards change, to contemplation, where serious attention is given towards the costs and benefits of change, through to preparation, where planning occurs. The final stage is maintenance, where the individual actively works to sustaining change. MI pays particular attention to acknowledging the stages of behavioural change and refrains from pushing people towards adjusting behaviours until the individual is willing.

MI is a collaborative rather than prescriptive approach, in which the focus is to evoke the person's own motivation and resources for change by supporting clients to explore and resolve ambivalence (Rollnick & Miller, 1995). Underlying MI is an implicit belief that each individual has such motivation and resources to change, and that evocation rather than persuasion serves best in resolving ambivalence (Rollnick & Miller, 1995). The process avoids direct confrontation and challenging, preferring to acknowledge clients' perspectives at all times. MI can be integrated within such other therapeutic processes of clarifying commitment and insight, identifying client-relevant goals, identifying barriers towards reaching established goals and heightening relapse prevention in an individualised manner.

MI is a flexible and client-responsive approach that is ideal for adapting to UHR populations, where the clinical diversity and needs of clients are extremely heterogeneous (Leicester, Phillips, Francey, Yung & McGorry, 2003). MI is particularly adaptable to adolescent populations where ambivalence and defiance is common. As such, an approach that minimises overt challenging and confrontation can serve well to enhance engagement (Baer & Peterson, 2002). In addition, MI has been demonstrated to be effective within indicated prevention contexts, such as for reducing alcohol-related incidents in adolescents (Monti et al., 1999). However, Bellack and Gearon (1998) suggest that the level of client-centred focus for self-exploration may need to be adapted for people struggling with abstraction, introspection and other high level cognitive tasks. They recommend that a somewhat more directive style could be incorporated, so that the therapist is more leading in exploration of adverse consequences of sustained substance misuse.

Miller and Rollnick (2002) emphasise the importance of understanding the guiding principles of MI, rather than approaching it as a strictly defined sequence of techniques. The guiding principles include:

1. Empathy. Be empathic by acknowledging and respecting the client's perspective without judgement. This includes acknowledging ambivalence, which is considered normal within behavioural change. This is not to condone substance use, but promote acceptance and understanding.
2. Develop discrepancy. Discrepancies between the way the clients perceive themselves and the way they actually are should be highlighted by the therapist. This can take place by exploring the costs of the substance use and identifying past, present and future goals. If the discrepancy is highlighted, the individual will endeavour to change in order to remove the tension (Elkins et al., 2004). In essence, highlighting the discrepancy between beliefs and behaviour can be a powerful factor towards motivating change.

3. Roll with resistance. Arguing is counterproductive towards addressing ambivalence or productive change and places engagement of the client at great risk. Rolling with resistance is an important acknowledgement of the client's perspective and techniques such as reflection and reframing are encouraged. The therapist can still invite new information and perspectives, for example via psychoeducation, but refrain from imposing these views. An important element of rolling with resistance is to be aware that resistance is a sign that the client sees the situation differently and a change in approach is most likely needed.

4. Support self-efficacy. The concept of self-efficacy refers to the client's own belief about his or her ability to accomplish certain tasks and goals. This is a key factor involved in decisions towards change and therapists can promote self-efficacy via reflection on past achievements and reinforcing that change is realistic and achievable.

Decision Grid

A valuable and collaborative technique within the framework of MI is to explore the client's perceived costs and benefits of the use and cessation of substances. It is important to allow sufficient time to generate a comprehensive account of these factors and reflection from previous sessions is certainly helpful. A 'Decision Grid' (Fig. 7.1) can be developed consisting of four quadrants, each of which is worked through individually so that careful attention is focused on numerous perspectives towards substance use. The recommended order for working through the cells is indicated, so that a cohesive flow can be maintained when exploring each perspective (Elkins et al., 2004; Hinton et al., 2002).

Miller and Rollnick (2002) suggest that the therapist works towards allowing the client to 'persuade' him/herself that there is substantial reason for change. The Decision Grid requires that the client focuses on his or her substance use in a structured and detailed manner and considers their use from a number of different perspectives. Following initial development of the grid, exploration and summary should work towards clients clarifying their position by defending the statements they have generated in a non-confronting manner (Elkins et al., 2004). The Decision Grid provides a platform from where clear decisions about goal setting can be made.

Collaboration and a client-focused perspective should continue to be central to the therapeutic process and an individualised approach should be adopted to clarify clients' goals and needs. Whilst treatment modules and methods will vary between services, we would advocate that a CBT approach is tailored towards reaching treatment goals and objectives.

1 Positive factors related to substance use.	4 Positive factors related to reducing or ceasing substance use.
3 Negative factors about continuing substance use.	2 Negative factors about stopping substance use.

Figure 7.1   Decision Grid

Relapse Prevention

It is normal for problematic substance use to relapse when treatment has ended (Elkins et al., 2004). Booster sessions towards the end of treatment are recommended, with a focus on reaffirmation of commitment towards client-generated goals and attention to maintain positive momentum. An extended treatment plan may also incorporate planned follow-up sessions after the core treatment phase, which serve to revise psychoeducation material, check on support resources and review threats to goal attainment (Elkins et al., 2004; Phillips & Francey, 2004).

Case example

Ben was a 17-year-old boy who was living with his family and had been unemployed since leaving school six months prior to referral. Initially Ben had consulted his local doctor about his lowered mood and was subsequently referred to our service. Upon assessment he reported experiencing approximately 10 months of lowered mood, decreased motivation and heightened irritability. He reported a range of sub-threshold psychotic symptoms, including regularly feeling as though others were able to know and alter his thoughts, mild paranoia and infrequent auditory hallucinations. Ben clearly stated that he was quite disturbed by these experiences and felt that his ability to control them was steadily decreasing. Ben was a regular cannabis user, smoking most nights of the week with his close friends for over two years. Initially he acknowledged cannabis may have adverse side effects such as mild paranoia, but felt that the source of problems was more related to unemployment and family conflict.

Ben was initially reluctant to discuss his experiences in detail and struggled with exploring stressors or difficulties, which may have been related to his depressive features and mental state concerns. He insisted that he just wanted to feel better and since we were the 'experts', we should be able to fix the situation. Ben's reluctance and ambivalence during the early stages of treatment were acknowledged and explored. He was soon able to begin discussing important changes and factors in his life, which were incorporated into developing his own explanatory model of his difficulties. Psychoeducation was incorporated from the start of therapy and created a safe environment to discuss issues that Ben often found difficult to explore, such as substance use, stress and managing distressing thoughts.

The Decision Grid was introduced after several sessions following agreement to explore Ben's substance use in more depth. This followed acknowledgement that his cannabis use 'may' be problematic for his mental health. Homework activities were gradually incorporated with a focus on monitoring and raising awareness of cognitive, emotional and environmental factors involved in cannabis use. The homework did not involve asking Ben to challenge or dispute negative thoughts or emotions, but focused on raising a detailed level of awareness of aspects connected with his cannabis use. These diary-based tasks became a rich source of information for the Decision Grid. He was initially surprised at being encouraged to openly discuss the positives surrounding drugs, since he was used to feeling quite defensive about his cannabis use. Ben identified that cannabis helped to relieve boredom, created laughter, bonded him closely with his friends and helped him to sleep. He was concerned that stopping smoking would jeopardise friendships, reduce regular activities, leave him with 'no interests', create boredom and would result in him spending more time at home. Ben was able to identify a range of negatives caused by cannabis, including financial burden, 'possibly' making his distressing thoughts worse, worsening his relationships with his family, creating the 'same old' routine and that he wasn't feeling the 'high' any more. He reported that stopping smoking would create an opportunity for new activities, potentially help his mental state, improve relationships with his family and increase his chances of finding employment.

Following the Decision Grid, goals were established around gaining employment as a mechanic and finding new activities outside the constant pattern of nightly cannabis use. Ben stated that he would start to consider discussion about reducing his cannabis intake, although he was uncertain about implementing strategies to do so. He was quite sceptical of straightforward distraction-based behavioural approaches for coping with urges or cravings. Whilst initially this may have been interpreted as ambivalence, it opened the door for Ben to consider other approaches that were more personalised to his needs. He discussed his aims to reduce smoking with friends and included them as a source of encouragement, rather than an element of life he feared jeopardising. The specific behavioural approaches that Ben found most appropriate included delaying the time of his first intake of cannabis for the evening, delaying the time between his 'pipes' and smoking smaller amounts. These initial steps could be gradually increased and since they were around controlling use rather than abstinence, he was able to observe improvements within the first week of implementation. Delaying his first pipe for the evening by 20 minutes and using marginally smaller amounts of cannabis gave Ben concrete evidence that he was able to make noticeable changes relatively quickly, without having a major impact on his life. This first period of small but steady change was invaluable because it gave Ben the confidence to commit to further adjustments he wanted in his life. Personal goals and ambitions such as gaining work within the automotive industry and returning to playing music with friends on a regular basis appeared to be more realistic.

During the following months therapy focused on managing distressing thoughts and associated anxiety, CBT targeting depressive thoughts and gaining employment. Over the period of six months Ben gained work as an apprentice mechanic, reduced his smoking to once weekly and recommenced playing the guitar. His psychotic-like symptoms reduced and Ben was effectively able to utilise both cognitive and behavioural techniques to identify and challenge distressing thoughts. Over a 12-month period Ben was able to clearly identify that increasing his cannabis use coincided with heightened irritability, lowered mood, an increase in disturbed cognitions and reduced motivation to work. This development in insight as to how Ben's substance use affected numerous aspects of his life became a very powerful motivator for an ongoing commitment to reduce and eventually cease cannabis use. Furthermore, he identified that ongoing cannabis use could jeopardise the goals he had already achieved which appeared central to sustaining his mental health.

Formulation

Ben commenced using cannabis in his early teens and the benefits he observed were immediate and powerful. Firstly, by being known to use cannabis he not only experienced social acceptance, he established an identity amongst his adolescent peers. He felt as though he was more than merely a follower and enjoyed developing his reputation as a 'smoker'. Ben did not notice adverse effects during his initial years of smoking; in fact, he enjoyed the sensations of intoxication, which usually occurred in relaxed social environments where friendships were formed and solidified around cannabis. He was not behaviourally challenging at school and generally got along well with teachers. During the early stages of his cannabis use he felt as though cannabis had only impacted positively on his quality of life.

During Ben's later years of secondary school a number of stressors emerged that were within the 'normal' realm of adolescent development. His ambivalence towards studies was beginning to be noticed by teachers and reported back to his parents. This resulted in a moderate level of tension at school and regular arguments at home. Ben was not used to being challenged and tended to react with a high level of defensiveness and, at times, verbal aggression, thus escalating the intensity and frequency of discordance with his parents. During this period he began experiencing heightened irritability, lowered mood and less enjoyment of regular activities such as social interaction. He believed this was due to the arguing and 'pressure' he felt he was under from family and school.

He would escape from both school and family by smoking cannabis with friends and eventually the friends would come to Ben's to smoke. Cannabis and friends became the source of many arguments with his family, but for Ben they were the only positives he could recognise. Paranoid beliefs began developing relating to questioning the motives of family members and rumination regarding what friends thought of him. These 'unusual' cognitive experiences began regularly eliciting extreme levels of anxiety and his ability to question his thoughts and reduce rumination was steadily decreasing. At times during these periods of heightened arousal he experienced brief auditory hallucinations, which were difficult to decipher, and concern that others such as friends may be able to somehow influence his distress. As changes in Ben's mental state intensified a familiar pattern of cannabis consumption, avoidance of family and withdrawal from school had set in.

A large part of the treatment focus was to develop further understanding regarding disparities between Ben's coping mechanisms and his ambitions. Only after considerable work around recognising maladaptive coping mechanisms, i.e. cannabis and avoidance, could discussion around ambitions commence. Whilst cannabis became a particular focus, the overall aims were to address the presenting distress and move towards developing his quality of life. As insight developed, motivation and confidence surrounding the possibility of change increased.

ACKNOWLEDGEMENTS

The author gratefully acknowledges the contributions of Leanne Hides, Kathryn Elkins, Lisa Phillips and Shona Francey. A very special thanks to all the clients, families and staff of the PACE Clinic.

REFERENCES

Adams, I.B. & Martin, B.R. (1996). Cannabis: Pharmacology and toxicology in animals and humans. *Addiction*, **91**, 1585–1614.
Addington, J. & Addington, D. (1998). Effect of substance misuse in early psychosis. *British Journal of Psychiatry*, **172** (Suppl. 33), 134–136.
Allebeck, P., Adamsson, C., Engstrom, A. & Rydberg, U. (1993). Cannabis and schizophrenia: A longitudinal study of cases treated in Stockholm County. *Acta Psychiatrica Scandinavica*, **88**, 21–24.
Arsenault, L., Cannon, M., Poulton, R., Murray, R., Caspi, A. & Moffitt, T.E. (2002). Cannabis use in adolescence and risk for adult psychosis: Longitudinal prospective study. *British Medical Journal*, **325**, 1212–1213.
Arseneault, L., Cannon, M., Witton, J. & Murray, R. (2004). Causal association between cannabis and psychosis: Examination of the evidence. *British Journal of Psychiatry*, **184**, 110–117.
Baer, J.S. & Peterson, P.L. (2002). Motivational interviewing with adolescents and young adults. In W.R. Miller & S. Rollnick (Eds), *Motivational Interviewing* (2nd edn, pp. 320–332). New York: Guilford Press.
Baker, A. & Hambridge, J. (2002). Motivational interviewing: enhancing engagement in treatment for mental health problems. *Behaviour Change*, **19**, 138–145.
Barondes, S.H. (1999). *Molecules and Mental Illness*. New York: Scientific American Library.
Barrowclough, C., Haddock, G., Tarrier, N., Lewis, S.N., Moring, J., O'Brien, R. et al. (2001). Randomized controlled trial of motivational interviewing, cognitive behavioural therapy and family intervention for patients with comorbid schizophrenia and substance use disorders. *American Journal of Psychiatry*, **158**, 1706–1713.

Bechdolf, A., Wagner, M. & Hambrecht, M. (2002). Psychological intervention in the pre-psychotic phase: Preliminary results of a multicentre trial. *Acta Psychiatrica Scandinavica*, **104**, 41.

Bellack, A.S. & Gearon, J.S. (1998). Substance abuse treatment for people with schizophrenia. *Addictive Behaviours*, **23**, 749–766.

Bersani, G., Orlandi, V., Kotzalidis, G.D. & Pancheri, P. (2002). Cannabis and schizophrenia: Impact on onset, course, psychopathology and outcomes. *European Archives of Psychiatry and Clinical Neuroscience*, **252**, 86–92.

Bien, T.H., Miller, W.R. & Tonigan, J.S. (1993). Brief interventions for alcohol problems: A review. *Addiction*, **88**, 315–336.

Birchwood, M. (2000). The critical period for early intervention. In M. Birchwood, D. Fowler & C. Jackson (Eds), *Early Intervention in Psychosis* (pp. 28–63). Chichester, UK: Wiley.

Blanchard, J.J., Brown, S.A., Horan, W.P. & Sherwood, A.R. (2000). Substance use disorders in schizophrenia: Review, integration and a proposed model. *Clinical Psychology Review*, **20**, 207–234.

Bovasso, B.B. (2001). Cannabis abuse as a risk factor for depressive symptoms. *American Journal of Psychiatry*, **158**, 2033–2037.

Boyle, M.H. & Offord, D.R. (1991). Psychiatric disorders and substance use in adolescence. *Canadian Journal of Psychiatry*, **36**, 699–705.

Bradley, A. & Toohey, B. (1998, February). *Individualised Assessment and Treatment Planning for Dual Diagnosis Clients: A Practical Model for Clinicians*. Workshop presented at Having it both ways: problematic drug and alcohol use and mental illness, Melbourne, Australia.

Brook, J.S., Cohen, P. & Brook, D. (1998). Longitudinal study of co-occurring psychiatric disorders and substance use. *American Academy of Child & Adolescent Psychiatry*, **37**, 322–330.

Cantor-Graae, E., Nordstrom, L.G. & McNeil, T.F. (2001). Substance abuse in schizophrenia: A review of the literature and a study of correlates in Sweden. *Schizophrenia Research*, **48**, 69–82.

Cantwell, R., Brewin, J., Glazebrook, C., Dalkin, T., Fox, R., Medley, I. et al. (1999). Prevalence of substance misuse in first-episode psychosis. *British Journal of Psychiatry*, **174**, 150–153.

Cleghorn, J.M., Kaplan, M.D., Szechtman, B., Szetchman, H., Brown, G.M. & Franco, S. (1991). Substance use and schizophrenia: Effect on symptoms but not neurocognitive function. *Journal of Clinical Psychiatry*, **52**, 26–30.

Degenhardt, L. (2003). Editorial: The link between cannabis use and psychosis: Furthering the debate. *Psychological Medicine*, **33**, 3–6.

Degenhardt, L., Hall, W. & Lynskey, M. (2003). Testing hypotheses about relationships between cannabis use and psychosis in Australia. *Drug and Alcohol Dependence*, **71**, 37–48.

DeQuardo, J.R., Carpenter, C.F. & Tandon, R. (1994). Patterns of substance abuse in schizophrenia: nature and significance. *Journal of Psychiatric Research*, **28**, 267–275.

Derogatis, J.R. (1983). *SCL-90-R: Administration, Scoring and Procedures Manual – II*. Towson: Clinical Psychometric Research.

DiClemente, C.C. & Prochaska, J.O. (1998). Toward a comprehensive, transtheoretical model of change: Stages of change and addictive behaviours. In W.R. Miller & N. Heather (Eds), *Treating Addictive Behaviours* (2nd edn, pp. 3–24). New York: Plenum Press.

DiClemente, C.C. & Velasquez, M.M. (2002). Motivational interviewing and the stages of change. In W.R. Miller & S. Rollnick (Eds), *Motivational Interviewing* (2nd edn, pp. 201–221). New York: Guilford Press.

Drake, R.E., Bartels, S.J., Teague, G.B., Noordsy, D.L. & Clarke, R.E. (1993). Treatment of substance abuse in severely mentally ill patients. *Journal of Nervous and Mental Disease*, **18**, 606–611.

Drake, R.E., Mercer-McFadden, C., Mueser, K.T., McHugo, G.J. & Bond, G.R. (1998). Review of integrated mental health and substance abuse treatment for patients with dual disorders. *Schizophrenia Bulletin*, **24**, 589–608.

Edwards, J. & McGorry, P.D. (2002). *Implementing Early Intervention in Psychosis*. London: Martin Dunitz.

Elkins, K., Hinton, M. & Edwards, J. (2004). Cannabis and psychosis. In J.F.M. Gleeson & P.D. McGorry (Eds), *Psychological Interventions in Early Psychosis: A Treatment Handbook* (pp. 137–156). Chichester, UK: Wiley.

Fergusson, D.M., Horwood, L.J. & Swain-Campbell, N.R. (2002). Cannabis use and psychosocial adjustment in adolescents and young people. *Addiction*, **97**, 1123–1135.

Fergusson, D.M., Horwood, L.J. & Swain-Campbell, N.R. (2003). Cannabis dependence and psychotic symptoms in young people. *Psychological Medicine*, **33**, 15–21.

Fowler, I.L., Carr, V.J., Carter, N.T. & Lewin, T.J. (1998). Patterns of current and lifetime substance use in schizophrenia. *Schizophrenia Bulletin*, **24**, 443–455.

French, P. & Morrison, A.P. (2004). *Early Detection and Cognitive Therapy for People at High Risk of Developing Psychosis: A Treatment Approach*. New York: Wiley.

Griffiths, J.D., Cavanagh, J. & Oates, J. (1972). Paranoid episodes induced by drugs. *Journal of the American Medical Association*, **205**, 39–46.

Hall, W. (1998, February). *Cannabis Use and Psychosis*. Keynote address from Having it both ways: Problematic drug and alcohol use and mental illness, Melbourne, Australia.

Hall, W., Degenhardt, L. & Teeson, M. (2004). Cannabis use and psychotic disorders: An update. *Drug and Alcohol Review*, **23**, 433–443.

Hamera, E., Schneider, J.K. & Deviney, S. (1995). Alcohol, cannabis, nicotine and caffeine use and symptom distress in schizophrenia. *Journal of Nervous and Mental Disorders*, **183**, 559–565.

Henquet, C., Krabbendam, L., Spauwen, J., Kaplan, C., Lieb, R., Wittchen, H. et al. (2005). Prospective cohort study of cannabis use, predisposition for psychosis and psychotic symptoms in young people. *British Medical Journal*, **330**, 11.

Hides, L., Lubman, D.I. & Dawe, S. (2004). Models of co-occurring substance misuse and psychosis: are personality traits the missing link? *Drug and Alcohol Review*, **23**, 425–432.

Hinton, M., Elkins, K., Edwards, J. & Donovan, K. (2002). *Cannabis and Psychosis: An Early Psychosis Treatment Manual*. Melbourne: EPPIC.

Horowitz, M.J. (1969). Flashbacks: Recurrent intrusive images after the use of LSD. *American Journal of Psychiatry*, **126**, 565–569.

Hutchison, G. & Lee, D. (2002). Substance use is related to increased duration of untreated psychosis. *Acta Psychiatrica Scandinavica*, **106** (Suppl. 413), 74.

Jackson, H.J., McGorry, P.D. & Dudgeon, P. (1995). Prodromal symptoms of schizophrenia in first episode psychosis: Prevalence and specificity. *Comprehensive Psychiatry*, **36**, 241–250.

Johns, L.C., Cannon, M., Singleton, N., Murray, R.M., Farrell, M., Brugha, T. et al. (2004). Prevalence and correlates of self-reported psychotic symptoms in the British population. *British Journal of Psychiatry*, **185**, 289–305.

Kessler, R., McGonagle, K.A., Zhao, S., Nelson, C.B., Hughes, M., Eshleman, S. et al. (1994). Lifetime and 12-month prevalence of DSM-III-R psychiatric disorders in the United States: results from the National Comorbidity Study. *Archives of General Psychiatry*, **51**, 8–19.

Kendler, T.M., Gallagher, T.J., Abelson, J.M. & Kessler, R.C. (1996). Lifetime prevalence, demographic risk factors, and diagnostic validity of nonaffective psychosis as assessed in a US community sample. *Archives of General Psychiatry*, **53**, 1022–1031.

Khantzian, E.J. (1997). The self-medication hypothesis of substance use disorders: A reconsideration and recent applications. *Harvard Review of Psychiatry*, **4**, 231–244.

Kovasznay, B., Fleischer, J., Tanenberg-Karant, M., Jandorf, L., Miller, A.D. & Bromet, E. (1997). Substance use disorder and the early course of illness in schizophrenia and affective psychosis. *Schizophrenia Bulletin*, **23**, 195–201.

Leicester, S., Phillips, L., Francey, S., Yung, A. & McGorry, P. (2003, September). *DSM-IV Axis 1 Disorders in Individuals at High-risk for Psychosis and Implications for Treatment Planning*. Paper presented at the 14th International Symposium for the Psychological Treatment of Schizophrenia and Other Psychosis, Melbourne, Australia.

Linszen, D.H., Dingemans, P.M. & Lenior, M.E. (1994). Cannabis abuse and the course of recent-onset schizophrenic disorders. *Archives of General Psychiatry*, **51**, 273–279.

Linszen, D. & Lenior, M. (1999). Early psychosis and substance use. In P.D. McGorry & H.J. Jackson (Eds), *The Recognition and Management of Early Psychosis: A Preventive Approach* (pp. 363–375). UK: Cambridge University Press.

Lynskey, M.T., Coffey, C., Degenhardt, L., Carlin, J.B. & Patton, G. (2003). A longitudinal study of the effects of adolescent cannabis use on high school completion. *Addiction*, **98**, 685–692.

Macleod, J., Oakes, R., Copello, A., Crome, I., Egger, M., Hickman, M. et al. (2004). Psychological and social sequelae of cannabis and other illicit drug use by young people: A systematic review of longitudinal, general population studies. *Lancet*, **363**, 1579–1588.

McCreadie, R.G. (2002). Use of drugs, alcohol and tobacco by people with schizophrenia: Case-control study. *British Journal of Psychiatry*, **181**, 321–325.

McGorry, P.D. (1995). Psychoeducation in first-episode psychosis: A therapeutic process. *Psychiatry*, **58**, 313–328.

Miller, P., Lawrie, S.M., Hodges, A., Clafferty, R., Cosway, R. & Johnstone, E.C. (2001). Genetic liability, illicit drug use, life stress and psychotic symptoms: Preliminary findings from the Edinburgh study of people at high risk for schizophrenia. *Social Psychiatry and Psychiatric Epidemiology*, **36**, 338–342.

Miller, T., Zipursky, R.B., Perkins, D., Addington, J., Woods, S.W., Hawkins, K.A. et al. (2003). The PRIME North America randomized double-blind clinical trial of olanzapine versus placebo in patients at risk of being prodromally symptomatic for psychosis II. Baseline characteristics of the 'prodromal sample'. *Schizophrenia Research*, **61**, 19–30.

Miller, W.R. (1983). Motivational interviewing with problem drinkers. *Behavioural Psychotherapy*, **1**, 147–172.

Miller, W.R. & Rollnick, S. (2002). What is motivational interviewing? In W.R. Miller & S. Rollnick (Eds), *Motivational Interviewing* (2nd edn, pp. 33–42). New York: Guilford Press.

Monti, P.M., Colby, S.M., Barnett, N.P., Spirito, A., Rohsenow, D.J., Myers, M. et al. (1999). Brief intervention for harm reduction with alcohol-positive older adolescents in a hospital emergency department. *Journal of Consulting and Clinical Psychology*, **67**, 989–994.

Olin, J.T. & Keating, C. (1998). *Rapid Psychological Assessment*. Canada: Wiley.

Patton, G.C., Coffey, C., Carlin, J.B., Degenhardt, L., Lynskey, M. & Hall, W. (2002). Cannabis use and mental health in young people: cohort study. *British Medical Journal*, **325**, 1195–1198.

Pencer, A. & Addington, J. (2003). Substance use and cognition in early psychosis. *Journal of Psychiatry and Neuroscience*, **28**, 48–54.

Phillips, L.J., Curry, C., Yung, A.R., Yuen, H.P., Adlard, S. & McGorry, P.D. (2002). Cannabis use is not associated with the development of psychosis in an 'ultra' high-risk group. *Australian and New Zealand Journal of Psychiatry*, **36**, 800–806.

Phillips, L.J. & Francey, S.M. (2004). Changing PACE: Psychological Interventions in the Prepsychotic Phase. In J.F.M. Gleeson & P.D. McGorry (Eds), *Psychological Interventions in Early Psychosis: A Treatment Handbook* (pp. 23–40). Chichester, UK: Wiley.

Prochaska, J.O., DiClemente, C.C. & Norcross, J.C. (1992). In search of how people change: applications to the addictive behaviours. *American Psychologist*, **47**, 1102–1114.

Rabinowitz, J., Bromet, E.J., Lavelle, J., Carlson, G., Kovasznay, B. & Schwartz, J.E. (1998). Prevalence and severity of substance use disorders and onset of psychosis in first-admission psychotic patients. *Psychological Medicine*, **28**, 1411–1419.

Ries, R. (1993). Clinical treatment matching models for dually diagnosed patients. *Psychiatric Clinics of North America*, **16**, 165–175.

Robins, L.N. & Regier, D.A. (1991). *Psychiatric Disorders in America: The Epidemiologic Catchment Area Study*. New York: Free Press.

Rollnick, S. & Miller, W.R. (1995). What is MI? *Behavioural and Cognitive Psychotherapy*, **23**, 325–334.

Rorstad, P. & Checinski, K. (1996). *Dual Diagnosis: Facing the Challenge*. UK: Wynne Howard Publishing.

Rumbold, G.R. & Hamilton, M. (1998). Addressing drug problems: The case for minimisation. In M. Hamilton, A. Kellehear & G. Rumbold (Eds), *Drug Use in Australia* (pp. 130–144). Oxford, UK: Oxford University Press.

Smart, R.G. & Ogbourne, A.C. (2000). Drug use and drinking among students in 36 countries. *Addictive Behaviours*, **25**, 455–460.

Smit, F., Bolier, L. & Cuijpers, P. (2004). Cannabis use and the risk of later schizophrenia: A review. *Addiction*, **99**, 425–430.

Sorbara, F., Liraud, F., Assens, F., Abalan, F. & Verdoux, H. (2003). Substance use and the course of early psychosis: A 2-year follow-up of first-admission subjects. *European Psychiatry*, **18**, 133–136.

Stefanis, N., Hanssen, M., Smyrnis, N., Avramopolous, D., Evdokimidis, I., Verdoux, H. et al. (2001). Evidence that three dimensions of psychosis have a distribution in the general population. *Psychological Medicine*, **32**, 347–358.

Teeson, M., Hall, W., Lynskey, M. & Degenhardt, L. (2000). Alcohol and drug use disorders in Australia: Implications of the National Survey of Mental Health and Wellbeing. *Australian and New Zealand Journal of Psychiatry*, **34**, 206–213.

Van Mastright, S., Addington, J. & Addington, D. (2004). Substance misuse at presentation to an early psychosis program. *Social Psychiatry and Psychiatric Epidemiology*, **39**, 69–72.

Van Os, J., Bak, M., Hanssen, M., Bijl, R.V., de Graaf, R. & Verdoux, H. (2002). Cannabis use and psychosis: A longitudinal population-based study. *American Journal of Epidemiology*, **156**, 319–327.

Verdoux, H., Gindre, C., Sorbara, F., Tournier, M. & Swendsen, J.D. (2003a). Effects of cannabis and psychosis vulnerability in daily life: An experience sampling test study. *Psychological Medicine*, **33**, 23–32.

Verdoux, H., Sorbara, F., Gindre, C., Swendsen, J. & Van Os, J. (2003b). Cannabis use and dimensions of psychosis in a non-clinical population of female subjects. *Schizophrenia Research*, **59**, 77–84.

Weiser, M., Knobler, H.Y., Noy, S. & Kaplan, Z. (2002). Clinical characteristics of adolescents later hospitalized for schizophrenia. *American Journal of Medical Genetics*, **114**, 949–955.

Zammit, S., Allebeck, P., Andreason, S., Lundberg, I. & Lewis, G. (2002). Self reported cannabis use as a risk factor for schizophrenia in Swedish conscripts of 1969: Historical cohort study. *British Medical Journal*, **325**, 1199–1201.

CHAPTER 8

Addressing Attenuated Symptoms in 'At Risk' Clients

Samantha E. Bowe, Paul French and Anthony P. Morrison

This chapter aims to outline the use of cognitive therapy (CT) with individuals at high risk of developing psychosis, and specifically addresses working with attenuated symptoms. Attenuated symptoms can be defined as sub-clinical levels of positive symptoms (e.g. paranoia, hearing voices), as experienced in the prodromal phase, which put an individual at high risk of developing psychosis. The treatment of attenuated symptoms is extremely important as most of the high-risk trials are finding that the attenuated symptom group make up around 80% of their total cohort.

French and Morrison (2004) developed the cognitive approach to addressing attenuated symptoms discussed in this chapter. This approach has been evaluated in a randomised controlled trial (RCT; Morrison et al., 2004). Consequently, this approach is being used by the Early Detection and Intervention Team (EDIT) based in Salford, UK. The primary role of the EDIT service is to identify individuals who are at high risk of making transition to psychosis, and to deliver CT to prevent, or delay, transition. Such a service is also beneficial in reducing duration of untreated psychosis (DUP). For example, if an individual becomes psychotic, he or she can be immediately referred to a specialist mental health team, thus improving prognosis in the longer term.

This chapter begins by proposing a rationale for using CT with at-risk individuals. It then considers common presenting problems relevant to this client group, and how to formulate attenuated symptoms. Cognitive and behavioural intervention strategies to address attenuated symptoms are then outlined. Finally, a brief discussion on working with core beliefs in connection with attenuated symptoms is provided, along with a chapter summary and conclusions.

Working with People at High Risk of Developing Psychosis: A Treatment Handbook.
Edited by J. Addington, S.M. Francey and A.P. Morrison. © 2006 John Wiley & Sons, Ltd.

A RATIONALE FOR THIS APPROACH

Why Use CT with 'At Risk' Clients?

The efficacy of cognitive behavioural therapy for first episode psychosis and chronic psychotic symptoms has been demonstrated in a number of randomised control trials (RCTs) (Drury, Birchwood, Cochrane & MacMillan, 1996; Kuipers et al., 1997; Sensky et al., 2000; Tarrier et al., 1998). This suggests that if CT is effective at reducing distress associated with established psychotic symptoms, it is likely to be useful for those experiencing attenuated psychotic experiences. Further support for using CT with at-risk clients is provided by the evidence that cognitive behavioural monitoring of prodromal signs can facilitate relapse prevention (Birchwood et al., 1989). Moreover, the provision of CT to clients at significant risk of relapse is effective at reducing relapse rates and the number of hospital admissions (Gumley et al., 2003). This implies that CT is also likely to be useful to individuals at risk of developing psychosis who experience brief limited intermittent psychotic symptoms (BLIPS), which spontaneously remit within a week without anti-psychotic medication. Furthermore, mood related symptoms are common in prodromal states (Birchwood, 1996) and CT has been demonstrated to be an effective treatment for anxiety (Clark, 1986) and depression (Hollon, DeRubeis & Evans, 1996). Therefore, it is likely to be a helpful intervention to address common emotional disorders present in high-risk individuals.

Yung and colleagues (1998) found that 40% of individuals considered to be at high risk of psychosis made transition to psychosis over a 12-month period. Evidently, based on this finding, there will be a substantial number of individuals at risk of psychosis who will not go on to develop frank psychosis over a 12-month period, and will fall into the 'false-positive' category. CT in this early stage seems like a more ethical alternative to medical interventions (e.g. neuroleptic medication), which are commonly associated with side effects such as weight gain, sexual dysfunction and involuntary movements. The ethical debate regarding medical interventions such as neuroleptic medication for at-risk clients has been expanded upon elsewhere (Bentall & Morrison, 2002). Suffice it to say here that in addition to ethical concerns regarding medical interventions, as CT involves targeting difficulties from a shared 'problem list', it is likely to be a useful intervention for individuals who fall into this 'false-positive' category and do not go on to make transition to psychosis in a 12-month period. Further support for using CT with clients at high risk of developing psychosis comes from the results of a RCT outlined below.

The EDIE Study: RCT Results

The EDIE study was a RCT set up to evaluate the effectiveness of CT for the prevention of psychosis in people at high risk. Although previous research (McGorry et al., 2002) demonstrated that a combination of medication and psychological intervention (CBT) can delay the onset of frank psychosis six months post treatment, it is difficult to determine what specific contribution each intervention made in delaying onset. The EDIE study identified at-risk individuals, between the ages of 16 and 36, using Yung et al.'s (1998) approach. In brief, individuals were considered at risk if they reported BLIPS, which lasted less than a week and spontaneously resolved without anti-psychotic medication, or if they reported attenuated symptoms. BLIPS and attenuated symptoms were assessed using cut offs on the Positive and Negative Syndrome Scale (PANSS) (Kay, Fiszbein & Opler, 1987), since specific measures for at-risk clients were not available at the time. Individuals were also considered at risk if they themselves had a diagnosis of schizotypal personality disorder or had a first-degree relative with a history of psychosis, accompanied by a recent deterioration in functioning. A recent deterioration was assessed using the General Health Questionnaire (GHQ; Goldberg & Hillier, 1979) and the Global Assessment of Functioning (GAF; APA, 1994).

Following assessment, 58 participants were considered at high-risk of developing psychosis and were randomly allocated to either the monitoring group or the CT plus monitoring group. Results demonstrated that a six-month CT intervention was effective in reducing transition to psychosis over a 12-month period. Six per cent of individuals in the CT group made transition to psychosis, compared to 22–30% in the monitoring alone group (depending on the operational definition of transition), suggesting that CT alone can prevent or delay the onset of psychosis. CT also reduced the severity of attenuated symptoms over a 12-month period. Furthermore, the study had a high rate of consent (95%) and low drop out rate (14%), indicating that it is an acceptable intervention for this client group.

COMMON PRESENTING PROBLEMS IN 'AT RISK' CLIENTS

Individuals at risk of psychosis commonly present to therapy with a range of different problems; some of these are psychosis related, but there are many other common problems. Typically these include: anxiety, depression, social phobia, substance misuse, isolation and social withdrawal, inactivity and trauma related phenomena such as Post-traumatic stress disorder (PTSD). However, although attenuated symptoms are not of psychotic severity, or necessarily present on a daily basis, these experiences can be confusing and distressing, often resulting in help-seeking behaviour. At first clients typically keep their problems to themselves and do not share their concerns with family and friends due to stigma and fear. However, at the point at which their experiences interfere with other aspects of their lives such as college, and interpersonal relationships, this can trigger help-seeking which may be initiated by the individual or their family. A frequent conceptualisation of their experiences is that they are fearful of impending madness.

Engaging 'At Risk' Clients in Therapy

Although high-risk individuals are often help-seeking, engagement difficulties may still arise for a variety of reasons. Consequently, it is important to take steps to facilitate the engagement process. Using a problem-orientated approach facilitates engagement early on in therapy. It is important to work on what the client identifies as a problem, rather than the therapist assuming what the focus should be. Although individuals are considered at risk of psychosis due to anomalous experiences such as attenuated symptoms, this is not necessarily what the client will decide to prioritise on his or her problem list. Clients typically have a number of difficulties identified on their 'problem list'. If one of their therapy goals can be achieved quickly and successfully engagement can be enhanced. A positive experience of therapy can increase a client's hopes about achieving future goals.

In terms of practical issues, seeing clients in less stigmatising locations such as colleges, youth centres and GP surgeries is preferable to mental health settings, which could be associated with impending madness. It is worth asking clients about their previous contacts with, and attitudes to, services, which may impact upon the therapeutic relationship.

With regard to the therapy sessions, ensure the pacing of the sessions is appropriate for clients, and avoid the use of jargon as much as possible. Although agenda setting is an important part of structuring CT sessions, therapists should be flexible and not stick to rigid formats at the expense of engagement. In addition, therapists should be mindful that attenuated symptoms may impact upon engagement and the therapeutic relationship. As attenuated symptoms may influence communication or information processing, therapists should provide regular summaries of the material covered in sessions to ensure both client and therapist understand what has been covered.

The type of attenuated symptoms experienced may have direct implications on engagement. For example, if a client is suspicious about friends, family and work colleagues, it is likely that the client also has suspicions about the therapist. Even if engagement appears to be strong, the therapist should always enquire about whether he or she has similar thoughts about the therapist. If suspicion about the therapist is identified, then it is important to collaboratively look at ways of managing this difficulty. Providing clients with a copy of any case notes written in sessions can be helpful in making the therapy process more transparent and decrease levels of suspiciousness.

Furthermore, it may be worth considering having a regular item on the agenda regarding suspicious thoughts about the therapist. Ensuring that examples are identified and tackled facilitates engagement and reduces the likelihood of clients dropping out of therapy due to their suspicions. Asking for feedback at the end of each session on what was helpful and unhelpful about a session is also valuable on picking up on any engagement problems.

In the initial stages of therapy, it may be necessary to incorporate aspects of case management and crisis intervention to enhance engagement. As high-risk individuals are typically not in secondary care, they are unlikely to have any other professionals involved to assist them with practical issues such as housing. In such circumstances it is useful to address these difficulties while emphasising that moving onto structured therapy would be beneficial at a later date.

FORMULATION

When using CT to address attenuated symptoms, and other difficulties experienced by at-risk clients, it is essential that intervention strategies are formulation driven. As anomalous experiences such as psychotic symptoms and attenuated symptoms lie on a continuum with normal experiences, existing psychological models can be used to formulate attenuated symptoms. Formulating with at-risk clients is discussed below, followed by a brief description of psychological models of psychosis, along with case examples of formulating attenuated symptoms.

Formulating with 'At Risk' Clients

Ideally, a preliminary formulation of a client's presenting difficulties should be achieved by the end of the second session. At this stage, a simple maintenance formulation of a presenting difficulty, or recent example, is sufficient. Over subsequent sessions more information can be gathered and a more comprehensive, longitudinal formulation can be developed, which explains in more detail the relationship between various current problems the client is experiencing and his or her life experiences and long-standing beliefs. Formulating at this early stage can enhance engagement and communicates that the therapist has listened to the client and understood the client's difficulties. Formulation of presenting difficulties must be done collaboratively with the client, with the therapist explicitly requesting feedback at each stage to ascertain whether or not it makes sense. Essentially, the formulation should provide the client with an explanation of his or her current difficulties, which can then be used to guide the intervention. This explanatory framework can contribute towards 'normalising' a person's experiences.

A longitudinal formulation should clearly map out the cognitive, emotional and behavioural aspects of a client's difficulties, along with maintaining factors (e.g. safety behaviours and selective attention). Essentially, it should conceptualise the following: what problems the client is experiencing, how they are maintained, what is the relationship between different problems, why these problems developed and why certain interventions are likely to be effective.

Psychological Models of Psychosis

A number of models explaining positive symptoms of psychosis have been proposed (Bentall, 1990; Chadwick & Birchwood, 1994; Garety, Kuipers, Fowler, Freeman & Bebbington, 2001; Morrison, 1998, 2001; Morrison, Haddock & Tarrier, 1995). Within our work at the EDIT service, when formulating attenuated symptoms we tend to use Morrison's (2001) integrative cognitive model of hallucinations and delusions. When formulating voice hearing specifically, Morrison's (1998) maintenance model of auditory hallucinations is commonly utilised.

Morrison's (1998) model is based on cognitive models of panic and anxiety (Clark, 1986; Salkovskis, 1991) to explain the factors involved in the maintenance of auditory hallucinations. In agreement with other authors (Barrett & Etheridge, 1992; Romme & Escher, 1989; Romme, Honig & Escher, 1992), Morrison (1998) argues that auditory hallucinations are a 'normal' experience, which can be precipitated by a wide variety of internal and external triggers (e.g. stress, sleep deprivation). Often the hallucination is perceived and misinterpreted as threatening an individual's physical or psychological integrity (e.g. 'I must be mad', or 'I must obey else they will hurt me'). Such misinterpretations lead to an increase in physiological arousal and negative mood, which in turn increases the hallucinations, thus resulting in a vicious circle. Concurrently, the misinterpretation of the hallucination leads to safety behaviours (e.g. hypervigilance), which maintain the process by increasing the occurrence of auditory hallucinations, and preventing the opportunity to disconfirm the misinterpretation. This model is illustrated in Figure 8.1 below.

Morrison's (2001) integrative cognitive model of delusions and auditory hallucinations implies that it is the interpretation of an intrusion (e.g. hearing a voice or a paranoid thought) that is important. Essentially, a person is seen to be psychotic if he or she endorses a culturally unacceptable interpretation of an intrusion (e.g., perceiving hearing your first name on TV as evidence that everyone is talking about you). It is also argued that similar processes are involved in the development of non-psychotic disorders. Consequently, the model

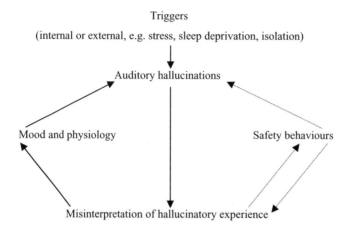

Triggers
(internal or external, e.g. stress, sleep deprivation, isolation)

Auditory hallucinations

Mood and physiology   Safety behaviours

Misinterpretation of hallucinatory experience

Figure 8.1   A cognitive model of auditory hallucinations. From Morrison (1998). A cognitive analysis of the maintenance of auditory hallucinations: are voices to schizophrenia what bodily sensations are to panic? *Behavioural and Cognitive Psychotherapy*, **26**, 289–302

encompasses key aspects of the Wells and Matthew's (1994) S-REF (self-regulatory executive function) model of emotional dysfunction which presents a framework for understanding how cognitive processes and structures interact in the maintenance of non-psychotic emotional disorders. Morrison (2001) proposes that these culturally unacceptable interpretations of intrusions will be maintained by safety behaviours (e.g. selective attention), beliefs about information processing strategies (declarative beliefs), faulty self-knowledge (meta-cognition), social knowledge, mood and physiology. This model is illustrated below in Figure 8.2 along with a client-friendly version (Figure 8.3).

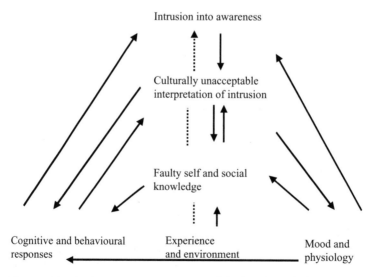

Intrusion into awareness

Culturally unacceptable
interpretation of intrusion

Faulty self and social
knowledge

Cognitive and behavioural   Experience   Mood and
responses   and environment   physiology

Figure 8.2   An integrative cognitive model of auditory hallucinations and delusions. From Morrison (2001). The interpretation of intrusions in psychosis: an integrative cognitive approach to hallucinations and delusions. *Behavioural and Cognitive Psychotherapy*, **29**, 257–276

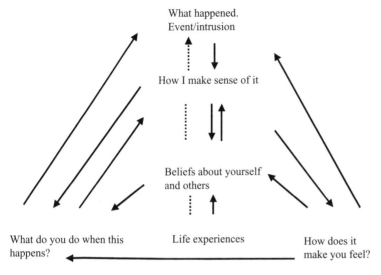

Figure 8.3   A client-friendly version of Morrison's (2001) model of psychosis. From The interpretation of intrusions in psychosis: an integrative cognitive approach to hallucinations and delusions. *Behavioural and Cognitive Psychotherapy*, **29**, 257–276

Formulating Attenuated Symptoms

To illustrate formulating attenuated symptoms the following case examples outline the different levels of formulation that are arrived at in therapy.

Case example

John was referred to the EDIT service due to hearing voices. He was distressed by this experience and although it hadn't happened for a few weeks, he was worried that it would happen again and continue. He also described distressing intrusive thoughts and anxiety. In the first therapy session we developed a simple maintenance formulation of his voice-hearing experience using Morrison's (1998) auditory hallucination model (illustrated in Figure 8.4).

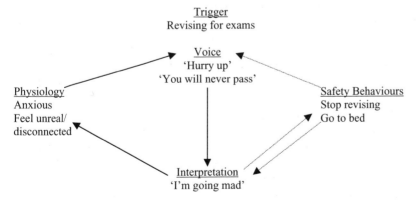

Figure 8.4   Maintenance formulation of hearing voices

Event	Thought/interpretation	Emotion	Behaviour
Tea tastes funny at work	They are poisoning me	Anxiety	Pour tea away Hypervigilant for signs of who is responsible

Figure 8.5   Formulation of recent example of paranoia

Case example

Susan was referred to the EDIT service due to paranoia and suspiciousness. She prioritised paranoia on her problem list, as it was interfering with her interpersonal relationships. Her relationship with her boyfriend was deteriorating, along with her relationships with friends and work colleagues. She was also experiencing distress associated with social anxiety and low mood. In the first few therapy sessions we tried to make sense of her experiences by formulating recent examples of suspiciousness and paranoia (illustrated in Figure 8.5). Further into therapy a longitudinal formation was developed using Morrison's (2001) cognitive model of psychosis (see Figure 8.6).

INTERVENTION STRATEGIES FOR ATTENUATED SYMPTOMS

Normalising

As mentioned previously in this chapter, it is now widely accepted that psychotic experiences lie on a continuum with normal experiences. This viewpoint is a consequence of substantial evidence that psychotic experiences such as hearing voices are not uncommon in the general population. There is also evidence that providing clients with a normalising rationale may be particularly effective for psychotic clients who experience auditory hallucinations (Sensky et al., 2000).

Consequently, it logically follows that providing normalising information plays a vital role in CT for at-risk clients as it challenges catastrophic appraisals of attenuated symptoms (e.g. fears of going mad). Furthermore, normalising experiences, such as hearing voices, can increase an individual's understanding of what is happening and reduce stigma and distress.

Informing clients that people in the general population have similar experiences can be helpful. Posey and Losch (1983) conducted a study on 375 undergraduate students and found that 36% regularly heard their name being called out loud when nobody was present, and 39% reported hearing their own thoughts out loud. The annual incidence of experiencing hallucinations is estimated at 4–5% (Tien, 1991). Translating this information into specific figures for your country can be very helpful in making the person believe that such experiences are relatively common.

Providing clients with information on the links between trauma and voice hearing can be helpful. For instance, Romme and Escher (1989) found that 70% of voice hearers began to experience voices following traumatic and stressful life events such as bereavement, and concluded that voice hearing was a normal reaction to stress and part of the coping process. The research literature also associates auditory hallucinations with child abuse (Ross, Anderson & Clark, 1994), bereavement (Grimby, 1993), solitary confinement (Grassian, 1983), and being taken hostage (Siegel, 1984). With regard to unusual beliefs, Cox and

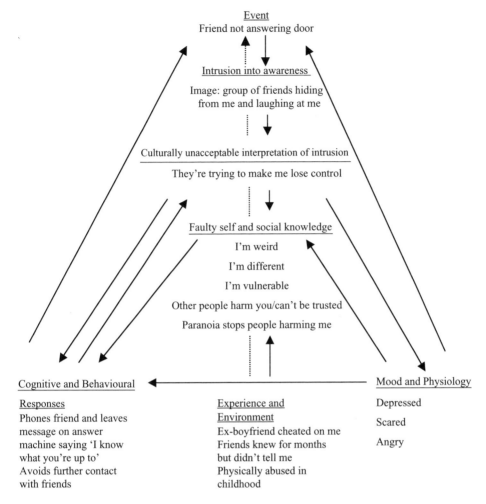

Figure 8.6 A longitudinal formulation of paranoia

Cowling (1989) found that many people in the normal population believe in unscientific phenomena. For instance, they reported that more than 50% believed that thought transference could occur between two people and that they could predict something is going to happen before it actually does.

Cognitive Intervention Strategies to Address Attenuated Symptoms
Generating Alternative Explanations

In the early stages of psychosis, an individual may not have fully explored explanations for anomalous experiences. Some individuals may be preoccupied with thoughts about impending madness whereas others may be uncertain about the possible causal explanations. Facilitating the client to generate a range of possible explanations for his or her attenuated symptoms, and then, in a structured manner, evaluating the supporting and counter evidence for each explanation, is a very useful intervention. Clearly, this technique is not unique to at-risk clients and is used when working with a number of different disorders (Beck, Rush, Shaw & Emery, 1979; Greenberger & Padesky, 1995; Wells, 1997). Similar to working with clients with anxiety disorders or established psychosis, generating alternative explanations for experiences can reduce distress and encourage people at risk of psychosis to evaluate the accuracy of their initial interpretations. The aim is to generate alternative explanations that are less distressing and more accurate (or consistent with the evidence gathered). If someone has a current explanation that he or she believes accounts for his/her experiences, it is important to evaluate the advantages and disadvantages of such an interpretation before generating alternatives and examining evidence.

It is essential to spend time generating an exhaustive list of possible explanations. This process should be done using guided discovery (the Socratic Method), asking patients questions to help them generate options and reach their own conclusions. For each of the explanations, conviction ratings should be established. Using a 0–100 percentage scale is preferable to a 0–10 scale as it is more sensitive to measuring change in conviction. Clear anchor points should be provided to the client (e.g. 0 = do not believe this at all; 100 = believe it to be absolutely true, without any doubt). This is illustrated in Figure 8.7.

Generating Evidence for and against Intrusive Thoughts

Generating supporting and counter evidence for intrusions can be an effective strategy when targeting attenuated symptoms in therapy. It is again important that Socratic dialogue is used when reviewing the evidence. Once the therapist and client have reviewed the evidence for the intrusion (e.g. a paranoid thought), it is useful to arrive at a balanced thought that takes account of all the evidence generated.

Case example

Julie was a 22-year-old woman who was referred to the EDIT service due to distress associated with low levels of paranoia. She found it difficult to leave the house as she believed everyone was laughing at her. During a therapy session, Julie and her therapist generated evidence for and against a paranoid thought she experienced whilst out. This is illustrated in Figure 8.8.

Working with Meta-cognitions in Relation to Attenuated Symptoms

As discussed previously in this chapter, meta-cognitions are implicated in the maintenance of anxiety disorders, psychotic experiences and attenuated symptoms. Wells (1995) proposes that meta-cognitive beliefs comprise of: beliefs about thought processes (e.g. 'I have a poor memory'); beliefs about the content of thoughts (e.g. thinking something bad will mean it will happen); and beliefs about the advantages and disadvantages about particular types of thinking.

Meta-cognitions in relation to the development of psychosis are important for a number of reasons. The existing literature shows that it is not unusual for individuals with psychosis to report positive effects of voice hearing (e.g. voices keeping them company; Miller, O'Connor & DiPasquale, 1993). Also, it is not uncommon for people with psychosis to have

Experience/intrusion	Hearing a voice in my head whispering 'shut up'
Current explanation for intrusion	I am going mad/it's caused by stress
Current emotions associated with this belief	Scared/happy

All possible explanations:

Explanation for intrusion	Belief rating (0–100) 0 = this is not the reason I am having this thought 100 = this is definitely the reason I am having this thought	Associated mood
Stress	40%	Relieved
I'm going mad	65%	Scared
Something is trying to make me lose control	25%	Frightened
Ghost	35%	Scared
Anxiety	30%	OK

Evidence for and against a belief

Belief to be examined	It's caused by stress
Associated mood	Relief as I could control stress
Belief rating	40%

Evidence for	Evidence against
Had lots of changes in my life around that time	Felt excited at the time
Not getting on with parents	
Had just moved in with boyfriend	
Had just started college course	
Was feeling anxious meeting new people	
I heard a voice six months ago when I felt stressed out doing exams	
I was having lots of headaches which may indicate I was stressed	
Felt tired all the time	
Wanted to spend more time on my own	
Maybe it's possible to feel excited at the same time as being stressed out	

Belief rating (re-rated)	85%
Alternative belief	Maybe I heard a voice because I was feeling stressed due to so many changes in my life. Perhaps I didn't notice I was feeling stressed because I was excited about positive changes like moving in with my boyfriend and starting college.
Associated mood	Relaxed and relieved

Figure 8.7 Generating alternative explanations for voice hearing.

Experience/intrusion	Walking down the street and noticing people in cars looking at me. Image of people laughing
Current explanation for intrusion	Everyone is laughing at me. Others are out to get me
Current emotions associated with this belief	Anxiety/sadness
Thought to be tested:	Everyone is laughing at me
Conviction = 80%	
Evidence for	Evidence against
I saw someone looking at me from their car	Maybe they were looking at people walking past as they were stuck in traffic
They laughed with the passenger in the car	I've noticed I look at people when I'm in a car at traffic lights because I'm a bit bored
	Maybe they were laughing at a joke
	Maybe they were laughing at something funny on the radio

Conclusion: It was probably a coincidence, they were probably laughing at something else, like a joke, rather than at me.
Conviction in original belief = 40%

Figure 8.8   Considering evidence for and against a paranoid thought

positive beliefs about delusions (e.g. paranoid beliefs providing excitement or grandiose beliefs making them feel special). It has also been suggested that delusions may also be protective and defend against self-blame (Bentall, Kinderman & Kaney, 1994). Furthermore, Morrison, Wells and Nothard (2000) found that positive beliefs about unusual experiences were the best predictor of a predisposition to hallucinate in the general population. Positive beliefs about unusual experiences, therefore, appear to be a maintenance factor as they increase the frequency of anomalous experiences.

Negative beliefs about unusual experiences also play a role in maintaining psychotic and attenuated symptoms. In their study, Freeman and Garety (1999) found that the majority of people with persecutory delusions experienced meta-worry concerning the controllability of delusional ideas. Furthermore, Baker and Morrison (1998) found that individuals with psychosis experiencing auditory hallucinations scored higher on meta-cognitive beliefs about controllability and danger associated with particular types of thoughts. It is likely that as an individual progresses closer to making transition to frank psychosis, he or she develops negative interpretations of attenuated symptoms. Such interpretations may relate to fears of 'losing control' or 'going mad' or from perceiving the experiences as coming from an external, powerful source (e.g. spirits possessing them).

Due to the reasons outlined above, a thorough assessment of meta-cognitions in relation to attenuated symptoms should be carried out. This can be done using established CT techniques such as the downward arrow technique. The use of self-report measures can also provide valuable information. In the EDIT service we routinely use the meta-cognitions questionnaire (MCQ; Cartwright-Hatton & Wells, 1997), the Interpretation of Voices Inventory (Morrison et al., 2002), and the Beliefs about Paranoia Scale (Morrison et al., 2005).

In CT for at-risk clients, targeting such meta-cognitions (e.g., beliefs about attenuated symptoms) is essential in reducing frequency of, and distress associated with, attenuated symptoms. Established CT techniques, such as generating alternative explanations, evaluating evidence, behavioural experiments and considering advantages and disadvantages of meta-cognitions, can all be used to address meta-cognitive beliefs.

Clearly, other aspects of CT may have resulted in a reduction of distress and frequency of attenuated symptoms. However, it is essential that meta-cognitions associated with a reoccurrence of attenuated symptoms are also addressed, as an individual may still hold beliefs that these experiences are in some way catastrophic. For example, in the case illustrated earlier, the use of normalising information and generating alternative explanations for voice hearing were effective in modifying the belief that hearing voices means 'I am going mad'. We also established how he would interpret and respond to a recurrence of voice hearing: it is normal to hear voices and a recurrence would be interpreted as a sign of increased stress and appropriate stress management techniques would be used. However, on further

Belief to be tested Conviction for belief tested = 60%	Others will notice I'm hearing a voice and think I'm mad
Evidence for	Evidence against
Perhaps I act differently when it happens as things around me feel like they are going faster than me	I am pretty sure I act the same as usual (70%) but I've always been on my own when it's happened
*I sit down when it happens (until it goes away)	Other people can't hear the voice
	My friend came round just after I heard the voice as she didn't notice anything different about me
	I sit down a lot at work
	Work colleagues wouldn't really make anything of me sitting down
	If it happened out of work and I sat down, people might think I was feeling dizzy or sick
	I know someone who hears a voice and I can't tell when she is or isn't hearing it
Conclusion: If I hear the voice again, other people would be unlikely to notice and therefore would not think I had gone mad	
Conviction for belief tested = 10%	

*Indicates one of his safety behaviours which was later worked on in therapy.

Figure 8.9

exploration we established that if he were to hear voices again, he would know he was not mad, but other people would notice a change in him and believe he was going mad. Clearly, meta-cognitions such as this catastrophic interpretation of a recurrence of voice hearing could exacerbate the situation and lead to increased levels of distress. Evidently, this would need to be targeted to influence long-term change. Figure 8.9 demonstrates how generating supporting and counter evidence can be useful in achieving this.

If this client were still experiencing hallucinatory phenomena, then it would also have been possible to conduct a behavioural experiment to test his prediction; for example, the use of video feedback, following induction of the problematic experience, could have helped him to evaluate his assumptions about behaving differently and appearing visibly 'mad'.

Behavioural Intervention Strategies Addressing Safety Behaviours Associated with Attenuated Symptoms

Based on empirical evidence, cognitive models of anxiety disorders imply that people routinely adopt certain safety behaviours to prevent a feared catastrophe (Clark, 1986; Salkovskis, 1991, 1996; Wells, 1995). For instance, a person with panic disorder, who interprets his or her legs feeling wobbly as evidence that he or she will collapse, may hold on to a railing to prevent this from happening. As outlined in Morrison's (1998) cognitive model of voices, and integrative model of psychosis (2001), safety behaviours play a role in maintaining distress in psychosis. For instance, a person may interpret hearing a voice as meaning he or she will lose control and attempt to prevent this by staying in the house and going to bed. In line with the anxiety disorders literature, evidence suggests that dropping safety behaviours associated with voice hearing in psychosis can decrease distress levels (Nothard, Morrison & Wells, 2005). It therefore follows that safety behaviours play a role in maintaining distress associated with attenuated symptoms in at-risk individuals (French & Morrison, 2004).

Wells (1997) has identified a number of different ways in which safety behaviours maintain beliefs about, and dysfunctional interpretations of, intrusions:

- Safety behaviours can maintain distress by exacerbating bodily symptoms.
- Non-occurrence of feared outcomes can incorrectly be attributed to the use of safety behaviours rather than to the fact that it would not have happened anyway.
- Certain safety behaviours such as hypervigilance to danger may increase exposure to danger-related information, which may strengthen negative beliefs.
- Safety behaviours may contaminate social situations and affect interactions in a manner consistent with negative appraisals.

When working with at-risk clients, a thorough assessment of safety behaviours in relation to attenuated symptoms must be undertaken. Figure 8.10 illustrates examples of safety behaviours. When introducing the concept of safety behaviours the use of metaphors, such as the use of garlic, crucifixes and holy water to avoid harm by vampires, can be helpful (for more details, see Morrison et al., 2004; Wells, 1997).

Once safety behaviours have been identified, behavioural experiments to test out their utility in the short and long term are very useful. Behavioural experiments manipulating

Event	Interpretation/feared catastrophe	Safety behaviour
Walked past a bus stop and people laughed	People are talking about me	Cross over the road and walk really fast Hypervigilance
Hear a voice saying 'hurry up'	I'm going mad	Rest/sit down Slow down activities
Visual hallucination of a dog in the garden	I'm losing control	Shut curtains Stop going into the garden
Woman looked at me in the street	She knows I'm mad	Head down Clench fists

Figure 8.10 Examples of safety behaviours in relation to attenuated symptoms

safety behaviours facilitate disconfirmation of dysfunctional interpretations of attenuated symptoms. When setting up such an experiment it is important to establish specifically what the client predicts will happen if he or she drops the safety behaviour, so he or she can use the information gathered from the experiment to test out his or her prediction explicitly. Sometimes it can be useful to go out into the feared situation with a client to observe safety behaviours. This can provide the therapist with valuable information.

Case example

A client was afraid of going out, due to fears that other people would look at him and subsequently find out there was something wrong with him. During a therapy session it was established that one of his safety behaviours was hypervigilance, which was described as being fairly discrete. However, it was not until the therapist observed the client in the feared situation that it became obvious that his hypervigilance would be extremely noticeable to other people. When he was scanning for danger his movements became much exaggerated, turning his head from left to right, with his back up against a wall, and when somebody walked past he would hide around the side of a building. Clearly, this was making him look suspicious and drawing a great deal of attention and making it very likely that other people would look at him and assume something was wrong with him. In these circumstances, utilising cognitive techniques looking at the evidence for and against people looking at him would have been pointless, before addressing the safety behaviours per se.

These behaviours were initially discussed in therapy with the client being asked to comment on how he would react if he were to notice someone engaging in similar activities whilst out walking. The client was then asked to undertake a behavioural experiment of going for a walk and during this walk he was instructed to do his usual behaviours for five minutes, then increase these behaviours for five minutes and finally drop them altogether for five minutes. During this time he was asked to mentally note how many people looked at him and what their reactions were.

Subsequently this information was incorporated into the formulation and this enabled him to recognise the fact that perhaps some of his behaviours, which initially had been designed to help, had now become unhelpful and were maintaining aspects of his belief.

WORKING WITH CORE BELIEFS

When formulating using Morrison's (2001) model of hallucinations and delusions, core beliefs are identified within the faulty self and social knowledge section of the model.

Identifying core beliefs can be helpful in contributing to clients' understanding of why their difficulties developed. Although the identification of core beliefs is essential when formulating a client's difficulties, it is not necessarily vital to target them directly in therapy. Developing a formulation with a client, which incorporates core beliefs, may be sufficient in demonstrating why his or her difficulties have arisen. However, for some clients their core beliefs may be influential in maintaining their interpretations of attenuated symptoms, or may leave them significantly more at risk of future relapses. Under such circumstances CT techniques to modify core beliefs may be necessary. A common example of a core belief that people at risk of psychosis share is that they are 'different'. This can be the result of early experiences and/or traumatic events such as sexual abuse. If an idiosyncratic formulation indicates that working on core beliefs is necessary, clinicians should apply the usual established techniques to do so. Such techniques include generating evidence for and against to evaluate the beliefs, role-play, positive data logs and continua methods (Padesky, 1994). For a full account of working on core beliefs, see French and Morrison (2004).

CONCLUSIONS

Working with people with attenuated psychotic symptoms using CT has been shown to be effective in reducing transition to psychosis. CT is an acceptable intervention for this population, and has far less risk of side effects than anti-psychotic medication; it is also likely to be useful to those people defined as at ultra-high risk, but who never would go on to develop a psychotic disorder (the false positives). Interventions with this group of patients should be collaborative and use guided discovery, and intervention strategies should be targeted at achieving goals that are set in relation to a shared problem list. Cognitive and behavioural strategies should be selected on the basis of an idiosyncratic case formulation that is based on a cognitive model. Common change methods include normalising the experience, evaluating advantages and disadvantages of ways of thinking, considering evidence for and against thoughts, generating alternative explanations and behavioural experiments. These are useful tools for reducing distress and improving quality of life with people experiencing attenuated psychotic symptoms.

REFERENCES

American Psychiatric Association (1994). *Diagnostic and Statistical Manual of Mental Disorders* (3rd edn, revised). Washington, DC: Author.
Baker, C.A. & Morrison, A.P. (1998). Cognitive processes in auditory hallucinations: Attributional biases and metacognition. *Psychological Medicine*, **28**, 1199–1208.
Barrett, T.R. & Etheridge, J.B. (1992). Verbal hallucinations in normals. I: People who hear voices. *Applied Cognitive Psychology*, **6**, 379–387.
Beck, A.T., Rush, A.J., Shaw, B.F. & Emery, G. (1979). *Cognitive Therapy of Depression*. New York: Guilford Press.
Bentall, R.P. (1990). The illusion of reality: A review and integration of psychological research on hallucinations. *Psychological Bulletin*, **107**, 82–95.
Bentall, R.P., Kinderman, P. & Kaney, S. (1994). The self, attributional processes and abnormal beliefs: Towards a model of persecutory delusions. *Behaviour Research and Therapy*, **32**, 331–341.
Bentall, R.P. & Morrison, A.P. (2002). More harm than good. The case against using antipsychotic drugs to prevent severe mental illness. *Journal of Mental Health*, **11**, 351–365.

Birchwood, M. (1996). Early intervention in psychotic relapse: Cognitive approaches to detection and management. In G. Haddock & P.D. Slade (Eds), *Cognitive Behavioural Interventions with Psychotic Disorders* (pp. 171–211). London: Routledge.

Birchwood, M., Smith, J., Macmillan, F., Hogg, B., Prasad, R., Harvey, C. et al. (1989). Predicting relapse in schizophrenia: The development and implementation of an early signs monitoring system using patients and families as observers. *Psychological Medicine*, **19**, 649–656.

Cartwright-Hatton, S. & Wells, A. (1997). Beliefs about worry and intrusions: The meta-cognitions questionnaire and its correlates. *Journal of Anxiety Disorders*, **11**, 279–296.

Chadwick, P. & Birchwood, M. (1994). The omnipotence of voices: A cognitive approach to auditory hallucinations. *British Journal of Psychiatry*, **164**, 190–201.

Clark, D.M. (1986). A cognitive approach to panic disorder. *Behaviour Research and Therapy*, **24**, 461–470.

Cox, D. & Cowling, P. (1989). *Are You Normal?* London: Tower Press.

Drury, V., Birchwood, M., Cochrane, R. & Macmillan, F. (1996). Cognitive therapy and recovery from acute psychosis: I. Impact on psychotic symptoms. *British Journal of Psychiatry*, **169**, 593–601.

Freeman, D. & Garety, P.A. (1999). Worry, worry processes and dimensions of delusions: An exploratory investigation of a role for anxiety processes in the maintenance of delusional distress. *Behavioural and Cognitive Psychotherapy*, **27**, 47–62.

French, P. & Morrison, A.P. (2004). *Early Detection and Cognitive Therapy for People at High Risk of Developing Psychosis: A Treatment Manual*. Chichester, UK: Wiley.

Garety, P.A., Kuipers, E., Fowler, D., Freeman, D. & Bebbington, P.E. (2001). A cognitive model of positive symptoms of psychosis. *Psychological Medicine*, **31**, 189–195.

Goldberg, D.P. & Hillier, V.F. (1979). A scaled version of the general health questionnaire. *Psychological Medicine*, **9**, 139–145.

Grassian, G. (1983). The psychopathology of solitary confinement. *American Journal of Psychiatry*, **140**, 1450–1454.

Greenberger, D. & Padesky, C.A. (1995). *Mind Over Mood: A Cognitive Treatment Manual for Clients*. New York: Guilford Press.

Grimby, A. (1993). Bereavement among elderly people: Grief reactions. *Acta Psychiatrica Scandinavica*, **87**, 72–80.

Gumley, A.I., O'Grady, M., McNay, L., Reilly, J., Power, K. & Norrie, J. (2003). Early intervention for relapse in schizophrenia: Results of a 12-month randomised control trial of cognitive behaviour therapy. *Psychological Medicine*, **33**, 419–431.

Hollon, S.D., DeRubeis, R.J. & Evans, M.D. (1996). Cognitive therapy in the treatment and prevention of depression. In P.M. Salkovskis (Ed.), *Frontiers of Cognitive Therapy* (pp. 293–317). New York: Guilford Press.

Kay, S.R., Fiszbein, A. & Opler, L.A. (1987). The positive and negative syndrome Scale (PANSS) for schizophrenia. *Schizophrenia Bulletin*, **13**, 261–276.

Kuipers, E., Garety, P., Fowler, D., Dunn, G., Bebbington, P., Freeman, D. et al. (1997). The London–East Anglia randomised control trial of cognitive-behaviour therapy for psychosis. I: Effects of the treatment phase. *British Journal of Psychiatry*, **171**, 319–327.

McGorry, P.D., Yung, A.R., Phillips, L.J., Yuen, H.P., Francey, S., Cosgrave, E.M. et al. (2002). Randomised control trial of intervention designed to reduce the risk of progression to first-episode psychosis in a clinical sample with subthreshold symptoms. *Archives of General Psychiatry*, **59**, 921–928.

Miller, L.J., O'Connor, E. & DiPasquale, T. (1993). Patients attitudes to hallucinations. *American Journal of Psychiatry*, **150**, 584–588.

Morrison, A.P. (1998). A cognitive analysis of the maintenance of auditory hallucinations: Are voices to schizophrenia what bodily sensations are to panic? *Behavioural and Cognitive Psychotherapy*, **26**, 289–302.

Morrison, A.P. (2001). The interpretation of intrusions in psychosis: An integrative cognitive approach to hallucinations and delusions. *Behavioural and Cognitive Psychotherapy*, **29**, 257–276.

Morrison, A.P., Bentall, R.P., French, P., Walford, L., Kilcommons, A., Knight, A. et al. (2002). A randomised control trial of early detection and cognitive therapy for preventing transition to psychosis in high risk individuals: Study design and interim analysis of transition rate and psychological risk factors. *British Journal of Psychiatry*, **181**, 78–84.

Morrison, A.P., French, P., Walford, L., Lewis, S.W., Kilcommons, A., Green, J. et al. (2004). Cognitive therapy for the prevention of psychosis in people at ultra-high risk: Randomised control trial. *British Journal of Psychiatry*, **185**, 291–297.

Morrison, A.P., Gumley, A.I., Schwannauer, M., Campbell, M., Gleeson, A., Griffin E. et al. (2005). The beliefs about paranoia scale: Preliminary validation of a metacognitive approach to conceptualising paranoia. *Behavioural and Cognitive Psychotherapy*, **33**, 153–164.

Morrison, A.P., Haddock, G. & Tarrier, N. (1995). Intrusive thoughts and auditory hallucinations: A cognitive approach. *Behavioural and Cognitive Psychotherapy*, **23**, 265–280.

Morrison, A.P., Wells, A. & Nothard, S. (2000). Cognitive factors in predisposition to auditory and visual hallucinations. *British Journal of Clinical Psychology*, **39**, 67–78.

Nothard, S., Morrison, A.P. & Wells, A. (2005). *The Role of Safety Behaviours in the Maintenance of Negative Beliefs and Distress Associated with the Experience of Hearing Voices.* Manuscript submitted for publication.

Padesky, C.A. (1994). Schema change processes in cognitive therapy. *Clinical Psychology and Psychotherapy*, **1**, 267–278.

Posey, T.B. & Losch, M.E. (1983). Auditory hallucinations of hearing voices in 375 normal subjects. *Imagination, Cognition and Personality*, **2**, 99–113.

Romme, M.D. & Escher, S.D. (1989). Hearing voices. *Schizophrenia Bulletin*, **15**, 209–253.

Romme, M.D., Honig, E. & Escher, S.D. (1992). Hearing voices. *Schizophrenia Bulletin*, **15**, 209–215.

Ross, C.A., Anderson, G. & Clark, P. (1994). Childhood abuse and positive symptoms of schizophrenia. *Hospital and Community Psychiatry*, **45**, 489–491.

Salkovskis, P.M. (1991). The importance of behaviour in the maintenance of anxiety and panic: A cognitive account. *Behavioural Psychotherapy*, **19**, 6–19.

Salkovskis, P.M. (1996). *Frontiers of Cognitive Therapy.* New York: Guilford Press.

Sensky, T., Turkington, D., Scott, J.L., Scott, J., Siddle, R., O'Carroll, M. et al. (2000). A randomised control trial of cognitive-behavioural therapy for persistent symptoms in schizophrenia resistant to medication. *Archives of General Psychiatry*, **57**, 165–172.

Siegel, R.K. (1984). Hostage hallucinations. *Journal of Nervous and Mental Disease*, **172**, 264–271.

Tarrier, N., Yusupoff, L., Kinner, C., McCarthy, E., Gledhill, A., Haddock, G. et al. (1998). A randomised control trial of intense cognitive behaviour therapy for chronic schizophrenia. *British Medical Journal*, **317**, 303–307.

Tien, A.Y. (1991). Distributions of hallucinations in the population. *Social Psychiatry and Psychiatric Epidemiology*, **26**, 287–292.

Wells, A. (1995). Meta-cognition and worry: A cognitive model of generalised anxiety disorder. *Behavioural and Cognitive Psychotherapy*, **23**, 301–320.

Wells, A. (1997). *Cognitive Therapy for Anxiety Disorders.* London: Wiley.

Wells, A. & Matthews, G. (1994). *Attention and Emotion: A Clinical Perspective.* Hove, UK: Erlbaum.

Yung, A., Phillips, L.L., McGorry, P.D., McFarlane, C.A., Francey, S., Harrigan, S. et al. (1998). A step towards indicated prevention of schizophrenia. *British Journal of Psychiatry*, **172**, 14–20.

CHAPTER 9

Brief Limited Intermittent Psychotic Symptoms (BLIPS): A Cognitive Behavioural Approach to Formulation and Intervention

Andrew I. Gumley

INTRODUCTION

There has been considerable debate as to the validity of the prodrome in first episode psychosis. The initial prodrome is an evasive concept, illusive to systematic characterisation (Moller & Husby, 2000): the 'will-o'-the-wisp'[1] of psychosis research, so to speak. It is a largely retrospective construct derived from phenomenological research into the subjective experiences of very early psychosis (e.g. Cutting, 1985; Docherty, Van Kammen, Siris & Marder, 1978; Freedman, 1974; Freedman & Chapman, 1973; McGhie & Chapman, 1961; Moller & Husby, 2000). These studies have shown that individuals become aware of subtle but significant cognitive perceptual changes prior to the onset of psychosis, and that these experiences include feelings of self-consciousness, de-realisation, heightened awareness, attentional difficulties and perceptual disturbance. Recently, Moller and Husby (2000) extracted eight dimensions of self-experienced cognitive perceptual changes during the prodromal stages of psychosis. The most commonly occurring experiences included changes in perception of the self (e.g. feeling unreal or changed, feeling like a spectator), preoccupation with unusual ideas (e.g. being absorbed in one's own thoughts, rumination) and 'neurotic-like experiences' (including depression, anxiety and suicidal ideation). Many participants also reported having been fearful of losing control of, or being unable to monitor, their own thoughts. These experiences have been termed 'basic symptoms' by Huber, Gross, Schuttler and Linz in 1980. They were operationalised by Gross, Huber, Klosterkötter and

---

[1] 'Something that misleads or deludes; an illusion.' Oxford English Dictionary, 2004.

Working with People at High Risk of Developing Psychosis: A Treatment Handbook.
Edited by J. Addington, S.M. Francey and A.P. Morrison. © 2006 John Wiley & Sons, Ltd.

Linz (1987) through the development of the Bonn Scale for Assessment of Basic Symptoms (BSABS).

In a prospective study of these basic symptoms, Klosterkötter, Hellmich, Steinmeyer and Schultze-Lutter (2001) were able to follow up 160 participants over an average of nine and a half years from an initial sample of 695 individuals referred for assessment of prodromal symptoms. Of this group, 110 showed evidence of disturbance according to the BSABS. According to DSM-IV criteria, 79 patients (49.4%) were diagnosed with schizophrenia in the follow-up period. The general predictive accuracy of initial BSABS prodromal symptoms was investigated for those who had at least one BSABS prodromal symptom. Of the 79 participants who developed symptoms which met DSM-IV criteria for schizophrenia, 77 had reported at least one prodromal symptom, whereas only 33 of the 81 patients who did not meet criteria for schizophrenia had shown at least one BSABS prodromal symptom. Therefore, the sensitivity (the ability to correctly predict when psychosis will occur) of at least one BSABS prodromal symptom to schizophrenia was 98% and the specificity (the ability to correctly predict when psychosis will not occur) was 59%. On the other hand, McGorry (1998) has argued that prior to the first episode of psychosis the range of signs and symptoms are so diverse that the 'psychotic prodrome' has limited predictive power to first episode psychosis. For example, the number of BSABS prodromal symptoms assessed in the Klosterkötter et al. (2001) study was 66. McGorry and Singh (1995) have suggested the term 'at risk mental state' (ARMS) as a more appropriate descriptive term which describes a sub-clinical clustering of symptoms and experiences, which, whilst regarded as a risk factor for subsequent psychosis, does not imply an inevitable transition to acute psychosis.

THE 'AT RISK MENTAL STATE' (ARMS)

Alison Yung, Patrick McGorry and colleagues (Yung & McGorry, 1996; Yung, Phillips, Yuen & McGorry, 2004; Yung et al., 2003) have made progress in developing operational criteria to identify three subgroups of individuals hypothesised to be at ultra high risk (UHR) of developing psychosis. The first group are those individuals with attenuated, low-level or sub-clinical positive psychotic symptoms (AS) including ideas of reference, odd beliefs or magical ideation, perceptual disturbance, paranoid ideation, odd thinking and speech, or odd behaviour or appearance, which occur several times per week. These individuals have experienced AS for greater than one week but less than five years, and would not meet criteria for schizotypal personality disorder. Group two are those individuals defined by the presence of either transient psychotic symptoms (BLIPS: Brief Limited Intermittent Psychotic Symptoms), where the symptoms are of psychotic intensity, have occurred in the last year, but the duration is less than one week and the symptoms resolve spontaneously. Group three are those individuals with 'trait plus state risk factors'; that is, individuals diagnosed with a schizotypal personality disorder (DSM-IV) or a first degree relative with a DSM-IV psychotic disorder, who have had a significant decrease in mental state or functioning maintained for at least one month but no longer than five years. Those with a significant decrease in mental state or functioning in the last year but with subsequent recovery would also be considered as meeting 'at risk' criteria.

In reality, there appears to be considerable overlap between these three groups (Yung et al., 2003, 2004). In a group of 104 individuals, 69 met criteria for AS, 29 met criteria for BLIPS and 39 met criteria for 'trait plus state risk'. As one can see from Figure 9.1

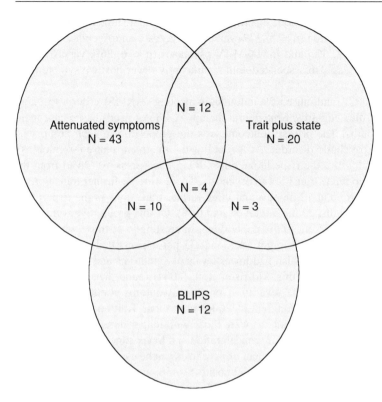

Figure 9.1 Number of participants meeting each criterion. From Yung et al. (2004). Risk factors for psychosis in an ultra high-risk group: psycho-pathology and clinical features. *Schizophrenia Research*, **67**, 131–142.

above, although none of these individuals meet criteria for a psychotic disorder, they are nevertheless a complex group.

For example, over half of the BLIPS group (n = 17) also met criteria for AS (n = 10), 'trait and state' (n = 3) and both AS and 'trait plus state' (n = 4). Morrison and colleagues (2004) used the same criteria to identify a cohort of 58 individuals. No overlap between the subgroups was reported. Most met criteria for AS (n = 48, 83%), followed by BLIPS (n = 6, 10%) then trait plus state (n = 4, 7%). In this sample, Morrison et al. (2002) reported that these participants reported high levels of worry about the controllability of their own thoughts, less cognitive confidence, greater negative beliefs about thoughts (including superstitiousness), greater cognitive self-consciousness and greater sensitivity to rejection and criticism compared to a non-patient control sample.

Yung et al. (2004) found that of the total group of 104, 29 (27%) went on to meet criteria for a psychotic disorder at six months, and 36 (35%) at 12 months. Morrison and colleagues (2004) followed up their participants in the context of a randomised controlled trial comparing cognitive therapy with treatment as usual over 12 months. Three criteria for transition were documented: a symptomatic transition based on severity of PANSS (Positive and Negative Syndrome Scale) positive scale score, a pragmatic clinical transition criterion determined by prescription of antipsychotics and a diagnostic transition determined by the presence of probable DSM-IV psychotic disorder. Transition in the treatment as usual group was higher for PANSS transition (n = 5, 22% versus n = 2, 6%), antipsychotic transition (n = 7, 30% versus n = 2, 6%) and for DSM-IV psychosis (n = 6, 26% versus n = 2, 6%). Cognitive therapy was also associated with significantly fewer positive symptoms at 12 months.

McGorry et al. (2002) randomised 59 individuals meeting (ARMS) criteria to either low dose risperidone plus cognitive behavioural therapy (CBT) or needs based case management over 12 months. The primary outcome was the proportion in each group who made transition to a psychotic disorder. At the end of the treatment phase (six months), three (10%) individuals from the risperidone plus CBT group versus 10 (36%) from the case management group made transition to psychosis. There were no further transitions in the case management group at 12 months and three further transitions in the risperidone plus CBT group at 12 months, giving a total of six (19%). Of this group, five were either non-adherent or partially adherent to the risperidone. Interestingly, of those who refused randomisation but accepted follow-up, an additional 33 participants had a lower rate of transition at 12 months (18%) but also had lower levels of symptoms and disability prior to randomisation. Consistent with this, Morrison et al. (2004) found that, controlling for interim psychological treatment, the severity of positive symptoms at entry to the study predicted transition to psychosis. Yung et al. (2004) found that Trait and AS subgroups were more likely to make the transition, as were those with longer duration of symptoms prior to referral, higher depression, lower concentration and lower functioning.

To summarise, ARMS for the development of psychosis can be clearly identified. Those with more severe, albeit attenuated, lower level positive symptoms are at much higher risk of transition into psychosis (Cornblatt et al., 2003; Morrison et al., 2004; Yung et al., 2004). In addition, it is clear that this is a period characterised by high levels of negative affect and emotional distress (Yung et al., 2004). Phenomenological studies tell us how individuals begin to experience themselves as detached and changed, and, indeed, their own thoughts as uncontrollable (Moller & Husby, 2000; Morrison et al., 2002). These individuals also show much higher levels of interpersonal sensitivity, and fear of rejection and criticism from others (Morrison et al., 2002).

LESSONS FROM RELAPSE DETECTION STUDIES

Studies investigating the prediction and prevention of relapse amongst individuals with established psychotic disorders could shed an interesting light on the findings described above. Early signs of relapse are characterised by high levels of emotional distress including anxiety, fear, depression, suicidal thinking, shame, embarrassment and hopelessness. Yet emotional or dysphoric symptoms of relapse are poor predictors of recurrence of psychosis. Only when low-level psychotic symptoms are included in the definition of early signs of relapse can early 'prodromal' signs reliably predict the recurrence of psychosis. This suggests that the emotional distress seen during early relapse is a response to the re-emergence of low-level psychotic symptoms. This emotional distress is likely to be cognitively mediated. For example, fear of losing control, puzzlement and perplexity, and fear of going crazy are common characteristic experiences associated with early signs of relapse (Hirsch & Jolley, 1989). These appraisals represent individuals' cognitive response to the possible recurrence of psychosis (Birchwood, 1995; Gumley, White & Power, 1999) and are understandable given the experiences of psychosis and often reported trauma associated

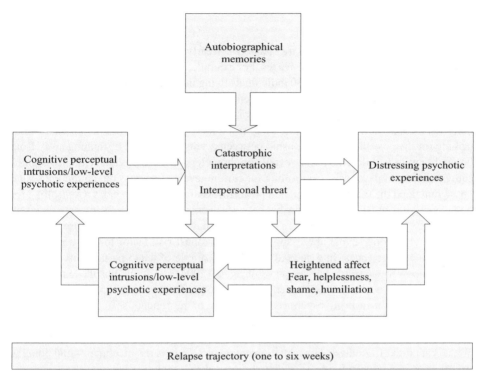

Figure 9.2 A cognitive behavioural conceptualisation of ARMS for relapse

with hospitalisation (Morrison, Frame & Larkin, 2003). Indeed, such appraisals are likely to be informed by pertinent autobiographical memories and experiences. Further compounding these threat appraisals, the experience of psychosis also encapsulates feelings of loss, entrapment, humiliation and defeat (Iqbal, Birchwood, Chadwick & Trower, 2000). Therefore both anxiogenic and depressogenic appraisals are relevant to individuals' cognitive responses to the threat of recurrence of psychosis. This is consistent with relapse phenomenology where both symptoms of anxiety and depression are commonplace. Figure 9.2 illustrates this cognitive behavioural conceptualisation of the recurrence of psychosis. Similarly, early signs of recurrence can be considered as an ARMS.

AT RISK MENTAL STATE (ARMS) AND THE EARLY SOCIAL ENVIRONMENT

Individuals who are at risk of developing psychosis tend to have experienced problematic early social environments (e.g. Spauwen, Krabbendam, Lieb, Wittchen & van Os, 2004; van Os, 2004; van Os, Pedersen & Mortensen, 2004) or potentially traumatic events (e.g. Bebbington et al., 2004; Janssen et al., 2004). These events may operate to undermine optimal social, emotional and cognitive development of the person via the violation of important attachment and bonding experiences, thus undermining the person's ability to reflect on their own cognitive processes, regulate affect and mentalise the beliefs and intentions of others.

Trauma

Epidemiological studies have shown a link between early childhood trauma and the development of distressing psychotic experiences. For example, Bebbington et al. (2004) identified psychiatric disorders amongst 8 580 individuals living in the UK. Compared to respondents with other psychiatric disorders, the prevalence of lifetime victimisation amongst people with a definite or probable psychosis was elevated. These experiences included sexual abuse, bullying, local authority care, running away from home and being a victim of assault. Controlling for the possible interrelationship between events, sexual abuse, running away from home, being in a children's home, expulsion, homelessness and assault remained significant predictors of psychosis. Controlling for current levels of depression, childhood sexual abuse remained the most significant and powerful risk factor for psychosis. Controlling for both depression and the interrelationship between events, sexual abuse, being expelled from school and experiencing assault were predictors of having psychosis. Therefore these data show that childhood sexual abuse appears to be a robust risk factor for the development of psychotic experiences. In a general population sample of 4 045 participants who were followed up over two years, Janssen and colleagues (2004) also found that the experience of childhood sexual abuse was associated with psychosis. This relationship remained despite different ways of measuring psychosis. In addition, more frequent sexual abuse was associated with greater risk of developing psychosis and having 'Need for Care' as measured by the Camberwell Assessment of Need (Slade, Phelan, Thornicroft & Parkman, 1996). What is apparent from these data is that severe disruption in early attachments and bonding experiences increases individuals' vulnerability to developing psychosis.

Urbanicity

In a five-year prospective study of 2 548 adolescents, Spauwen et al. (2004) found that 17.3% (n = 441) had had at least one psychotic experience. They found that growing up in an urban area was associated with an increased risk of expression of psychosis or mania even after controlling for gender, socio-economic status, family history of psychosis and any adolescent psychiatric diagnosis. In a three-year study of the total Swedish population aged between 25 and 65 (4.4 million), Sundquist, Frank and Sundquist (2004) found an incidence of 6 163 cases of first episode psychosis. They found that increasing levels of urbanisation were associated with increased rates of psychosis. Those living in the most densely populated areas had a 66–77% increase in risk of developing psychosis. Van Os et al. (2004) found that in a population-based Danish cohort study of 1 020 063 people, the effect of family history on later risk of schizophrenia increased with the level of urbanicity; that is, between 20–35% exposed to both factors had developed schizophrenia because of the interaction of these two causes. Van Os (2004) argues that individuals with increased genetic liability to psychosis may have less opportunity to modify unusual or psychotic experiences in an (urban) environment with high levels of social fragmentation and low levels of social control, in combination with the lack of perceived safety and increased social stress associated with living in inner city environments. In relation to environmental safety and threat, Janssen and colleagues (2004) found that perceived ethnic discrimination was linked to the subsequent development of delusional persecutory ideation in a three-year study of the Dutch general population (n = 4 076). In summary, it can be argued that individuals who are at UHR of developing psychosis are likely to bring with them experiences of living in a stressful and fragmented social environment characterised by increased interpersonal threat.

BRIEF LIMITED INTERMITTENT PSYCHOTIC SYMPTOMS

Therefore it could be hypothesised that the psychological vulnerabilities to the development of BLIPS include sexual abuse, disrupted attachments and bonds (e.g. running away from home, being in a children's home, expulsion, homelessness), family history and urbanicity, all of which are known to increase risk of developing an ARMS for psychosis. In the context of increased environmental stress, negative life events and increased emotional reactivity, material from underlying cognitive/emotional schemata may overwhelm the person's ability to reflect on and monitor their own cognitive perceptual experiences (self-reflectiveness and metacognitive monitoring). Fonagy, Gergely, Jurist and Target (2002) have previously argued that self-reflective capacity is acquired via secure early attachment bonds and fine-tuned through childhood and adolescent and peer relationships. Conversely, lack of self-reflective capacity has its origins in problematic early experiences, particularly insecure attachment bonds. Vulnerability to increased risk of developing psychosis may be mediated by a fragile or under-developed self reflective capacity that has its origins in early childhood and adolescent adversity. In the context of high levels of negative affect, this loss of self-reflectiveness and metacognitive monitoring may produce an ARMS for psychosis. For example, Bak and colleagues (2003) found that those individuals with ARMS for psychosis that had a need for care were more likely to use symptomatic coping and report stronger feelings of loss of control over psychotic experiences. Symptomatic coping is a coping strategy characterised by going along with or indulging in psychotic experiences: i.e. a failure in self-reflective mentalisation. This lack of self-reflectiveness is also a construct found within the Beck Cognitive Insight Scale (BCIS; Beck, Baruch, Balter, Steer & Warman, 2004). Beck and colleagues formulated insight in psychosis as the person's metacognitive ability to reflect upon, correct and re-evaluate her/his beliefs and interpretations. Reduced self-reflectiveness as measured by the BCIS was associated with more severe hallucinations, delusions and thought disorder.

Loss of self-reflectiveness may, in the context of high levels of negative affect, predispose individuals to experience intrusive cognitive events as externally caused. In addition, negative cognitive interpersonal schema may predispose individuals to being oversensitive to interpersonal threat. In this context paranoia can be conceptualised as an evolved mental state designed to enable the person to detect interpersonal threat and respond rapidly to a perceived threat. Therefore, this paranoid state of mind is designed to view others as threatening, to see interpersonal mistrust and vigilance as an adaptive and helpful survival strategy, to jump to conclusions quickly and in coming to a conclusion be more confident and self-certain than others.

The approach to cognitive therapy for BLIPS described below is guided by the theoretical conceptualisation illustrated in Figure 9.3, and focuses upon the immediate alleviation of emotional distress associated with BLIPS. Furthermore, the approach attempts to address the underlying negative cognitive interpersonal schemata whilst enhancing the person's ability to reflect upon her/his own cognitive perceptual experiences, and, where relevant, the mental states of others. Therefore, according to this conceptualisation, cognitive behavioural

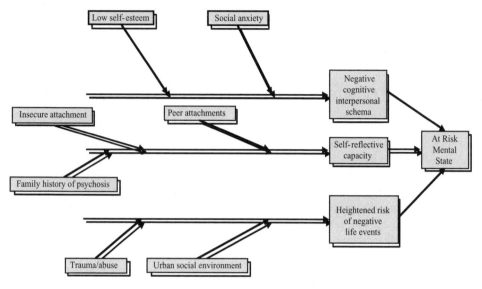

Figure 9.3   Developmental model of evolution of ARMS

psychotherapy aimed at facilitating the person's recovery from BLIPS and in preventing a future recurrence needs to focus on the development of her/his self-reflective capacity. This is achieved through the development of a collaborative therapeutic relationship that allows exploration of the person's early experiences, cognitive interpersonal schema and enduring adaptive and maladaptive behavioural strategies.

COGNITIVE THERAPY FOR BLIPS

During or in response to brief or transient psychotic symptoms, individuals report very high levels of emotional distress which are congruent with their catastrophic appraisals of the personal, social and vocational/educational implications of their psychotic experience(s). The following case scenario illustrates this point.

Case example

Jenny is a 25-year-old married mother of two. She has a history of post-natal depression following the birth of her last child two years previously. She had been seeing her GP on a regular basis since that time. During that period she had been experiencing continuing depressed mood and recurring intrusive and unwanted thoughts. She was referred to our service following a brief period of hearing command hallucinations telling her to harm her child. These hallucinations resolved spontaneously.

> It was awful, I thought I was going to harm the weans, it was like this battle going on in my head. I thought I was going mad, that I would end up in hospital . . . I know this woman who lives in the estate. She's in and out of hospital all the time. She looks weird, like she's on drugs or something. Everyone laughs at her. I could see myself ending up like her, except I'd be worse.

There are two key sets of appraisals linked to Jenny's experience of auditory hallucinations. First is her primary appraisal of the command hallucinations themselves; that is that she is fearful she might act on these and harm her children ('*I thought I was going to harm the weans, it was like this battle going on in my head*'). Second are her secondary appraisals that she is going mad and that she will end up in hospital ('*I could see myself ending up like her, except I'd be worse*'). Supporting these secondary appraisals is her experiential evidence of stereotypes of madness.

Style of Therapy

Cognitive therapy is collaborative, problem orientated, focused and formulation driven. These are key elements that characterise cognitive therapy in response to BLIPS.

Problem List

Therapy and therapist activity is licensed by the client's problem list. The role of the therapist in the early stages of engagement is to focus on the identification of clients' overt problems alongside their cognitive, affective, interpersonal and behavioural dimensions. Careful descriptive characterisation of clients' problems enables the evolution of a micro-level formulation describing the nature of clients' difficulties. Careful problem analysis also enables the development of shared goals. The relationship between clients' problems and their goals facilitates the negotiation of the key tasks of therapy. This mutuality between goals and tasks is central to the development of a strong, early working alliance.

Formulation

Case formulation is tailored according to the therapist's intentions, the client's interpersonal and recovery style and the timing or phase in therapy. It evolves throughout therapy and is seen as a live, creative and ongoing process. It is not an event that is delivered to the patient by the therapist in a static or one-dimensional manner. Case formulation during the engagement phase is designed to capture important emotional meanings and consolidate the development of therapeutic alliance. Narrative is emphasised as a means of capturing important meanings and overcoming paranoid states of mind or an avoidant/sealing over recovery styles. In this sense the therapist is attempting to activate the client's own attachment system by providing meaningful representations of the client's experience, which capture implicational/emotional rather than intellectual levels of meaning (Teasdale & Barnard, 1993). Case formulation is also sensitive to connecting information together on an 'as required' basis. For example, when working on alliance the therapist will attempt to incorporate meanings that are relevant to alliance, whereas when working with interpersonal schema the formulation will connect the client with relevant experiences (e.g. early trauma) and interpersonal responses (e.g. compliance and subjugation).

This layering of formulation throughout the process of therapy is central to tracking client progress and recovery, appropriately pacing therapy and timing specific interventions. The emphasis on narrative formulation corresponds with important exercises during therapy, which focus on the development of an integrated and coherent self-reflective stance and the crafting of a revised and self-accepting narrative. A brief example of a narrative-based formulation is given below.

Dear Jenny

It was difficult for you to seek help for your distressing experiences. You felt ashamed of your thoughts and fearful of becoming mentally ill and being entrapped by psychiatric services. Despite this you have sought help and have worked hard to develop a trusting alliance. Recently you were able to reflect on how difficult it was for you to feel safe during our initial sessions. You were frightened that I would be disapproving or critical, or even hostile and rejecting, in response to talking about your distressing experiences. In developing a sense of trust you have begun to learn that many of the experiences, including intrusive thoughts and voice hearing, are known to occur relatively frequently in the general population. However, you have also begun to reflect on how, when you experience these intrusions, you also experience highly self-critical thoughts that make you feel frightened and ashamed. Perhaps a way forward for us is to think about how you could respond to these self-critical thoughts in a way that alleviates those distressing feelings.

Therapist

Case formulation also provides a conceptual framework to represent individuals' psychological difficulties and provides the basis for assessment and therapy planning. Persons (1989) conceptualises psychological problems as occurring at two levels: the **overt difficulties** and **underlying psychological mechanisms**. Overt difficulties are the problems that clients present with such as depression, interpersonal problems, procrastination, social anxiety or body image. Overt difficulties can be broken down into their component parts, including specific emotions (e.g. embarrassment, fear and shame), behaviours (e.g. pleasing others, avoidance, passivity) and thoughts (e.g. views of self, others, world and future). **Underlying psychological mechanisms** are the hypothesised psychological structures, processes or difficulties that underlie and cause overt difficulties. In this way the case formulation can help make problems appear more cohesive and coherent in that an understanding of the underlying processes can help to synthesise a number of problems in few problem areas with a common underlying mechanism. The formulation can further highlight the connection between these problem areas. In particular a developmental case formulation regarding the genesis of particular difficulties can provide a comprehensive and manageable framework for the understanding of complex difficulties that might appear extremely overwhelming and all-engulfing. Another important constructive component of any case formulation is the clear implication for treatment and specific intervention strategies and techniques. Case formulation aims to help a person to prioritise what feels most important or essential at the time – and it will also highlight connections and interdependence between emotions and certain interactions or behaviours that will help to prioritise certain areas for intervention. It will often appear that treatment progress is not achieved within an anticipated time frame or that patients might find it a lot harder than expected to make certain agreed changes or to implement particular strategies. These road-blocks are important markers to refine and re-evaluate both the formulation and the related intervention strategies as they occur for a reason.

The therapist needs to carefully consider the specific aims of the case formulation at that point in therapy. For example, the aim may be to improve engagement and alliance, to capture important experiential meanings, to elucidate underlying psychological processes, to make links between current experiences and historical events from early development or to provide a basis for treatment planning. The therapist will find it helpful to reflect on their specific aims at that point in therapy and thus select the best approach to develop and communicate a formulation based on (a) the specific goal of formulation and (b) how much affect the client is able to tolerate by communicating significant and emotionally salient meanings.

Clearly, within the context of a person's problem list and individualised case conceptualisation there are a range of evidence-based techniques and strategies available to cognitive therapists that have been designed to alleviate trauma, anxiety, depression and other problems. Cognitive therapy for individuals presenting with and recovering from BLIPS is driven by their problem list, goals and formulation. Below are some specific strategies which have been found to be useful in this population.

Acute Phase Interventions

Immediately and in response to BLIPS the therapist is faced with a number of therapeutic tasks and priorities. These are to optimise engagement and to reduce the overall levels of emotional distress. These tasks can be accomplished in a number of ways, including through validation of the person's emotional distress, where possible decatastrophising and normalising her/his psychotic experiences, and identifying and addressing the person's beliefs about madness, stigma and hospitalisation. Following this acute phase of intervention, the therapeutic tasks evolve towards developing a reflective understanding of the development of BLIPS. This involves the development of a coherent narrative that incorporates and integrates important cognitive, emotional, behavioural and interpersonal factors that may have contributed to the evolution of BLIPS. Second, the therapist may work with the person to identify and resolve emotional distress, providing the opportunity for the person to strengthen existing or develop helpful coping strategies. Finally, in order to develop the person's resilience to future episodes, it may be important to develop an understanding of the nature of longer term vulnerability to the recurrence of BLIPS. This phase focuses on understanding the evolution of problematic cognitive interpersonal schemata. In particular, the therapist and client may work together to understand how these schema have influenced the person's reactions to her/his own thoughts and experiences and her/his interpersonal coping strategies.

Engagement

Individuals experiencing BLIPS access health and other services in a variety of ways. It may be that the person is seeking help after experiencing recent BLIPS. In this case the goal of seeking help may be to seek reassurance, to prevent recurrence, to develop a greater understanding of BLIPS or to address an underlying issue that the person considers causative to the episode. On the other hand, a person may be seeking help at the request of her/his family or loved ones. In this case she/he may therefore feel ambivalent about seeking help. It is clearly important therefore to clarify a person's reasons for seeking help in order to develop an early conceptualisation of her/his personal goals and expectations of therapy.

The process of engagement following BLIPS may well be difficult where (a) individuals perceive negative consequences to disclosing the contents of their experience (for example, being hospitalised or being told that they have schizophrenia), (b) the individual feels ashamed or embarrassed by the contents of her/his thoughts or by the nature of her/his behaviour during BLIPS, and/or (c) the person has continuing AS such as paranoia and suspiciousness. A person may well have sought help on previous occasions and have negative experiences of the consequences of seeking help. For example, many individuals with ARMS will not be able to access routine community mental health services because they have not been 'ill enough'. On the other hand, some clinicians may have attributed their psychotic experiences to having 'borderline personality disorder' and therefore have told the person that she/he is not ill. In other cases, the person may have been admitted to an acute psychiatric ward for a brief period and may be fearful of this happening again. Therefore, during the initial stages of engagement there are a number of key questions that may be useful.

Have you sought help before?
    Where was that? What happened? How did you feel about that?
How did you feel about coming here today?
    What was the hardest thing about coming here? In what way were you
    worried/anxious/uneasy? Did you have positive feelings about coming here today?

These broad questions, with their associated probes, give the therapist an opportunity to clarify any misapprehensions about the therapist's power (e.g. to hospitalise), intention (e.g. to medicate) or role (e.g. to tell the person's family about the contents of discussion). The specific probes also facilitate the opportunity for the development of a fresh and relatively unprocessed discourse relating to the person's own feelings and experiences. Individuals' emotional responses surrounding help seeking often provide important data as to the nature of their interpersonal experiences and underlying cognitive interpersonal schema. The transcript below gives an example of this process.

Therapist: What were your feelings about coming here today?
Client: Hmmm. I don't know really. I want to speak to someone but... {three-second
            pause} I was really nervous coming here today, a bit embarrassed really. I felt
            a bit stupid, I guess.
Therapist: What made you feel stupid about coming here?
Client: Talking to someone, telling somebody what I've been feeling.... {four-second
            pause} sometimes I think I'm going mental.
Therapist: Can you tell me more about that?
Client: It's like this stuff that goes on in my head when I get stressed out. I'm not really
            sure what's going on. My doctor sent me to [place] and they said there was
            nothing wrong with me, but I couldn't tell them how I was feeling properly.
Therapist: Why was that?
Client: I didn't know what they would do about it. Maybe they would put me in
            hospital or something.
Therapist: So you get worried about people reacting badly to your problems so it's
            difficult to talk. You felt nervous coming here today but you've made it.
            Perhaps we could talk a bit more about the kinds of things that have been
            upsetting you.

Engagement during BLIPS is also potentially challenging. The person may well be highly disorientated, fearful, paranoid, hostile and/or angry. This may well be the case where friends, family or even the police have brought the person to the clinic for an emergency assessment. In this case emotional distress is likely to be high, thus making the process of engagement and the evolution of a therapeutic discourse extremely difficult. Therefore, when intervening during an acute phase of BLIPS, therapeutic tasks are prioritised according to the careful assessment and identification of evidence of risk of harm to self and/or harm to others. Once these priorities have been addressed, treatment can move to addressing other therapy priorities including the evolution of a reflective discourse, the development of a formulation, reducing personal vulnerability to further BLIPS and the facilitation of emotional recovery and well-being.

Decatastrophising Psychotic Experiences

An important process in engagement is the normalisation of psychotic experiences. A central aim of proving a normalising rationale is to begin to develop a coherent, compassionate and accepting explanation of the person's psychotic experiences within a non-threatening and open discourse. Therefore in order to establish the person's perspective and starting point for normalising information, the therapist enquires not only as to the nature of psychotic experiences but also their content and idiosyncratic meanings. Problems can occur during this process; for example, providing a normalising rationale for an extremely distressing event might be experienced by the person as a minimising of their distress or the emotional importance of the event. Therefore a critical skill of the therapist is to seek opportunities to validate the individual's experiences and responses. This process can be facilitated by the careful development of a timeline examining the interaction between life events and daily hassles and their affective and cognitive impact. The following case scenario illustrates this point.

Case example

Jack, a 22-year-old single man studying computer design at a local college, was referred by a liaison CPN following attendance at a local accident and emergency department. He gave a three-day history of acute paranoia and was offered psychiatric admission. After one night, Jack's distress and paranoia was observed to reduce significantly and he was discharged from the inpatient unit and referred for follow-up. Jack had believed that the police, colleagues at work and family were trying to kill him. When seen two days later for follow-up, he was less sure about this but remained suspicious of others, particularly their motives to undermine, criticise or make a fool of him. Jack was particularly distressed after the night spent in the acute psychiatric ward and had begun to worry that he was mentally ill.

Jack described always having been anxious and awkward in the company of others. He described having feelings of anxiety and embarrassment in social situations and would often endure the company of others at college. In the last few months, he described a number of stressful events including failing a project in college and subsequently splitting up with a girlfriend. The failed paper led to feelings of inadequacy and failure. He felt highly self-conscious and felt that some other people in his class enjoyed his failure and found it funny. He described feelings of anger and humiliation. This happened during a period of high stress as he and his girlfriend were having frequent arguments. The split, although reasonably amicable, emphasised existing feelings of failure and loneliness. He imagined people laughing at him and criticising him. In the weeks before his BLIPS he had become increasingly self-conscious, anxious and angry and had used cannabis. He felt that this relaxed him more. One week before his BLIPS, Jack had accessed some pornographic websites. Jack described feeling ashamed of himself, seeing himself as despicable and unlovable. He began to worry that his use of the internet was being monitored and that the police would arrest and detain him.

The therapist noted strong feelings of shame, humiliation, embarrassment and fear that permeated the discourse. In order to address his catastrophic appraisals of mental illness and support the process of engagement, the therapist discussed the pre-existing social anxiety that Jack seemed to describe. The therapist provided Jack with information in social anxiety in order to check out whether the experiences of social anxiety matched his own. The therapist began to propose that given Jack's long-standing feelings of social anxiety it was understandable in the context of the significant and sustained feelings of stress that this sensitivity to criticism became magnified, disproportionate and distressing, hence suggesting a link between social anxiety and paranoia.

Developing an Image of BLIPS

Developing an image of BLIPS allows the person to reflect upon the experience and incorporate information that may not have been processed. In addition, it allows the therapist and client to explore hypotheses concerning the psychological factors involved in the development of BLIPS. Similarly, this process allows the therapist and client to develop a representation of ARMS for BLIPS recurrence, thus facilitating preventative interventions, adaptive coping strategies and help seeking. Figure 9.4 provides a framework to explore the development of BLIPS, focusing on salient events and meanings connected to the development of negative affect, loss of self-reflectiveness and the evolution of psychotic experiences. This also gives a fine-grained analysis of the development of BLIPS that can provide a framework for supporting the person in identifying and being mindful of recurrences of ARMS in the future.

Developing a Compassionate View of Psychotic Experiences

The therapist works carefully throughout this process to promote a compassionate state of mind towards the self and one's experiences. Gilbert (2005) has illustrated that a caregiving mentality underpins the communication of compassion, and in this context there are a number of salient competencies including 'protecting the self from threats, not being a threat to oneself, helping, soothing, sending signals that indicate acceptance and positive affect – warmth' (p. 39). During therapy the therapist supports the client in promoting such a state of mind through helping shape, model, encourage and develop a kindly, caring, empathic, soothing and warm cognitive response to distressing psychotic experiences.

Recovery and Staying Well

The Paranoid Mind

A major potential obstacle to recovery and vulnerability to recurrence of BLIPs is the presence of continuing low-level feelings of paranoia, vigilance, suspiciousness and interpersonal threat appraisal. There is a need to explore, understand and narrate the person's experiential framework, which guides her/his awareness, interpretation and response to

ESTABLISH DATE OF BLIPS

ESTABLISH ONSET OF EARLY SIGNS OF BLIPS

CHOOSE EVENT DURING PERIOD BETWEEN ONSET OF EARLY SIGNS AND BLIPS
Prototypic questions:
When talking about this period, is there a particular memory that comes to mind?
At what point did this occur?
Are there other events which come to mind?

ESTABLISH TIMELINE FOR EVENTS IN RELATION TO ONSET OF EARLY SIGNS AND
BLIPS

ESTABLISH EVENT ASSOCIATED WITH 'HOT' COGNITIONS
Prototypic questions:
Which of these events distressed you most?
If only one of these events occurred, which would have been the most upsetting?
Why is that?

ELICIT MEMORIES AND IMAGES ASSOCIATED WITH THE EVENT
Prototypic questions:
What was so upsetting about that?
Are there thoughts and images which come to mind?
Can you describe these?

GUIDED DISCOVERY TO ESTABLISH MEANING
What does that event mean to you?
What was the worst thing about that?

ELICIT COGNITIONS RELATED TO SELF, AND SELF IN RELATION TO PSYCHOSIS
What does it say about your experience?
Do you still think that?
How does it make you feel about your experience?

LINK EVENT AND MEANING THROUGH COGNITIVE, PERCEPTUAL AND
PHYSIOLOGICAL EXPERIENCES
When you think about that now, how do you feel? (Probe cognitive, perceptual and physical
experience)
What do/did you notice about your thoughts?
What do/did you notice about your body?

FORMULATE AND SUMMARISE BY LINKING EVENT, INTERNAL EXPERIENCES,
BELIEFS AND EMOTIONAL/BEHAVIOURAL SEQUELAE

Figure 9.4   Reflecting on the evolution of BLIPS

interpersonal threat. In this context the paranoid mind could be conceptualised as an evo-
lutionarily adaptive state of mind designed to favour survival, but may achieve this goal at
the cost of affiliation, proximity seeking and kinship. The paranoid mind could be conceptualised as having the following characteristics.

The Paranoid Mind is Strategically Deployed

It could be argued that paranoia represents a strategic cognitive response to the perception of interpersonal threat. In a factor analytic study, Morrison et al. (2005) investigated beliefs about paranoia. Using a 31-item questionnaire, in a sample of 317 undergraduates, they found four empirically distinct constructs: beliefs about paranoia as a survival strategy, positive beliefs about paranoia, normalising beliefs about paranoia and negative beliefs about paranoia. Beliefs about paranoia as a survival strategy are exemplified by the following examples: 'paranoia is useful for avoiding trouble' or 'being paranoid or suspicious keeps me safe from harm'. Survival beliefs were associated with more frequent paranoid thoughts and negative beliefs were associated with the distress arising from delusional ideation. These findings help us reflect on how individuals' survival beliefs might be activated by an interpersonally threatening situation. Thus being in a threatening situation (e.g. meeting a friend in an unknown pub) activates survival beliefs (e.g. watch out for untrustworthy people in strange situations) thus generating vigilance for threat, heightened self-focus, suspicious appraisals and external personal attributions.

The Paranoid Mind Makes Decisions Quickly

Numerous studies have shown consistently that individuals with persecutory paranoia have a reasoning style characterised by 'jumping to conclusions' (reviewed by Dudley & Over, 2003; Garety & Freeman, 1999). Generally, individuals with delusions come to decisions more quickly and do so on less evidence compared to controls. Such biases in data gathering and decision making have been reported in individuals with spider phobias (de Jong, Mayer & van-den-Hout, 1997) and individuals who are anxious about their health (de Jong, Haenen, Schmidt & Mayer, 1998). Dudley and Over (2003) have argued that heightened levels of threat awareness increase the sense that a threat exists. The tendency to engage in confirmatory reasoning and jump to conclusions about threat is therefore likely to be protective. Disconfirmatory reasoning, whilst more effective in decision making, takes longer and is an inefficient strategy to deal with threat. In other words, better to jump to conclusions that a threat exists and react even if this means getting it wrong than come to a considered and logical decision that there is no threat, and get it wrong. False positives are therefore less costly in terms of survival than false negative.

The Paranoid Mind is Concerned with External Personal Threat

Individuals with persecutory paranoia attend to interpersonal threat-related stimuli (Fear, Sharp & Healy, 1996; Kaney & Bentall, 1989), recall more threat-related information (Bentall, Kaney & Bowen-Jones, 1995; Kaney, Wolfenden, Dewey & Bentall 1992) and tend to view not only themselves, but others as vulnerable to threat (Kaney, Bowen-Jones, Dewey & Bentall, 1997). When making inferences about positive and negative events, individuals attribute the cause of negative events to other people, whereas depressed patients attribute the cause to self (reviewed by Bentall, Corcoran, Howard, Blackwood & Kinderman, 2001). Such attentional and inferential biases are consistent with a model of paranoia as a state of mind designed to detect interpersonal threat.

Of course there are important costs to the paranoid mind. Paranoia is a distressing experience associated with feelings of vulnerability to harm by others. The paranoid mind is less concerned with mentalising complex affects and intentions than detecting interpersonal threat. In relation to this, there is some evidence that persons who are experiencing acute persecutory paranoia have difficulties understanding the intentions of others, in other words they have a theory of mind or mentalisation difficulty (Corcoran, Cahill & Frith, 1997; Corcoran, Mercer & Frith, 1995; Craig, Hatton, Craig & Bentall, 2004; Frith & Corcoran, 1996; Herold, Tényi, Lénard & Trixler, 2002; Langdon, Coltheart, Ward & Catts, 2002; Pickup & Frith, 2001; Randall, Corcoran, Day & Bentall, 2003).

Problems with the Term Paranoia

During the process of seeking help, individuals' concerns regarding interpersonal threat may have been attributed to being paranoid. Often this is felt to be minimising, pathologising or invalidation of the person's experience. Therefore, it is important to agree terms with respect to how the term paranoia is understood. It could be that the therapist chooses to avoid use of the term. However, we have found it to be extremely useful to explore the meaning of the term with the person. The process of exploring the meanings attached to the term paranoia can lead to the development of a rich narrative. Often individuals will describe associations with the drug-using culture (e.g. 'being para'), associations with mental illness or more idiosyncratic associations with weakness or defectiveness. Indeed, depending how an individual responds to the question 'What do you understand by the term paranoia?' can have a marked influence over the structure of the unfolding discourse. For example:

Therapist: What do you understand by the term paranoia?
Client: Well, it's a sign of weakness, isn't it? I've never had it myself, but if you let anyone see that you're paranoid you are buggered, aren't you? They'll be straight in there!
Therapist: Can you tell me what you mean 'straight in there'?
Client: They'll have you; you'll get a right good kicking.
Therapist: Okay, so you've said paranoia is a sign of weakness. Can you tell me anything else about what you understand by the word?
Client: Well, put it this way. If you are like in a group like a motorcycle gang or something and you do something wrong and then they chuck you out and then you are on the outside and you don't feel cocky any more and they can attack you because like you're on the outside of the group now, and that is what paranoid is, eh?

In this more extreme example of the beginnings of a discourse on paranoia, the client creates an edifice of paranoia as a sign of weakness and therefore vulnerability to attack, and a sign of being on the outside and a loss of confidence. In creating such an edifice it then becomes difficult for the client and therapist to maintain a collaborative discourse, given that the current meaning framework compels the client to reject the term in relation to her/his life experience. Instead the therapist may explore experiences of interpersonal threat and how the person has maintained resilience and strength in the face of adversity. In so doing the therapist may work carefully to develop a developmental and life history view of interpersonally threatening events alongside a careful description of the cognitive, emotional and behavioural consequences of these events. In this sense the therapist always maintains the stance that specific meanings in relation to interpersonal threat are products that have arisen from the complex interplay of life events, interpersonal relationships and interactions accounting for how the person and significant others have interacted within that framework over time. The short transcript illustrated above is contextualised by the following case description.

Case example

Bill is 20 years old and grew up in a small tenement flat in the centre of Glasgow in a family of eight. Bill never met his father. His mother had to work long hours and he does not report many positive memories of loving or caring behaviour. One older sister living in the house brought him up. He had four older brothers, three of whom have long-standing drug problems. He has one younger sister and one younger brother. A family friend, who has since been imprisoned, sexually abused Bill until his mid-teens. During this period Bill developed a number of problems in terms of poor school attendance, drug using and antisocial behaviour. Bill left home at 16 and over the last four years has spent much of his life homeless. During that period Bill learned to be suspicious of the motives of others and has maintained a hostile approach to others he doesn't know. Over this period, he has never discussed his experiences or feelings with others. In the year before referral to the service Bill had his first stable relationship and his girlfriend became pregnant. Bill was referred following a brief but extreme episode of persecutory paranoia characterised by beliefs that mafia gangs were trying to kill him and his girlfriend, and that information about him was being communicated on the TV and radio.

Working with the Personal Distress of the Paranoid Mind

Given this way of conceptualising paranoia, the therapist aims to work carefully with the person to help them become aware of the attributes of the paranoid mind. The therapist can explore the advantages and disadvantages of the person's experience of paranoia. The therapist may focus on ways in which paranoia has been helpful in the person's life and the life situations or interpersonal relationships that have prompted this response. In doing this, the therapist begins to chart the relationship between life events and situations, interpersonal relationships and the development of a paranoid state of mind. In so doing, the therapist encourages the client to reflect upon her/his experiences and to consider the strategic or survival value of paranoia in her/his social and emotional context. This gives the therapist valuable opportunity to validate the person's experience and also provides a normalising and accepting narrative of the development and context of paranoia. In doing this, the therapist is attempting to encourage the development of a metacognitive stance: that is the ability to reflect on and judge one's own thinking and feelings. By doing this the therapist can then gently encourage the person to consider the negative consequences of paranoia in terms of her/his own emotional well-being, her/his feelings of closeness, warmth and affiliation with others and her/his ability to trust and understand others. In this way the interplay between events (e.g. being bullied at school), beliefs (e.g. people are untrustworthy), emotions (e.g. fear, anxiety, embarrassment) and interpersonal coping behaviours (e.g. avoidance, suspiciousness and vigilance, jumping to conclusions) can be formulated and understood. Figure 9.5 below gives a diagrammatical formulation of the maintenance of the paranoid mind using Bill's experiences as an example.

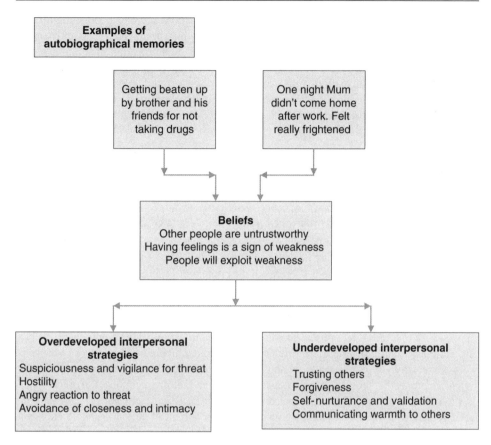

Figure 9.5   Diagrammatical formulation of paranoid mind

In this way the therapist is able to illustrate how the person's beliefs about others concerning mistrust, dangerousness and exploitation are embedded in important and emotionally salient life experiences. This is an important part of the process of validation and support. The therapist is also able to help communicate a warm, compassionate and kindly understanding of the evolution of paranoid beliefs. In addition, the interplay between the person's beliefs and her/his interpersonal coping gives her/him the opportunity to explore how interpersonal strategies have become overdeveloped or underdeveloped and how these strategies may unintentionally distort interpersonal experiences, prevent the development of trust and maintain feelings of loneliness, isolation, vulnerability and threat. In undertaking this process of formulation it may be important to attune to the developmental context of paranoia – particularly the person's care-giving environment, trauma, abuse and peer attachments.

The therapist might consider then a range of possible strategies to support the person in developing trust and reducing vulnerability. A therapist may work to craft new beliefs with the person, for example, 'Some people might be trustworthy', 'I can cope with threats from others', 'I can look after my girlfriend'. These new beliefs might be investigated and strengthened through a range of evidence-based strategies such as historical testing of old and new beliefs, use of continuum, the use of behavioural experiments to strengthen new beliefs, notebooks to collect evidence for and against old and new beliefs, monitoring interpersonal strategies such as jumping to conclusions (whilst noting both costs and benefits to self and others) and addressing traumatic imagery or memories that maintain negative interpersonal schemata. In addition, this approach to conceptualising paranoia opens up important possibilities in exploring the use of compassionate mind training in supporting the development of an accepting, compassionate care-giving mentality to address persecutory states of mind (Gilbert & Irons, 2005).

CONCLUSIONS

Responding to BLIPS is an important but potentially complex clinical priority. Many in-dividuals who present with BLIPS do so in the context of AS such as suspiciousness and paranoia. In addition, epidemiological research shows that those who are at ultra high risk of developing psychosis, including those who present with BLIPS, may be more likely to have experienced negative interpersonal events in the context of familial or social fragmentation (Bebbington et al., 2004; Janssen et al., 2004; Spauwen et al., 2004; van Os et al., 2004). Risk of transition to psychosis via BLIPS with or without AS can therefore be conceptualised in developmental terms. Negative life events and adverse social and familial circumstances may operate to undermine optimal social, emotional and cognitive development of the per-son via the violation of important primary and peer attachment and bonding experiences. This process may undermine the person's metacognitive capacity to reflect on their own cognitive processes, regulate intense negative affects and inhibit mentalisation of the beliefs and intentions of others. Therefore, in responding to BLIPS the clinical priorities are the development of a therapeutic alliance through the agreement of mutually shared goals and tasks, the decatastrophisation and normalisation of distressing psychotic experiences and the alleviation of emotional distress. In so doing, the therapist and client can work together to develop a self-reflective understanding of the emergence of BLIPS, thus enabling the development of a mindful, self-accepting awareness of the experiences associated with the development of BLIPS. In terms of further recovery, therapists may want to consider sup-porting, where relevant, the development and evolution of negative interpersonal schema that prevent recovery and increase vulnerability to transition. One novel way of character-ising such negative interpersonal schema is through the conceptualisation of the paranoid mind as a state of mind, which has been evolved to enhance early detection of interpersonal threat, minimisation of danger and increased survival.

REFERENCES

Bak, M., Myin-Germeys, I., Hanssen, M., Bijl, R., Vollebergh, W., Dellespaul, P. et al. (2003). When does experience of psychosis result in a need for care? A prospective general population study. *Schizophrenia Bulletin*, **29**, 349–358.

Bebbington, P.E., Bhugra, D., Brugha, T., Singleton, N., Farrell, M., Jenkins, R. et al. (2004). Psy-chosis, victimisation and childhood disadvantage: Evidence from the second British National Survey of Psychiatric Morbidity. *British Journal of Psychiatry*, **185**, 220–226.

Beck, A.T., Baruch, E., Balter, J.M., Steer, R.A. & Warman, D.M. (2004). A new instrument for measuring insight: the Beck Cognitive Insight Scale. *Schizophrenia Research*, **68**, 319–329.

Bentall, R.P., Corcoran, R., Howard, R., Blackwood, N. & Kinderman, P. (2001). Persecutory delusions: A review and theoretical integration. *Clinical Psychology Review*, **21**, 1143–1192.

Bentall, R.P., Kaney, S. & Bowen-Jones, K. (1995). Persecutory delusions and recall of threat-related, depression-related, and neutral words. *Cognitive Therapy and Research*, **19**, 445–457.

Birchwood, M. (1995). Early intervention in psychotic relapse: Cognitive approaches to detection and management. *Behaviour Change*, **12**, 2–19.

Corcoran, R., Cahill, C. & Frith, C.D. (1997). The appreciation of visual jokes in people with schizophrenia: A study of 'mentalising' ability. *Schizophrenia Research*, **24**, 319–327.

Corcoran, R., Mercer, G. & Frith, C. D. (1995). Schizophrenia, symptomatology and social inference: Investigating 'theory of mind' in people with schizophrenia. *Schizophrenia Research*, **17**, 5–13.

Cornblatt, B.A., Lencz, T., Smith, C.W., Correll, C.U., Auther, A.M. & Nakayama, E. (2003). The schizophrenia prodrome revisited: A neurodevelopmental perspective. *Schizophrenia Bulletin*, **29**, 633–651.

Craig, J.S., Hatton, C., Craig, F.B. & Bentall, R.P. (2004). Persecutory beliefs, attributions and theory of mind: Comparison of participants with paranoid delusions, Asperger's syndrome and healthy controls. *Schizophrenia Research*, **69**, 29–33.

Cutting, J. (1985). *The Psychology of Schizophrenia*. Edinburgh: Churchill Livingstone.

De Jong, P.J., Haenen, M.A., Schmidt, A. & Mayer, B. (1998). Hypochrondriasis: the role of fear confirming reasoning. *Behaviour Research and Therapy*, **36**, 65–74.

De Jong, P.J., Mayer, B. & van-den-Hout, M. (1997). Conditional reasoning and phobic fear: Evidence for a fear confirming pattern. *Behaviour Research and Therapy*, **35**, 507–516.

Docherty, J.P., Van Kammen, D.P., Siris, S.G. & Marder, S.R. (1978). Stages of onset of schizophrenic psychosis. *American Journal of Psychiatry*, **135**, 420–426.

Dudley, R. & Over, D.E. (2003). People with delusions jump to conclusions: A theoretical account of research findings on reasoning of people with delusions. *Clinical Psychology and Psychotherapy*, **10**, 263–274.

Fear, C.F., Sharp, H. & Healy, D. (1996). Cognitive processes in delusional disorder. *British Journal of Psychiatry*, **168**, 61–67.

Fonagy, P., Gergely, G., Jurist, E.L. & Target, M. (2002). *Affect Regulation, Mentalization, and the Development of the Self.* New York: Other Press.

Freedman, B.J. (1974). The subjective experience of perceptual and cognitive disturbances in schizophrenia: A review autobiographical accounts. *Archives of General Psychiatry*, **30**, 333–340.

Freedman, B.J. & Chapman, L.J. (1973). Early subjective experience in schizophrenic episodes. *Journal of Abnormal Psychology*, **82**, 45–54.

Frith, C.D. & Corcoran, R. (1996). Exploring 'theory of mind' in people with schizophrenia. *Psychological Medicine*, **26**, 521–530.

Garety, P.A. & Freeman, D. (1999). Cognitive approaches to delusions: A critical review of theories and evidence. *British Journal of Clinical Psychology*, **38**, 113–154.

Gilbert, P. (Ed.) (2005). *Compassion: Conceptualisations, Research and Use in Psychotherapy.* London: Brunner-Routledge.

Gilbert, P. & Irons, C. (2005). Focussed therapies and compassionate mind training for shame and self attacking. In P. Gilbert (Ed.), *Compassion: Conceptualisations, Research and Use in Psychotherapy* (pp. 263–325). London: Brunner-Routledge.

Gross, G., Huber, G., Klosterkötter, J. & Linz, M. (1987). *BSABS: Bonn Scale for Assessment of Basic Symptoms.* Heidelberg, Germany: Springer Verlag.

Gumley, A.I., White, C.A. & Power, K.G. (1999). An interacting cognitive subsystems model of relapse and course of psychosis. *Clinical Psychology and Psychotherapy*, **6**, 261–278.

Herold, R., Tényi, T., Lénard, K. & Trixler, M. (2002). Theory of mind deficit in people with schizophrenia during remission. *Psychological Medicine*, **32**, 1125–1129.

Hirsch, S.R. & Jolley, A.G. (1989). The dysphoric syndrome in schizophrenia and its implications for relapse. *British Journal of Psychiatry*, **155** (Suppl. 5), 46–50.

Huber, G., Gross, G., Schuttler, R. & Linz, M. (1980). Longitudinal studies of schizophrenic patients. *Schizophrenia Bulletin*, **6**, 592–605.

Iqbal, Z., Birchwood, M., Chadwick, P. & Trower, P. (2000). Cognitive approach to depression and suicidal thinking in psychosis 2. Testing the validity of the social ranking model. *British Journal of Psychiatry*, **177**, 522–528.

Janssen, I., Krabbendam, L., Bak, M., Hanssen, M., Vollebergh, W., de Graaf, R. et al. (2004). Childhood abuse as a risk factor for psychotic experiences. *Acta Psychiatrica Scandinavica*, **109**, 38–45.

Kaney, S. & Bentall, R.P. (1989). Persecutory delusions and attributional style. *British Journal of Medical Psychology*, **62**, 191–198.

Kaney, S., Bowen-Jones, K., Dewey, M.E. & Bentall, R.P. (1997). Two predictions about paranoid ideation: Deluded, depressed and normal participants' subjective frequency and consensus judgments for positive, neutral and negative events. *British Journal of Clinical Psychology*, **36**, 349–364.

Kaney, S., Wolfenden, M., Dewey, M.E. & Bentall, R.P. (1992). Frequency and consensus judgements of paranoid, paranoid depressed and depressed psychiatric patients: Subjective estimates for positive, negative and neutral events. *British Journal of Clinical Psychology*, **31**, 85–87.

Klosterkötter, J., Hellmich, M., Steinmeyer, E.M. & Schultze-Lutter, F. (2001). Diagnosing schizophrenia in the initial prodromal phase. *Archives of General Psychiatry*, **58**, 158–164.

Langdon, R., Coltheart, M., Ward, P.B. & Catts, S.V. (2002). Disturbed communication in schizophrenia: The role of poor pragmatics and poor mind-reading. *Psychological Medicine*, **32**, 1273–1284.

McGhie, A. & Chapman, J. (1961). Disorders of attention perception in early schizophrenia. *British Journal of Medical Psychology*, **34**, 103–116.

McGorry, P. (1998). Preventive strategies in early psychosis: Verging on reality. *British Journal of Psychiatry*, **172**, 1–2.

McGorry, P. & Singh, B.S. (1995). Schizophrenic risk and possibility of prevention. In B. Raphael & G.D. Burrows (Eds), *Handbook of Studies in Preventative Psychiatry* (pp. 491–514). Amsterdam, Netherlands: Elsevier Science.

McGorry, P.D., Yung, A.R., Phillips, L.J., Yuen, H.P., Francey, S., Cosgrave, E.M. et al. (2002). Randomized controlled trial of interventions designed to reduce the risk of progression to first-episode psychosis in a clinical sample with subthreshold symptoms. *Archives of General Psychiatry*, **59**, 921–928.

Moller, P. & Husby, R. (2000). The initial prodrome in schizophrenia: Searching for naturalistic core dimensions of experience and behaviour. *Schizophrenia Bulletin*, **26**, 217–232.

Morrison, A.P., Bentall, R.P., French, P., Walford, L., Kilcommons, A, Knight, A. et al. (2002). Randomised controlled trial of early detection and cognitive therapy for preventing transition to psychosis in high-risk individuals. Study design and interim analysis of transition rate and psychological risk factors. *British Journal of Psychiatry*, **181** (Suppl.), **48**, s78–84.

Morrison, A.P., Frame, L. & Larkin, W. (2003). Relationships between trauma and psychosis: A review and integration. *British Journal of Clinical Psychology*, **42**, 331–353.

Morrison, A.P., French, P., Walford, L., Lewis, S.W., Kilcommons, A., Green, J. et al. (2004). Cognitive therapy for the prevention of psychosis in people at ultra-high risk: Randomised controlled trial. *British Journal of Psychiatry*, **185**, 291–297.

Morrison, A.P., Gumley, A.I., Schwannauer, M., Campbell, M., Gleeson, A., Griffen, E. et al. (2005). The beliefs about paranoia scale: Preliminary validation of a metacognitive approach to conceptualising paranoia. *Behavioural and Cognitive Psychotherapy*, **33**, 153–164.

Persons, J.B. (1989). *Cognitive Therapy in Practice: A Case Formulation Approach*. New York: Norton.

Pickup, G.J. & Frith, C.D. (2001). Theory of mind impairments in schizophrenia: Symptomatology, severity and specificity. *Psychological Medicine*, **31**, 207–220.

Randall, F., Corcoran, R., Day, J.C. & Bentall, R.P. (2003). Attention, theory of mind and causal attributions in people with persecutory delusions: A preliminary investigation. *Cognitive Neuropsychiatry*, **8**, 287–294.

Slade, M., Phelan, M., Thornicroft, G. & Parkman, S. (1996). The Camberwell Assessment of Need (CAN): Comparison of the assessment of staff and patients in the needs of the severely mentally ill. *Social Psychiatry and Psychiatric Epidemiology*, **31**, 109–113.

Spauwen, J., Krabbendam, L., Lieb, R., Wittchen, H.U. & van Os, J. (2004). Does urbanicity shift the population expression of psychosis? *Journal of Psychiatric Research*, **38**, 613–618.

Sundquist, K., Frank, G. & Sundquist, J. (2004). Urbanisation and incidence of psychosis and depression. *British Journal of Psychiatry*, **184**, 293–298.

Teasdale, J.D. & Barnard, P.J. (1993). *Affect, Cognition and Change: Re-modelling Depressive Thought*. Hillsdale, N.J.: Erlbaum.

Van Os, J. (2004). Does urban environment cause psychosis? *British Journal of Psychiatry*, **183**, 287–288.

Van Os, J., Pedersen, C.B. & Mortensen, P.B. (2004). Confirmation of synergy between urbanicity and familial liability in the causation of psychosis. *American Journal of Psychiatry*, **161**, 2312–2314.

Yung, A.R. & McGorry, P.D. (1996). The initial prodrome in psychosis: Descriptive and qualitative aspects. *Australian and New Zealand Journal of Psychiatry*, **30**, 587–599.

Yung, A.R., Phillips, L.J., Yuen, H.P., Francey, S.M., McFarlane, C.A., Hallgren, M. et al. (2003). Psychosis prediction: 12-month follow up of a high-risk ('prodromal') group. *Schizophrenia Research*, **60**, 21–32.

Yung, A.R., Phillips, L.J., Yuen, H.P. & McGorry, P.D. (2004). Risk factors for psychosis in an ultra high-risk group: Psychopathology and clinical features. *Schizophrenia Research*, **67**, 131–142.

CHAPTER 10

Working with Families Following the Diagnosis of an At Risk Mental State

April A. Collins and Jean Addington

Research and clinical experience repeatedly remind us that psychosis can, and often does, wreak havoc in families. There is substantial evidence in the literature which demonstrates that the responsibility of providing care for an adolescent or adult child with a psychotic illness can place the caregiver at risk for distress, anxiety, depression and economic strain (Barrowclough, Tarrier & Johnston, 1996; Scottish Schizophrenia Research Group, 1992; Szmukler et al., 1996a). The prevalence of associated psychological distress in caregivers is high, with 29–60% of samples having diagnosable psychiatric symptoms (Barrowclough & Parle, 1997; Birchwood & Cochrane, 1990). Similarly, distress and, at times, psychiatric morbidity have also been reported in the relatives of families at the first episode of psychosis (Addington, Coldham, Jones, Ko & Addington, 2003; Addington, McCleery & Addington, in press-b; Kuipers & Raune, 2000; Tennakoon et al., 2000). However, little is known about the specific ways in which families handle these strains, or what distinguishes those who competently manage these difficulties from those who collapse under the daily pressures.

There is compelling evidence that demonstrates (i) that psychosis has an impact on families, (ii) that families can influence the course and outcome of illness (Smith, Berthelsen & O'Connor, 1997), and (iii) that informal family caregivers provide the vast majority of care for those in the early phases of a psychotic illness. Consequently, working with families during what has come to be known as the time of "ultra high risk" (UHR) clearly deserves our attention. In keeping with the idea that early detection and intervention at the first episode may improve the course of schizophrenia for patients (Birchwood & MacMillan, 1993; McGlashan, 1998), the notion of intervention with families following the diagnosis of an "at risk mental state" (ARMS) may offer opportunities for secondary prevention. That is, working with families at this very early phase will allow us to begin to ask questions about which family factors might be protective for an individual who is at UHR of illness progression and which factors may assist with recovery efforts (McGorry, Yung & Phillips, 2003). It will also give us the opportunity to ask what underlies successful family adaptation

Working with People at High Risk of Developing Psychosis: A Treatment Handbook.
Edited by J. Addington, S.M. Francey and A.P. Morrison. © 2006 John Wiley & Sons, Ltd.

following the onset of a subclinical syndrome in an "at risk" population. More specifically, we need to try to identify and foster those key processes that enable families to successfully navigate through the crises and challenges that the diagnosis of an ARMS imposes. There is much to be learned from families who succeed that can inform our work with those who persistently struggle in their caregiving efforts (Robinson, 1996).

Since the literature is almost non-existent on the topic of intervention with families following the identification of an ARMS, the background for this chapter has drawn from a number of perspectives and thus represents the convergence of three lines of independent work. These are the recent outcome literature on first episode families, the construct of expressed emotion (EE), which has a well-established history in studies of families affected by severe and persistent mental illness (Goldstein & Miklowitz, 1995), and the theoretical framework of coping and adaptation (Folkman, 1997; Folkman, Chesney & Christopher-Richards, 1994a; Folkman, Chesney, Cooke, Boccellari & Cooke, 1994b; Folkman, Lazarus, Dunkel-Schetter, Delongis & Gruen, 1986; Lazarus & Folkman, 1984a). These have been used in the development of a framework to help guide our work with families. Case studies have been incorporated to highlight typical presenting problems and the strategies that have been used to help.

BACKGROUND

Psychosis and First Episode Families

To date, very few studies have examined the impact of first episode psychosis on families. Those which do indicate that there is a significant impact. For example, the Scottish Schizophrenia Research Group (McCreadie & Robinson, 1987; McCreadie et al., 1989) reported that at admission relatives' distress was significantly greater than that of a normal community sample. Seventy-seven percent of their sample of caregivers could be categorized as "psychiatric cases" on the General Health Questionnaire, and by 12 months, 40% of their families remained above the threshold for case identification. However, by 24-month follow-up, relatives showed no more distress than found in a normal community sample and this distress was associated with their ill relative's symptomatology (McCreadie et al., 1989). Addington et al. (in press-b) have reported three-year outcome data on 187 families in the Calgary Early Psychosis Program. Their results are notable for a number of reasons. First, they confirm that many families (47%) do experience moderate to severe levels of distress following the onset of the illness. By three years, although the distribution of distress among first episode families in their sample approximated general population norms, 26% were still endorsing moderate to severe levels of distress. It is noteworthy that in this study poor psychological well-being was best predicted by the family's appraisal of the impact of the illness and less by the severity of illness.

Expressed Emotion (EE)

The notion that family relationships may be one of the more powerful "environmental influences" that shape the course and outcome of schizophrenia has its roots in British social psychiatry (Collins, 2002). The construct of EE emerged from this literature and has been extensively studied over the last several decades (Barrowclough & Hooley, 2003; Kavanagh, 1992). EE is a construct which encompasses several key aspects of close interpersonal relationships. It reflects critical, hostile or emotionally over-involved attitudes on the part of family members towards a relative with a disorder or impairment. Moreover, within the context of a stress–vulnerability model, the patient's family home is viewed as an environment capable of influencing the illness for better or worse (Barrowclough & Hooley, 2003).

Much has been written on the evolution of EE. However, the current approach views the behavior of both patients and relatives as reactions to stress and their resultant attempts to cope. In so doing, it implicitly recognizes the role of two moderating variables: the interpretations that each person makes of the other's behavior and the coping skills that each brings to bear (Kavanagh, 1992). In support, research has demonstrated that those with higher levels of EE have increased burden and perceive themselves as coping less effectively (Barrowclough & Parle, 1997; Brewin, MacCarthy, Duda & Vaughn, 1991; Scazufca & Kuipers, 1996, 1998; Smith, Birchwood, Cochrane & George, 1993). What appears to be most important in EE is the appraisal the relative has of the patient's condition, rather than the actual deficits shown by the patient (Bentsen et al., 1998). Recent work has examined the concept of EE in first episode families in terms of incidence, and differences between high and low EE families (Heikkila et al., 2002; Raune, Kuipers & Bebbington, 2004). These research groups suggest that a carer appraisal model (Folkman & Lazarus, 1985) is helpful in understanding the development of EE (Barrowclough, Lobban, Halton & Quinn, 2001; Hooley & Campbell, 2002). For example, Raune et al. (2004) found that there was no association between EE and illness-related factors but that avoidant coping was the strongest predictor of EE during a first episode. This finding is consistent with the perception of high EE caregivers that their situational stress exceeds their coping capacity (Raune et al., 2004) and offers indirect support to the notion that maladaptive cognitive appraisals may maintain a high EE response (Barrowclough & Parle, 1997).

Coping and Adaptation

To better understand the coping within families we consider a well-established model of stress and coping (Folkman, 1997; Lazarus & Folkman, 1984b). Coping is defined as a person's constantly changing cognitive and behavioral efforts to manage specific external and/or internal demands that are appraised as taxing or exceeding the person's resources (Lazarus & Folkman, 1984a). External demands refer to the features of the event itself and internal demands refer to the emotional reactions a person has to the event. There are two styles of coping—problem focused and emotion focused (Folkman, Lazarus, Gruen & DeLongis, 1986; Lazarus, 1993). In problem-focused coping the individual uses cognitive and behavioral efforts directed at defining the problem, generating possible solutions, weighing the alternatives in terms of their costs and benefits, and choosing among them and acting. The purpose of emotion focused coping is to regulate stressful emotions by changing either (i) the way the stressful relationship with the environment is attended to by using strategies like avoidance, minimization, distancing, selective attention, and positive comparisons, or (ii) the way the encounter is construed, which mitigates the stress even though the actual event has not changed. This model of coping is process oriented in that it focuses on what a person thinks and does in a specific stressful encounter, and how this changes as the encounter unfolds (Lazarus, 1993). Coping is seen as being influenced by context; that is, it is influenced by a person's appraisal of the actual demands of the encounter and the resources available for managing them.

The approach makes a number of valuable contributions. It directs our attention away from the notion that coping is a static event that can be measured and fully understood cross-sectionally. Instead, coping is seen as a shifting process that occurs within a context and has the potential to change over time because what is attended to, and the threats themselves change (Lazarus, 1993). This, therefore, underscores the need to simultaneously focus on any co-occurring life events, as well as illness and treatment characteristics, because all are seen as potentially significant influences on a person's reaction to illness. For this reason, a comprehensive family assessment is an essential component of clinical work with UHR youth. In addition to offering salient collateral information about their child's premorbid level of function and the changes that have occurred, the assessment allows us to ask about what else has been happening in their lives. In our clinic, families dealing with the diagnosis of an ARMS in isolation has been the exception rather than the norm. Instead, our "typical family" has not only been dealing with the diagnosis that we have made, but has also been contending with a range of other issues. These have included pre-existing marital problems, personal mental health issues, other family members in crisis, and job loss. To ignore these other realities makes little sense. These issues need to be addressed alongside the challenges related to the diagnosis of an ARMS. If we failed to do so, our success in working preventatively with young UHR clients is likely to be limited.

Within this model there is also recognition that when people "cope" with a focal stressor, they are often coping not only with that stressor but also with a multiplicity of other challenges which may have been triggered by the initial problem (Lepore & Evans, 1996). For example, parents of children diagnosed with an ARMS have to cope over prolonged periods of time with multiple stressors related to caregiving and anxiety about their child's health and future. In addition, some, unfortunately, go on to contend with the reality that their child has converted to psychosis.

Effective coping implies a relationship between coping behaviors and various outcomes. Thus, the prime importance of appraisal and coping processes is that they affect or mediate adaptational outcomes (Lazarus & Folkman, 1984a). Individuals who use avoidant, emotion-focused coping strategies have more difficulty adapting to illness compared to those who use active problem-solving approaches (Carver et al., 1993; White, Richter & Fry, 1992). For example, avoidant coping strategies were related to higher distress, whereas problem-focused coping was related to lower levels of psychological distress in mothers of physically disabled children (Frey, Greenberg & Fewell, 1989; Miller, Gordon, Daniele & Diller, 1992).

Impact of Family Interventions

In the literature describing work with families with established psychotic illnesses, there is ample evidence demonstrating that long-term family treatment oriented toward educating families and improving their coping skills significantly delays but does not prevent relapse (Mari & Streiner, 1994; Pilling et al., 2002). Educationally based family interventions have also been found to reduce the incidence of hospitalization as well as bring about improvements in treatment adherence (Fadden, 1998). Family interventions for individuals with psychosis have been assessed either for their benefit in reducing relapse (Dixon & Lehman, 1995), or for their impact on family members (Barrowclough et al., 1996; Szmukler et al., 2003; Szmukler, Herrman, Colusa, Benson, & Bloch, 1996b). In fact, the evidence for the efficacy of family intervention has been substantive enough for it to be considered an evidence-based practice (Lehman et al., 2003).

Reports of intervention with first episode families are few, although some descriptions are available in the literature (Addington & Burnett, 2004; Addington et al., in press-a; Early Psychosis Prevention and Intervention Centre, 1997). Such programs offer a range of interventions that include psychoeducation but also focus on coping and adaptation. In our own work with first episode families, we have developed and described a recovery model that has its origins in the Calgary First Episode Program and has since been expanded for use in the First Episode Psychosis Program in Toronto, Canada (Addington et al., in press-a). In designing an optimal family program within a first episode service we were sensitive to the phase and stage of the illness. There are four stages to the recovery framework that was used to plan services for families: managing the crisis, initial stabilization and facilitating recovery, consolidating the gains, and prolonged recovery. Each stage has clearly articulated goals and associated interventions.

To date, only one study has reported on outcome. In a three-year uncontrolled trial of 187 first episode families, Addington et al. (in press-b) reported that over time families demonstrated improved psychological well-being and improved scores on the Experience of Caregiving Inventory (ECI; Szmukler et al., 1996a). Furthermore, this study demonstrated not only high acceptability of the intervention but also that a limited number of sessions were effective if they were offered over a longer period of time.

In addition to teaching families about the symptoms of psychosis, recovery, and the prevention of relapse using an early warning signs approach (McGorry, 1995), we must attend to the psychological well-being of family members and the coping processes that support it (Folkman & Greer, 2000). This is based on the belief that those families who are able to navigate the challenges that the illness imposes are in a better position to work with the treatment team to assist with the recovery efforts of their child, and are more likely to sustain their own personal well-being.

However, we also suggest that family approaches which simply provide new information to relatives and attempt to teach new skills are, at best, likely to confer modest benefit if they ignore the underlying complex belief systems that exist within families (Barrowclough & Hooley, 2003). It is likely that these belief systems will influence the ability of family members to engage with the treatment team to (i) protect against illness progression and (ii) facilitate the recovery of function and the resolution of emergent symptoms in their child. They are also likely to play a significant role in the ability of family members to develop and maintain their own psychological well-being in the face of a potentially serious illness in a child. The way in which families respond to the individual at risk may impact either positively or negatively on the young person's progress (Lobban, Barrowclough & Jones, 2003). Because ideas are likely to be influenced by cultural and social norms, relatives' beliefs are likely to play some role in shaping the beliefs and perceptions of the at risk person (Larsen & Opjordsmoen, 1996) and may thus further impact on the adaptive outcome for the individual at risk (Heijmans, deRidder & Bensing, 1999).

THE DEVELOPMENT OF A PROGRAM FOR FAMILIES FOLLOWING THE DIAGNOSIS OF AN AT RISK MENTAL STATE

The confluence of key constructs that have emerged in the family and first episode literature combined with the theoretical model of coping and adaptation provide a useful foundation upon which to develop a program for families of UHR individuals.

From this, we would suggest that there are three interdependent priorities for family work following the onset of the ARMS:

1. Management of the presenting problems in the young person with an ARMS (e.g., social withdrawal, reduced academic performance, attenuated positive symptoms).
2. Monitoring for the possible emergence of psychosis.
3. Development and maintenance of psychological well-being and adaptive functioning in family members.

The framework that we propose here is based on the recovery stage model developed by the Calgary and Toronto first episode groups (Addington et al., in press-a). The model we propose for working with UHR families addresses all three priorities stated above. There are four stages to the framework that can be used to plan services for UHR families. These are: Managing the Crisis, Developing an Explanation and Facilitating Recovery, Consolidating the Gains, and Conversion. Each stage has clearly articulated goals and associated interventions. In reality, however, families will not move smoothly through these four stages. Realistically, families will move in and out of crises. Hopefully, some families will not reach the fourth stage and, unfortunately, some families may not reach the third stage. Thus, in our family work we have to be aware of the movement back and forth between these different stages and be flexible in our approach.

Stage 1: Managing the Crisis

The first stage, following first contact with the service, involves engaging the client and family with the clinic and the person who will work specifically with the family. The essential steps of assessment and engagement begin at the time the family has first contact with the treatment team. However, as many families present in crisis, an initial response to this is required and will facilitate engagement with the family. During this phase of initial contact, families can present in a variety of ways. They may be confused and traumatized and have little or no real understanding of the changes that they have observed in their relative. Alternatively, families may minimize early problems and attempt to explain away early changes. They may argue with other family members regarding the best way to address the problem. Often the client is seen as demonstrating "bad" behavior or they are considered lazy, stubborn, hostile, or selfish. In our experience many families have felt overwhelmed by feelings of anger, guilt, and frustration following the recognition of an ARMS in their young relative. There are many ways in which clinicians can assist families to deal with this crisis phase. It is important for clinicians to listen to families' concerns, provide opportunities for ventilation, provide initial psychoeducation, and be available for frequent supportive contact with distressed families.

During and following the initial crisis, it is crucial that the treating team work hard to establish rapport with the family. The development of a strong therapeutic alliance with the family is a prerequisite so that they can then go on to work to establish goals for themselves as they relate to their role in the recovery efforts of their relative and their own well-being (Folkman & Greer, 2000). A sense of mastery can be promoted through knowledge acquisition and skill teaching but only if people are willing and able to hear and use the information that is offered.

The assessment of the family should include an evaluation of beliefs within the family about the causes of the ARMS, its ability to control the situation, the perceived benefits of recommended treatments, and perceived consequences to the person's life and how long the experience is likely to last. Families should be given support and assistance to manage their immediate concerns and offered an initial explanatory model of the ARMS. At the same time, it is important to begin to present more appropriate explanations if these are not present. This enables an alternate model to be considered rather than leaving an unchallenged lay model to become entrenched (McGorry, 1995).

An important part of the assessment is to consider whether the responses of the family to the situation are likely to alleviate or exacerbate problems or become problems themselves. This information can subsequently be used to develop an individualized sensitive and flexible plan of care for the family. It is important that clinicians do not assume that they know what matters to individual family members. Families approach the illness with their own internalized beliefs, histories, psychosocial, physical, and material resources, and expectations about the future. What matters to them may pertain to their relative's ARMS, to other areas of their life, or, most likely, some combination of both (Folkman & Greer, 2000). What is important now and what matters most needs to be concurrently defined by the family and the treatment team. This will allow us to help establish meaningful and realistic goals that can be agreed upon and linked to opportunities for mastery.

Finally at this first stage, it is necessary to begin to think about families who may have difficulty facilitating the recovery efforts of their relative and/or appear to be managing in ways that are detrimental to their own well-being. Additionally, there are often families who are struggling and present with more difficult or serious problems such as high levels of familial conflict, verbal or physical violence, or extreme levels of tension and distress. There may be multiple family members with psychosis or mental illness, a recent family history of suicide, or severe physical health problems in other members of the family. At times we are presented with families who have recently arrived from non-English speaking countries. The above are all examples of family issues not directly caused by the presenting problems or ARMS but which have a major effect on current problems and on the course of psychosis should it occur. We also have to be aware of the possibility that such family issues are risk factors for conversion in the vulnerable individual. The extent to which they can be addressed within a UHR clinic depends upon the training and experience of the family workers. It may require supervision from an experienced family therapist or even referral to another therapist. For the purpose of this chapter we will refer to such families as "high need". This group, in addition to the standard care offered to families, may require extra, more specialized, help from a family therapist.

Thus, the primary goals of this stage are to engage the family with the treatment team, develop a good working relationship, and begin a detailed assessment.

Table 10.1   Stage 1: Managing the crisis

Goals	Individual treatment
• Engage with the family • Develop a good working relationship • Collect a detailed collateral history and needs assessment • Help manage the crisis or confusion • Offer an initial explanatory model of the presenting problems • Identify high-need families	• Reasonably frequent contact • High support • Practical and emotional support to minimize the impact of the upheaval or trauma • Repeated and clear messages about managing current symptoms as well as potential psychotic symptoms and their treatment • Education about the role of the family in the treatment or monitoring process

Stage 2: Developing an Explanation and Facilitating Recovery

The second stage of this model is geared toward helping the family develop a good understanding and explanation for what has happened, and begin to focus on recovery. The goals of this stage are to continue to assess family functioning after the initial crisis has hopefully passed, to solidify the therapeutic alliance, and increase the family's knowledge of the ARMS. Specifically, we want to help the family understand the recovery process and raise awareness of early warning signs of developing psychosis or other psychiatric problems. Families need to understand the importance of monitoring for early symptoms of potential psychosis or other disorders in order to facilitate early intervention. They need to access and understand accurate information about the early warning signs of impending psychosis so that they can identify either a change or increase in the early symptoms should that happen.

Families are usually seeking explanations and addressing this involves helping them to develop an explanatory model for these early symptoms. Psychoeducation about the stress–vulnerability model of the development of psychosis is helpful in providing a framework to understand both symptoms and the rationale for interventions. Furthermore, family members need to minimize disputes about the young person's behavior and develop a consensus regarding the explanation for the change in behavior. Hopefully, this will help to avoid conflict and encourage family members to work together. Families need to learn what treatments are available and suitable for the young person in this early stage and what treatments might be available that will help prevent an exacerbation of these early subthreshold symptoms. Further information about appropriate sources of help and how to access appropriate treatment needs to be available.

It is at this stage that group work may be helpful. Groups can be short term offering information, education, and support. Groups help families to meet other families with similar problems. They provide opportunities for families to learn from each other's experience, and to share coping strategies and solutions to difficulties. They may help reduce the sense of isolation, shame, and stigma that often accompanies psychosis, and in this case, early signs of psychosis. Group work offers families the opportunity for open discussion and to exchange information with others, offering increased problem solving and increased

Table 10.2 Stage 2: Initial stabilization and facilitating recovery

Goals	Individual treatment
• Assess family functioning • Develop therapeutic alliance • Increase family's knowledge of psychosis • Help family to be able to identify early warning signs of psychosis or relapse of presenting symptoms • Develop a consensus among family members with respect to a shared explanatory model and/or formulation for presenting problems • Identify those with high-need and those with sustained patterns of interaction likely to interfere with patient outcome	• Support and education • Development of an explanatory model • Problem solving and coping strategies for the "at risk mental state" • Intensive work for high-need families *Group treatment* Short term Psychosis-education group

options. They can reinforce the education already received and offer support. It is essential, however, that the group leaders foster an interactive approach rather than a didactic one, so that families learn to be active participants in the process.

Again at this stage we must continue to ensure that the high-need families, and those families with sustained patterns of interaction which are likely to interfere with the patient's outcome, are engaged in specialized family care targeting the specific challenges that exist within the family. Thus, in summary in Stage 2, care for families can be offered individually or as a part of group treatment. The focus largely involves support, education, discussion about explanatory models, and coping strategies for dealing with problematic behaviors, attenuated symptoms, and other presenting problems.

Stage 3: Consolidating the Gains

The aim of the third stage is to consolidate the gains from the earlier stages. At this stage, families can be helped to incorporate knowledge learned in previous stages into their day-to-day practices. In addition, the individual may be involved in a program or intervention to promote recovery, or he or she may be involved only in a monitoring process around an increase in presenting symptoms. It may be that services outside of the specialized clinic are being used and the family needs to be aware of how these different services are proceeding. Both the family and client are taught to monitor for a worsening of symptoms or conversion to psychosis and how to implement strategies that have been identified as helpful in reducing symptoms and risk. It is also important that families are encouraged to continue to work on maintaining their own psychological well-being.

Individual treatment at this stage involves booster sessions with a focus on early warning signs and targeted problem solving. High-need families continue to receive more intensive family work from an expert family therapist. Finally, at this stage families are prepared for termination from the program. This is the final stage for many families and an appropriate focus is promoting and maintaining wellness for all family members.

Table 10.3   Stage 3: Consolidating the gains

Goals	Individual treatment
Assist family to: • Incorporate knowledge into day-to-day practices • Actively involve the client in a treatment program or in monitoring • Understanding risk of conversion or of presenting symptoms • Maintain personal psychological well-being	• Booster sessions • Family coping with a focus on staying well • Focus on early warning signs of symptom exacerbation • Targeted problem solving • More intensive family work from expert family therapist for high-need families • Termination

Table 10.4   Stage 4: Conversion

Goals	Individual treatment
• Changing expectations • Adapting to a less than full recovery • Psychoeducation • Coping with the transition to first episode services • Developing a hopeful consensus regarding long-term prognosis	• Work in this stage is individual and moves into the first episode program

Stage 4: Conversion to Psychosis

The final stage of the framework is only relevant for a proportion of families. Unfortunately for this group, a conversion to psychosis may mean transfer to a program appropriate for the treatment of a first episode of psychosis. There is little doubt that once the threshold is crossed and the individual converts to psychosis, there are painful and disorganizing consequences for the family. An extreme sense of loss can be expected. However, it is hoped that the family is better prepared for the development of psychosis and that earlier detection of psychosis has been possible resulting in less disruption to both the client and the family. Following the onset of a first psychotic episode, work for the family needs to be continued within early intervention programs or services where the focus will be on recovery from psychosis (Addington et al., in press-a).

THE APPLICATION OF THE FRAMEWORK TO CLINICAL CASES

The families that we have seen in our clinic have presented with a wide range of difficulties and issues. They have presented with concerns about declines in work, school, and social functioning that their relative has experienced. Behavioral problems are also commonly reported concerns. Changes in mood and the development of attenuated symptoms such as suspiciousness, poor reality testing, and religious preoccupation, when present, are usually particularly worrisome for families. In the following section, case examples of four different families are depicted. The presenting problems are reviewed and the framework outlined above is used to identify goals and interventions for each case study.

Worry About Genetic Risk

Case example

Thirteen-year-old Julie was referred to the UHR clinic by her mother, Marg, who suffers from schizophrenia. Marg was worried that Julie might be having early signs of developing psychosis. She was concerned about Julie's occasional defiant behavior, and that Julie was keeping her feelings bottled-up. Marg and Julie were seen individually and then together at the first appointment. During the meeting, it became apparent that Marg was extremely anxious and preoccupied with concerns about Julie's mental state. Marg was open about her own diagnosis of schizophrenia and informed us that her symptoms had increased over the last couple of weeks. The family assessment revealed that Marg was on a fixed income, had limited social support, and appeared to struggle in her parenting role with Julie. Marg could also be quite intrusive when Julie was in the room. Julie presented as a sullen and angry young woman. She either withdrew from conversations or was irritable and tested limits.

Following the initial assessment, the treatment team did not believe that Julie was experiencing any prodromal symptoms nor was there any decline in functioning. Julie herself expressed the need for some support. However, in view of her significant family history of schizophrenia and the clear difficulties in the parent–child relationship, we thought it would be appropriate to offer this family a range of services aimed at reducing the risk of the development of psychosis. The family worker met with Marg once a week for six weeks to discuss her concerns. During the course of their work together, it became clear that Marg was worried that Julie was ashamed of Marg's psychiatric illness, and felt somewhat threatened by her daughter's increasing independence. The family worker normalized Marg's concerns, and discussed the inherent difficulties involved in raising teenagers. The family worker encouraged Marg to set limits with Julie regarding appropriate behavior, and to foster Julie's budding autonomy by giving her some space. Marg was also referred to a parenting group in her community to further support her efforts in this area. In addition, Julie received weekly supportive therapy sessions in the clinic. Early sessions revolved around her embarrassment about having a mother with schizophrenia and with helping her to develop skills to allow better communication with her mother. Given the genetic risk, both Julie and her mother were given information about potential early warning signs of psychosis. The family continues to be seen at the clinic for regular monitoring and support.

This is an example of Stages 1 and 2 work focusing on psychoeducation to reduce stigma, early signs monitoring, and stress management and coping.

Too Much Stress

Case example

Brenda, who was 16, was referred to the clinic by a sexual assault counselor due to increased suspiciousness and self-harm behavior. Brenda met criteria for attenuated psychotic symptoms that did not appear (because of timing and content) to be a direct result of previous sexual abuse issues. Brenda's mother, Carol, was highly involved in Brenda's care and accompanied her daughter to all clinic appointments. Carol would often become tearful when discussing her current situation with clinic staff. She was very distressed by Brenda's condition and felt increasingly helpless. She also had no idea how to cope with Brenda's behavior. To add to her stress, Carol had two siblings with severe psychiatric illnesses. Not only did she have a caring role for them but it also increased her awareness of the possible negative outcomes for Brenda. Furthermore, due to general workplace conflict, she found her job to be highly stressful.

Given the severity of the anxiety that Carol was experiencing, the family worker contracted to meet with her twice weekly for the first two weeks. Despite the frequent contact, Carol would call the family worker between appointments and if she was not immediately available would call anyone in the clinic who would answer the phone. The initial challenge was to help Carol contain the crisis and develop some sense of control over the situation. This took several weeks of frequent regular contact with both the family worker and the treating physician. Eventually, Carol's distress settled enough that she began to process the information that was being provided to her about her daughter's ARMS. Carol's concerns were validated on an ongoing basis and the family worker helped her to develop coping strategies to deal with stress. Following contact with the family worker, Carol reported increased feelings of competence to deal with Brenda's behavior, and her tearfulness with clinic staff was greatly reduced.

However, this mother still regularly struggles. At times, it is difficult for her to hear the information that is being presented, especially when it requires thinking about changing her own behavior with respect to Brenda. Significant conflict continues to erupt between mother and daughter. The treatment team continues to work with Brenda, and the family worker meets with Brenda and her mother regularly in an attempt to problem solve with them around the issues that have arisen. The goal is to reduce the stress in the household and help both Brenda and her mother understand the ARMS.

This is an example of Stage 1 and 2 work—managing the crisis, initial stabilization, and developing coping. However, this mother has not made it to Stage 3.

Confusion

Case example

James is 18 and was referred to our clinic by his social worker for assessment of potential ideas of reference and paranoia. James refused to involve his father because he was afraid of being rejected by him. We worked with James and explored his fears while giving him the message that it was very important to involve families. Eventually James agreed to let us contact his father. We met with James' father on a few occasions to gather information both about the changes that he had seen in James and to understand more about the family.

Over the next few months James' symptoms increased in severity. Fortunately, as we had established a good working relationship with both James and his father, they were able to seek support as James' mental status deteriorated. James' father began to call quite regularly to discuss what was happening to his son. The father was quite distraught about his son's symptoms. He seemed in despair about the implications of the symptoms for James' future. He wanted to know if his son would be able to finish school and continue on to university and whether he would be able to get married and have a family. The father wondered whether there were other people like his son or if there was something that his family had done to cause James' unusual symptoms and behavior. The clinician provided information about the frequency of these symptoms in the general population, reassuring him that his son was not the only one who was dealing with these types of problems. The father had several sessions to explore any further questions, along with providing support during this tough time.

This is an example of Stages 1 and 2 offering psychoeducation, symptom monitoring, and support.

Conversion to Psychosis

Case example

Twenty-year-old Craig was referred to the clinic by his psychiatrist due to increased suspiciousness and unusual thought content. Craig's parents were concerned and frustrated with Craig's recent deterioration in social and occupational functioning. Specifically, Craig was unable to attend school or hold a job, refused to socialize with anyone outside his immediate family, and rarely left the house. His father asked clinic staff for guidance, as he was unsure whether he should push Craig to become more socially involved or just leave him alone. His inclination was to put pressure on his son rather than backing off.

The family worker met with Craig's parents on a weekly basis for the first couple of weeks to obtain a collateral history and a better understanding of them as a couple and as parents. Craig's difficulties were putting significant pressure on his parents, who at times were at odds with one another regarding how to manage issues that arose at home. The family worker contracted with the couple to meet together for four weekly sessions to provide information about ARMS and treatment options and to help them negotiate issues as they arose. Craig's parents met with the family worker, who spent time normalizing their feelings of frustration with their son's behavior, and provided psychoeducation about symptoms and the social and occupational difficulties that often accompany at risk mental states. Several months later Craig converted to a first episode of psychosis. The fact that his family had a pre-existing relationship with the treatment team, and had acquired knowledge about psychosis and treatments, allowed Craig and his family to identify the onset of psychosis and commence treatment with minimal delay.

This is an example of all four Stages.

CONCLUSION

Our knowledge about family intervention following the diagnosis of an ARMS at the present time is limited. However, as a first step in this area we have presented a framework for working with UHR families that is based on our research and clinical work with first episode families and from our clinical experience with UHR families. Our hope is that our early and ongoing work with UHR families will lead to a better understanding of the needs of, and effective interventions for, families supporting a young person at risk of psychosis. Further research is essential to develop and test important hypotheses concerning the role of families and family work in the prevention of psychosis in vulnerable young people.

REFERENCES

Addington, J. & Burnett, P. (2004). Working with families in the early stages of psychosis. In J. Glesson & P. McGorry (Eds), *Psychological Interventions for Early Psychosis 99–116*. Chichester, UK: Wiley.

Addington, J., Coldham, E., Jones, B., Ko, T. & Addington, D. (2003). The first episode of psychosis: The experience of relatives. *Acta Psychiatrica Scandinavica*, **108** (4), 285–289.

Addington, J., Collins, A., McCleery, A. & Addington, D. (in press-a). The role of family work in early psychosis. *Schizophrenia Research*.

Addington, J., McCleery, A. & Addington, D. (in press-b). Three year outcome of family work in an early psychosis program. *Schizophrenia Research*.

Barrowclough, C. & Hooley, J. (2003). Attributions and expressed emotion: a review. *Clinical Psychological Review*, **23** (6), 849–880.

Barrowclough, C., Lobban, F., Halton, C. & Quinn, J. (2001). An investigation of the models of illness carers of schizophrenia patients using the Illness Perception Questionnaire. *British Journal of Clinical Psychology*, **40** (Pt. 4), 371–385.

Barrowclough, C. & Parle, M. (1997). Appraisal, psychological adjustment and expressed emotion in relatives of patients suffering from schizophrenia. *British Journal of Psychiatry*, **171**, 26–31.

Barrowclough, C., Tarrier, N. & Johnston, M. (1996). Distress, expressed emotion and attributions in relatives of schizophrenia patients. *Schizophrenia Bulletin*, **22** (4), 691–702.

Birchwood, M. & Cochrane, R. (1990). Families coping with schizophrenia: Coping styles, their origins and correlates. *Psychological Medicine*, **20** (4), 857–865.

Birchwood, M. & MacMillan, F. (1993). Early intervention in schizophrenia. *Australian and New Zealand Journal of Psychiatry*, **27** (3), 374–378.

Brewin, C.R., MacCarthy, B., Duda, K. & Vaughn, C.E. (1991). Attribution and expressed emotion in the relatives of patients with schizophrenia. *Journal of Abnormal Psychology*, **100** (4), 546–554.

Carver, C.S., Pozo, C., Harris, S.D., Noriega, V., Scheier, M.F., Robinson, D.S. et al. (1993). How coping mediates the effect of optimism on distress: A study of women with early stage breast cancer. *Journal of Personality and Social Psychology*, **65** (2), 375–390.

Collins, A.A. (2002). Family intervention in early schizophrenia. In C. Shulz & R. Zipursky (Eds), *The Early Stages of Schizophrenia* (pp. 129–160). Washington: American Psychiatric Association.

Dixon, L.B. & Lehman, A.F. (1995). Family interventions for schizophrenia. *Schizophrenia Bulletin*, **21** (4), 631–643.

Early Psychosis Prevention and Intervention Centre (1997). *Working with Families in Early Psychosis* (No. 2 in a series of early psychosis manuals). Victoria: Psychiatric Services Branch, Human Services.

Fadden, G. (1998). Research update: psychoeducational family interventions. *Journal of Family Therapy*, **20**, 293–309.

Folkman, S. (1997). Positive psychological states and coping with severe stress. *Social Science and Medicine*, **45** (8), 1207–1221.

Folkman, S., Chesney, M.A. & Christopher-Richards, A. (1994a). Stress and coping in partners of men with AIDS. *Psychiatric Clinics of North America*, **17**, 35–55.

Folkman, S., Chesney, M.A., Cooke, M., Boccellari, A. & Cooke, M. (1994b). Caregiver burden in HIV+ and HIV− partners of men with AIDS. *Journal of Consulting and Clinical Psychology*, **62**, 746–756.

Folkman, S. & Greer, S. (2000). Promoting psychological well being in the face of serious illness: When theory, research and practice inform each other. *Psycho-oncology*, **9** (1), 11–19.

Folkman, S. & Lazarus, R.S. (1985). If it changes, it must be a process: Study of emotion and coping during three stages of a college examination. *Journal of Personality of Social Psychology*, **48** (1), 150–170.

Folkman, S., Lazarus, R.S., Dunkel-Schetter, C., DeLongis, A. & Gruen, R.J. (1986). Dynamics of a stressful encounter: Cognitive appraisal, coping, and encounter outcomes. *Journal of Personality and Social Psychology*, **50**, 992–1003.

Folkman, S., Lazarus, R.S., Gruen, R.J. & DeLongis, A. (1986). Appraisal, coping, health status and psychological symptoms. *Journal of Personality and Social Psychology*, **50**, 571–579.

Frey, K.S., Greenberg, M.T. & Fewell, R.R. (1989). Stress and coping among parents of handicapped children: a multidimensional approach. *American Journal of Mental Retardation*, **94**, 240–249.

Goldstein, M.J. & Miklowitz, D.J. (1995). The effectiveness of psychoeducational family therapy in the treatment of schizophrenic disorders. In W. Pinsof & L. Wynne (Eds). *Family Therapy Effectiveness: Current Research and Theory* (pp. 361–376). Washington: American Association for Marriage and Family Therapy.

Heijmans, M., deRidder, D. & Bensing, J. (1999). Dissimilarity in patients' and spouses representations of chronic illness: Exploration of relationship to patient adaptation. *Psychology and Health*, **14** (3), 451–466.

Heikkila, J., Karlsson, H., Taiminen, T., Lauerma, H., Ilonen, T., Leinonen, K.M. et al. (2002). Expressed emotion is not associated with disorder severity in first-episode mental disorder. *Psychiatry Research*, **111** (2–3), 155–165.

Hooley, J. & Campbell, C. (2002). Control and controllability: Beliefs and behavior in high and low expressed emotion relatives. *Psychological Medicine*, **32** (6), 1091–1099.

Kavanagh, D. (1992). Recent developments in expressed emotion and schizophrenia. *British Journal of Psychiatry*, **160**, 601–620.

Kuipers, E. & Raune, D. (2000). The early development of EE and burden in families of first onset psychosis. In M. Birchwood & D. Fowler (Eds), *Early Intervention in Psychosis: A Guide to Concepts, Evidence and Interventions* (pp. 128–140). Chichester, UK: Wiley.

Larsen, T.K. & Opjordsmoen, S. (1996). Early identification and treatment of schizophrenia: Conceptual and ethical considerations. *Psychiatry*, **59**, 371–380.

Lazarus, R. (1993). Coping theory and research: Past, Present and Future. *Psychosomatic Medicine*, **55** (3), 234–247.

Lazarus, R. & Folkman, S. (1984a). Coping and adaptation. In W.D. Gentry (Ed.), *The Handbook of Behavioral Medicine* (pp. 282–325). New York: Guilford Press.

Lazarus, R. & Folkman, S. (1984b). *Stress, Appraisal, and Coping*. New York: Springer Verlag.

Lehman, A.F., Buchanan, R.W., Dickerson, F.B., Dixon, L.B., Goldberg, R., Green Paden, L. et al. (2003). Evidence based treatment for schizophrenia. *Psychiatric Clinics North America*, **26** (4), 939–954.

Lepore, S.J. & Evans, G.W. (1996). Coping with multiple stressors in the environment. In M. Zeidner & N.S. Endler (Eds), *Handbook of Coping* (pp. 350–377). New York: Wiley.

Lobban, F., Barrowclough, C. & Jones, S. (2003). A review of the role of illness models in severe mental illness. *Clinical Psychological Review*, **23** (2), 171–196.

Mari, J.J. & Streiner, D. (1994). An overview of family interventions and relapse on schizophrenia: meta-analysis of research findings. *Psychological Medicine*, **24** (3), 565–578.

McCreadie, R.G. & Robinson, A.D. (1987). The Nithsdale Schizophrenia Survey. VI: Relatives' expressed emotion: Prevalence, patterns and clinical assessment. *British Journal of Psychiatry*, **150**, 640–644.

McCreadie, R.G., Wiles, D., Grant, S., Crockett, G.T., Mahmood, Z., Livingston, M.G. et al. (1989). The Scottish first episode schizophrenia study. VII: Two year follow-up. *Acta Psychiatrica Scandinavica*, **80** (6), 597–602.

McGlashan, T.H. (1998). Early detection and intervention of schizophrenia: Rationale and research. *British Journal of Psychiatry*, **172** (33), 3–6.

McGorry, P.D. (1995). Psychoeducation in first episode psychosis: A therapeutic process. *Psychiatry*, **58** (4), 313–328.

McGorry, P.D., Yung, A.R. & Phillips, L.J. (2003). The close in or ultra high risk model: A safe and effective strategy for research and clinical intervention in prepsychotic mental disorder. *Schizophrenia Bulletin*, **29** (4), 771–790.

Miller, A.C., Gordon, R.M., Daniele, R.J. & Diller, L. (1992). Stress, appraisal, and coping in mothers of disabled and nondisabled children. *Journal of Pediatric Psychology*, **17** (5), 587–605.

Pilling, S., Bebbington, P., Kuipers, E., Garety, P., Geddes, J., Orbach, G. et al. (2002). Psychological treatments in schizophrenia: I. Meta analysis of family intervention and cognitive behavior therapy. *Psychological Medicine*, **32** (5), 763–782.

Raune, D., Kuipers, E. & Bebbington, P.E. (2004). Expressed emotion at first episode: Investigating a carer appraisal model. *British Journal of Psychiatry*, **184**, 321–326.

Robinson, E. (1996). Causal attributions about mental illness: Relationship to family functioning. *American Journal of Orthopsychiatry*, **66** (2), 282–295.

Scazufca, M. & Kuipers, E. (1996). Links between expressed emotion and burden of care in relatives of patients with schizophrenia. *British Journal of Psychiatry*, **168** (5), 580–587.

Scazufca, M. & Kuipers, E. (1998). Stability of expressed emotion in relatives of those with schizophrenia and its relationship with burden of care and perception of patients' social functioning. *Psychological Medicine*, **28** (2), 453–461.

Scottish Schizophrenia Research Group (1992). The Scottish first episode schizophrenia study. VIII: Five year follow-up: Clinical and psychosocial findings. *British Journal of Psychiatry*, **161**, 496–500.

Smith, J., Berthelsen, D. & O'Connor, I. (1997). Child adjustment in high conflict families. *Child Care and Health Development*, **23** (2), 113–133.

Smith, J., Birchwood, M., Cochrane, R. & George, S. (1993). The needs of high and low expressed emotion families: A normative approach. *Social Psychiatry and Psychiatric Epidemiology*, **28** (1), 11–16.

Szmukler, G., Burgess, P., Herrman, H., Benson, A., Colusa, S. & Bloch, S. (1996a). Caring for relatives with serious mental illness: The development of the Experience of Caregiving Inventory. *Social Psychiatry and Psychiatric Epidemiology*, **31** (3–4), 137–148.

Szmukler, G., Herrman, H., Colusa, S., Benson, A. & Bloch, S. (1996b). A controlled trial of a counselling intervention for caregivers of relatives with schizophrenia. *Social Psychiatry and Psychiatric Epidemiology*, **31** (3–4), 149–155.

Szmukler, G., Kuipers, E., Joyce, J., Harris, T., Leese, M., Maphosa, W. et al. (2003). An exploratory randomized controlled trial of a support programme for carers of patients with a psychosis. *Social Psychiatry and Psychiatric Epidemiology*, **38** (8), 411–418.

Tennakoon, L., Fannon, D., Doku, V., O'Ceallaigh, S., Soni, W., Santamaria, M. et al. (2000). Experience of caregiving: Relatives of people experiencing a first episode of psychosis. *British Journal of Psychiatry*, **177**, 529–533.

White, N.E., Richter, J.M. & Fry, C. (1992). Coping, social support and adaptation to chronic illness. *Western Journal of Nursing Research*, **14**, 211–224.

CHAPTER 11

Group Therapy for People at High Risk of Developing Psychosis

Andreas Bechdolf, Verena Veith and Joachim Klosterkötter

Group therapy is widely used in the treatment of many mental disorders, including schizophrenia. Several meta-analyses have found that group therapy across a variety of settings, theoretical orientations, treatment models and disorders is as effective as individual therapy (Piper & Joyce, 1996; Tillitski, 1990). In addition to such advantages as cost-effectiveness and accessibility, group therapy provides participants with several opportunities for interpersonal and intrapersonal skills acquisition. First, the group may serve as a 'laboratory' environment for experimenting with new ways of communicating and interacting with others. Second, it is an ideal and relatively safe environment in which to practise interpersonal skills. Third, for many clients group therapy offers the opportunity to learn that they are not alone in their experiences and problems, thus normalising them. Finally, group treatment may increase awareness of others' needs and feelings, hence facilitating development of social perception skills.

This chapter will first present an overview of a comprehensive outpatient therapy programme, specifically designed for young people at high risk of developing psychosis, which is presently being offered in several centres across Germany. The chapter will then focus in more detail on the group therapy component of this programme, providing specific details on the structure of the therapy sessions and their respective treatment goals.

THE FRAMEWORK

The Early Recognition and Intervention Centre for Mental Crises (FETZ), a comprehensive outpatient prevention programme for persons at high risk of psychosis, offers individual therapy, short-term group therapy (15 sessions), computer-based cognitive training and three multifamily psychoeducation sessions over a 12-month time period. This programme, delivered across Germany via four specially designed clinical outpatient services, aims to provide a non-stigmatising setting for young people who are worried about their symptoms,

Working with People at High Risk of Developing Psychosis: A Treatment Handbook.
Edited by J. Addington, S.M. Francey and A.P. Morrison. © 2006 John Wiley & Sons, Ltd.

wish to receive treatment, and meet early initial prodromal state (EIPS) criteria. This criteria is defined by the presence of certain self-experienced cognitive and perceptual anomalies (i.e. 'basic symptoms' according to Huber & Gross, 1989) found to be predictive for transition to psychosis in 70% of cases within 5.4 years (Klosterkötter, Hellmich, Steinmeyer & Schultze-Lutter, 2001) and/or by a state-trait risk factor group similar to that as defined by Yung et al. (1998) and presented in Chapter 2.

The early intervention programme addresses cognitive difficulties, perceptual anomalies, negative symptoms, anxiety, depressive symptoms, family and occupational problems; all of which have been reported to occur frequently prior to first onset of positive psychotic symptoms (Häfner, Riecher-Rössler, Maurer, Fatkenheuer & Loffler, 1992; Klosterkötter et al., 2001). Drawing on established strategies of cognitive therapy for people with psychosis (Chadwick, Birchwood & Trower, 1996; Fowler, Garety & Kuipers, 1995; Kingdon & Turkington, 1994), the programme takes into account results from empirical studies of effective treatment strategies for first episode or recurrent schizophrenia, anxiety disorders and/or depressive symptoms (e.g. APA work group, 1998, 2000; Bustillo, Lauriello, Horan & Keith, 2001; Liebowitz, 1999). A modified vulnerability–stress–coping model for schizophrenia (Larsen, Bechdolf & Birchwood, 2003; Nuechterlein & Dawson, 1984; Zubin & Spring, 1977) serves as the global model for the FETZ intervention. The specific aims of the programme are to improve present symptoms, prevent social decline/stagnation and prevent or delay progression to psychosis. Improving coping resources and stress management are underlying strategies of the intervention.

FETZ Programme

In the FETZ programme, individual therapy is the central part of the early intervention programme and is divided into assessment/engagement, treatment and termination phases. During these phases a combination of psychoeducation and symptom-, stress- and crisis-management modules are adapted to the specific needs of each client. Additionally, there is a focus on the attributional styles that underpin the key problems. The therapy aims to establish a coherent understanding of the pre-psychotic state, which in turn is expected to enhance and protect self-esteem. Individuals are also offered computerised cognitive training, which is provided as a tool to address thought and perceptual anomalies directly. A brief psychoeducational multifamily intervention, primarily didactic, is offered to clients' carers and introduces the vulnerability–stress–coping model for the disorder and the rationale for early intervention. This type of psychoeducation aims to increase the family's understanding of the 'at risk mental state' (ARMS) and reduce interpersonal conflicts.

For the various stages and formats of therapy, a range of cognitive-behavioural strategies is utilised. Further details and case examples can be found elsewhere (Bechdolf, Maier, Knost, Wagner & Hambrecht, 2003; Bechdolf et al., 2005a, in press; Larsen et al., 2003).

GROUP THERAPY

Supplementing one another, group and individual therapies usually do not occur simultaneously. Skills acquired in the group programme can easily be employed in the client's subsequent individual therapy by either reinforcing or building upon skills. Typically, people join the group after they have participated in at least five individual therapy sessions. This procedure ensures that therapists are aware of the individual resources and difficulties of the clients, and allows common anxieties associated with joining a group to be addressed. At this stage of individual therapy, clients are usually provided with a preliminary formulation of their own ARMS. As a result of the aforementioned procedures, the majority of clients are able to develop some level of trust with their therapist and engage with the FETZ prevention programme.

Designed as a skills-training group, the group therapy allows members of the group to serve as peer models for dealing with stress, symptoms or perceived stigma. The group itself provides a forum for communicating about problems and beliefs associated with the ARMS in addition to a preliminary social network.

Therapists should be aware of possible negative attitudes about group therapy, which may be related to the client's negative experiences with interpersonal relationships, social anxiety, lack of self-confidence, and experiences with or even lay opinions of confrontational or exploratory group therapy. Consequently, we use normalising terms to describe the group therapy or parts of the intervention (e.g. 'self-confidence and interpersonal contact' for the therapy itself, 'mastery of difficult situations' for the problem-solving section of the programme). The aim is to reduce stigma and improve acceptance of the group approach.

Three Units of the Group Therapy

Unit 1: Positive Mood and Enjoyment

In order to promote group cohesion, increase self-confidence of the participants and reduce any anxiety associated with the group intervention itself, resources and pleasurable activities are the focus in the early stages of therapy. Here we address depression, not only as a common symptom in the prodromal phase, but also to help the client connect individual goals with important social skills such as those needed to experience a pleasurable activity, for example going to the cinema with a friend.

Unit 2: Social Perception and Social Skills Training

In this unit, the focus is on the perception of emotions and social situations and social skills training. The goals are to improve self-confidence and self-esteem, reduce interpersonal stress and help promote peer interaction and cultivate relationships.

Unit 3: Mastering Difficult Situations

This unit focuses upon current individual problems with opportunities for clients to apply a standardised problem-solving approach and practise newly acquired or improved social perception and behavioural skills. By this stage of therapy, group cohesion is well established, allowing participants to support each other in dealing with individual problems, unhelpful beliefs, stress, and stigma associated with the ARMS.

Objectives of the Group

In sum, the group therapy component of treatment aims to address the client's global functioning (i.e. symptoms, affect, engagement in activities), social functioning and coping skills. Specifically, Unit 1 serves to increase the level of pleasurable activities clients engage in, improve depressive symptoms and increase self-confidence and self-esteem. Unit 2 improves the clients' social and interpersonal skills, allowing for the resumption of personal relationships and improvement of familial relations. Finally, in Unit 3 clients improve existing coping skills (or learn new ones) allowing them to manage difficult situations effectively, thus reducing overall stress levels.

Characteristics of the Group Intervention

The FETZ group consists of 15 90-minute weekly group therapy sessions limited to six to eight participants. The first three sessions are open for new participants to join, after which the group is closed. In each session there is a 10-minute break at the end of the first hour. Two therapists lead the group, with one therapist assuming the main responsibility for each treatment session. The intervention uses a wide range of didactic and cognitive-behavioural strategies. Every session starts with a check-in, ends with a check-out, and utilises an agenda. A brief self-description of the participants' current mental state is always a part of these rounds. The check-in exercise can be used to connect specific experiences of individuals with the relevant group content. Feedback regarding weekly homework tasks and likes/dislikes of the session may be elicited for check-ins and check-outs. Expectations and contributions of clients, as well as theoretical models introduced by the therapists, are noted on a flipchart, which is always visible. A number of additional materials like handouts, work- and task-sheets are also used.

Generally, at the end of each session therapists provide participants with weekly homework assignments to connect the content of the group therapy to their daily lives. Homework is discussed at the beginning of the next group session. Each group session follows a detailed protocol containing the aims of the session, examples of interventions and typical responses for the therapist (Bechdolf et al., 2002).

CONTENTS OF EACH SESSION

In this section, each group session will be described in more detail. An overview of the sessions is presented in Table 11.1

Introduction

Session 1

There are numerous ways in which therapists introduce participants to each other and build group rapport. For example, therapists can pair up the participants and ask them to relate information to their partner who then introduces them to the larger group. Following introductions, participants' expectations of the group therapy are reviewed. Topics raised

Table 11.1 Session example of group therapy for people at high risk of psychosis

Unit	Session	Topic
	1	Introduction
Positive mood and enjoying	2	Scheduling and monitoring of pleasure activities I
	3	Scheduling and monitoring of pleasure activities II
	4	Scheduling and monitoring of pleasure activities III/ enjoyment
Training social perception and social skills	5	Social perception I
	6	Social perception II
	7	Acting self-confident
	8	Communication I
	9	Communication II
	10	Contact I
	11	Contact II
Mastering difficult situations	12	Problem solving
	13	Problem solving
	14	Problem solving
	15	Problem solving

include 'What is psychosis?', 'How can I plan my everyday life?', 'How can I explain my problems to others?' and 'How can I meet people?' Therapists introduce the group rationale and aims, and the programme schedule, linking the programme with the expectations of the participants so that it is clear which sessions may be most relevant for individual needs. Group rules are collaboratively established, which is crucial for developing the necessary atmosphere of trust and confidentiality. Rules relate to confidentiality, mutual respect for group members, giving feedback and using the group effectively, time commitment, and lateness or cancelling sessions.

Positive Mood and Enjoyment

Session 2: Scheduling and Monitoring of Pleasurable Activities I

This topic is elicited by discussion of individual experiences with depressed mood including brainstorming to share participants' coping strategies. The group then evaluates each strategy with respect to the degree of pleasure. The goal is for participants to learn that any pleasurable activity can help protect against low mood.

The link among pleasurable activity, thoughts and feelings is illustrated with the 'depression spiral' diagram. A list of common pleasurable activities is issued for participants to evaluate regarding subjective pleasure and frequency in their daily life. All pleasurable activities are divided into simple activities that do not require planning (e.g. going for a walk) and those that require planning (e.g. accompanying somebody to the cinema or joining a sports club). For the weekly homework task each participant chooses one or two activities from both categories, indicating on a worksheet the date they plan to carry them out along with affective state ratings immediately after completing each activity.

Session 3: Scheduling and Monitoring of Pleasurable Activities II

A review of the homework opens the session. Therapists emphasise the association between performing the activity completed for homework and the affective state. After establishing a rationale with the participants for classifying pleasurable activities as relaxing or active, progressive muscular relaxation (PMR) is taught. For the weekly task, each participant selects at least two easy-to-achieve activities with one being relaxing and one activating. Furthermore, each participant is encouraged to regularly engage in at least one easy-to-achieve pleasurable activity. PMR can be used at the end of any session where it seems appropriate.

Session 4: Scheduling and Monitoring of Pleasurable Activities III

In Session 4, therapists introduce the topic 'enjoyment', with a group discussion on requirements for enjoyment. The following attributes are presented – 'time', 'giving oneself permission to enjoy', 'full attention', and 'time limited' – and illustrated. An exercise related to enjoyment is given for homework. The next focus is on pleasurable activities that require preparation. Participants present an activity in which they would like to engage and with which they may have difficulty. The group generates solutions or preparatory steps to carry out the activity. Steps are assessed for expected difficulty. Typically participants identify steps that require social perception and social behaviour skills as being difficult. Steps that are evaluated as difficult are developed using role-plays, and then the activity is assigned as their weekly task.

Training Social Perception and Social Skills (Sessions 5–11)

Session 5: Social Perception I

The focus of this session is on the nature of social perception. Difficulties in this area are normalised, providing great relief to many participants. A discussion of the advantages and disadvantages of identifying one's emotions follow. Next, participants silently perform role-plays demonstrating one of the four major emotions (joy, rage/anger, sadness/grief, fear/uncertainty), with other group members identifying emotions portrayed followed by discussion of the emotional expression. The session ends with joint PMR practice.

Session 6: Social Perception II

In Session 6, through an examination of photographs representing social situations and specific affective states, everyone has the opportunity to describe the emotions depicted based on criteria established in the previous session such as facial expression, gestures and non-verbal interaction. The weekly task includes each participant selecting one or two emotions and monitoring a specific individual for this emotion. The session ends with discussion of experiences with the regularly performed pleasurable activity (Session 3) and group PMR practice.

Session 7: Acting Assertively

During this session, the therapists perform three role-plays in which the same situation is presented first in a non-assertive manner, then in an aggressive way and thirdly in an assertive manner. For example, actor A has reserved a seat for a long train journey. The train is very crowded and A's seat is occupied by person B. A asks B to leave the seat. Without knowing which version is being demonstrated, participants collect details of the different behaviour patterns in the three role-plays. Next, the group describes the characteristics (voice, modulation, content, gesture, facial expression) of the three versions and criteria for acting assertively are established (e.g. appropriate volume of voice, tone of voice, clear wording, use of the first person, eye contact, relaxed body posture, etc.). The therapists introduce further standard situations and the characteristics of corresponding assertive behaviour are defined by the group. Each participant practices assertive behaviour in role-plays while the remaining group members observe giving feedback based on the group's definitions. Participants are assigned a task whereby they distinguish among assertive, non-assertive or aggressive behaviours. They also keep a record of any situations in which they behaved assertively.

Session 8: Communication I

This session begins with an experiential exercise where members both receive and give praise. Members later share how it felt giving and receiving praise. After a small group exercise where members describe some of their own positive attributes, reactions to these exercises are processed in the larger group. Through role-play each participant has the opportunity to practise expressing positive feelings to another member with feedback being offered by observing group members. In a similar manner, the group develops helpful guidelines for expressing wishes. Again, performance of these guidelines is practised and monitored. For the weekly homework task, participants are asked to monitor and express positive feelings and wishes in appropriate situations.

Session 9: Communication II

In Session 9, therapists introduce the topic 'expressing negative feelings' by normalising both the occurrence of and difficulties with this. Work here is typical of assertiveness training. It is important that helpful guidelines for expressing negative feelings are developed by the group. Each participant is then allowed the opportunity to practise expressing negative feelings to another person using either a personal situation or an example suggested by the therapists, with the group members monitoring performance and offering feedback. The second topic, 'active listening', is introduced with the therapists role-playing a brief ineffective communication, demonstrating the importance of this skill for understanding one another. Guidelines for active listening are developed as a group task and practised in role-plays. For homework, participants are asked to monitor and express negative feelings (when appropriate).

Session 10: Contact I

The previous session set the stage for a focus on communicating with others and initiating social contact. The therapists start this session with two role-plays for establishing social contact; one modelling active listening skills, the other poor communication skills. The group uses the role-plays to develop helpful strategies to make a contact. Practice occurs through role-play in a typical situation introduced by therapists, with the others observing and offering feedback. As a weekly homework task, participants are asked to have short conversations with people they do not know well using the strategies developed in this session.

Session 11: Contact II

Participants practise 'making contact' in role-plays of specific, individually chosen situations derived from some of the 'pleasurable activities which require preparation' outlined in Session 3 (e.g. phoning a friend to arrange a trip to the cinema). Each participant role-plays his/her preferred individual activity, while the others observe and give feedback. As homework, participants are asked to perform their preferred individual activity. Finally, at the end of the session each client's experiences with the regularly performed pleasurable activity (cf. Session 3) are discussed.

Mastering Difficult Situations (Sessions 12–15)

Sessions 12–15 have a similar structure. The therapists collect the remaining topics from the list generated in Session 1 or others raised by clients to date, encouraging each client to present at least one relevant problem to the group. Each problem is reviewed using a typical problem-solving approach (i.e. describing the problem, collecting possible solutions, discussing possible solutions, selecting a solution, working out steps towards the solution, and role-playing key steps and their outcome). Furthermore, therapists encourage group validation of the presented experiences and elicit advice from peers regarding what to do. Presenting clients are asked to perform relevant steps of the problem-solving procedure as weekly homework tasks. If there is time left, PMR exercises, monitoring, and discussion of experiences with the regularly performed pleasurable activity (Session 3) are initiated. At Session 15, a celebration of the group's progress takes place (e.g. having cake and coffee together) and participants are asked to review the work done and give feedback regarding the programme.

Case example

Christina, a 25-year-old university student, presented with daily 'concentration problems' that had begun a few months earlier. She reported difficulties in thinking and perceptual anomalies. Her thoughts would disappear and at other times were confusing. In addition, Christina noted that reading had become much more difficult, suggesting impaired language comprehension. Christina described episodes of body numbness and said at times her body felt unreal. She appeared to be extremely sensitive to noises. The onset of the symptoms began after her father strangled her mother during a psychotic episode. Christina's father had a history of schizophrenia and had suffered from recurrent episodes for seven years. When Christina noticed her symptoms she reacted with anxiety and had periods of depression and resignation. Christina feared that she could also develop schizophrenia like her father and may thus become violent or feel 'outside of herself'. She felt insecure, withdrew from her friends and contacts, and feared that she might not pass her final exams. During the engagement phase, Christina expressed the following goals: 'to not lose control and become violent like my father', 'to cope better with my difficulties in thinking and manage the bodily sensations I experience', and 'feel prepared for stressful time periods during exam time'.

Over the course of the individual therapy, Christina noticed that she could influence her symptoms after monitoring them for some weeks. She also noted that by reducing stress factors (e.g. long study phases without intermission) and the application of protective factors (e.g. relaxing methods or planning work schedules), and rewarding herself with pleasurable activities, she could improve her symptoms. Individual therapy was augmented with psychoeducation to reduce Christina's fears of becoming psychotic like her father. Christina realised that many of her assumptions did not fit with the actual scientific results concerning schizophrenia; her symptoms, stress and protective factors differed substantially from her father's symptoms and behaviour. In this manner Christina developed a more realistic approach towards her symptoms, prognosis, and the possibilities of treatment and she felt less stigmatised as a result. Due to this strategy she also experienced an improvement in her thought and perceptual disturbances, as well as an improvement in her mood and anxiety symptoms. The exploration of her assumptions concerning deficits demonstrated that Christina linked the experience of thought and perceptual anomalies with the assumption of being 'out of order' or 'peculiar'. With the recognition and subsequent reduction of these dysfunctional assumptions and beliefs, Christina's resignation, anxiety and depressive symptoms further improved and she felt encouraged to seek social support and widen her social network.

During the group therapy process, Christina practised scheduling and monitoring of pleasurable activities, skills that were introduced during individual therapy. By practising role-plays, Christina learned to observe and to defend her interests and to be aware of her emotional state, which reduced both stress and her reaction to stress. The social skills training enabled Christina to develop more openness in communication and to build up continual contacts and establish a stable social network. She felt relief due to communication with clients who shared similar symptoms, experiences, beliefs and self-stigmatisations.

The computer-based cognitive training enabled Christina to work on her concentration and memory. She also learned that she could control her thoughts and perceptions. Although it was offered, family psychoeducation was not practical due to the long distance from her father's residence.

After one year of psychological therapy, the cognitive and perceptual disturbances, depersonalisation experiences, affective symptoms and social withdrawal noticeably improved (aim a). Social decline was prevented (aim b) and psychotic symptoms did not appear (aim c). Christina could predict risk situations earlier by monitoring the outbreak of symptoms and applying coping strategies effectively. She developed a detailed crisis management plan to cope with increasing symptoms. She established an adequate functional concept of the syndrome, which served as a basis for a coherent system of understanding. This understanding in combination with the acquired skills helped her to protect and enhance self-esteem and to reduce negative affective states and social withdrawal. Christina continued her university studies and had an optimistic outlook towards her future and her ability to cope with difficult life situations.

EVALUATION

The group therapy is undergoing evaluation as part of the FETZ prevention programme for clients in the EIPS in a randomized controlled, parallel group, four-centre trial (Bechdolf et al., 2005a,b, in press; Häfner et al., 2004; Ruhrmann, Schultze-Lutter & Klosterkötter, 2003). In the ongoing trial, clients are block-randomised to receive either a comprehensive cognitive behavioural therapy (CBT) intervention or 21 sessions of clinical management (CM) over a 12-month period (both treatment conditions incorporate elements of case management). Assessments take place at intake, post treatment and at month 24.

To date we can only report on a feasibility analysis, which was conducted for the first 12 participants randomised to CBT intervention (Bechdolf et al., 2005a, in press). From the initial sample, two subjects (16.8%) dropped out after one or more sessions and were lost to follow-up. Clinically and statistically significant pre- to post-treatment improvements were observed in the 10 participants who completed the intervention. Symptoms such as general psychopathology, basic symptoms and depression were significantly reduced by CBT, and global functioning (GAF; APA, 1994) significantly improved (p = 0.005). A descriptive analysis of transition rates to psychosis based on all data for all clients who gave informed consent to participate at the trial until October 16, 2003 (n = 123) indicated transition rates of 5.3% for the CBT group and 14.8% for the control group. Obviously conclusions cannot be drawn from these preliminary findings but they are promising.

CONCLUSION

In this chapter, we described group therapy for people at high risk of developing psychosis as part of a comprehensive outpatient early intervention programme. Preliminary evaluations of the total programme are encouraging in relation to the aims of the intervention, specifically, to improve present symptoms, to prevent social decline/stagnation and to prevent or delay progression to psychosis.

ACKNOWLEDGEMENT

The FETZ EIPS trial is supported by the German Research Network on Schizophrenia and funded by the German Federal Ministry for Education and Research BMBF (grant 01 GI 9935).

REFERENCES

American Psychiatric Association (1994). *Diagnostic and Statistical Manual of Mental Disorders* (4th edn). Washington, DC: Author.
APA work group (1998). American Psychiatric Association Practice Guidelines: practice guideline for the treatment of patients with panic disorder. *American Journal of Psychiatry,* **155** (Suppl. 5), 1–34.
APA work group (2000). American Psychiatric Association Practice Guidelines: practice guideline for the treatment of patients with major depressive disorder (rev. edn). *American Journal of Psychiatry,* **157** (Suppl. 4), 1–45.
Bechdolf, A., Knost, B., Maier, S., Schröder, C., Hambrecht, M. & Wagner, M. (2002). *Psychological Intervention for Persons at Risk of Psychosis in the Early Prodromal State* (2nd rev. edn). Unpublished Manual, University of Köln/Bonn, Germany.
Bechdolf, A., Maier, S., Knost, B., Wagner, M. & Hambrecht, M. (2003). *Psychological Intervention in the Early Prodromal State*. A case report. *Nervenarzt,* **5,** 436–439.

Bechdolf, A., Phillips, L.J., Francey, S.M., Leicester, S., Morrison, A.P., Klosterkötter, J., et al. (2005a). Recent approaches to psychological interventions for people at risk of psychosis. *European Archives of Psychiatry and Neuroscience.*

Bechdolf, A., Ruhrmann, S., Wagner, M., Kuhn, K.U., Jenssen, B., Bottlender, R. et al., (2005b). Interventions in the initial prodromal states of psychosis in Germany: Concept and recruitment. *The British Journal of Psychiatry*, **48** (Suppl.), 45–48.

Bechdolf, A., Veith, V., Schwarzer, D., Schorrmann, M., Stamm, E., Janssen, B. et al., (2005c). Cognitive-behavioural therapy in the pre-psychotic phase: An exploratory pilot study. *Psychiatry Research*, **136** (2–3): 251–255.

Bustillo, J.R., Lauriello, J., Horan, W.P. & Keith, S.J. (2001). The psychosocial treatment of schizophrenia: an update. *American Journal of Psychiatry*, **158**, 163–175.

Chadwick, P.D.J., Birchwood, M. & Trower, P. (1996). *Cognitive Therapy for Delusions, Voices and Paranoia.* Chichester, UK: Wiley.

Fowler, D., Garety, P. & Kuipers, E. (1995). *Cognitive Behaviour Therapy for People with Psychosis.* Chichester, UK: Wiley.

Häfner, H., Maurer, K., Ruhrmann, S., Bechdolf, A., Klosterkötter, J., Wagner, M. et al. (2004). Are early detection and secondary prevention feasible? Facts and visions. *European Archives of Psychiatry and Clinical Neuroscience*, **254**, 117–128.

Häfner, H., Riecher-Rössler, A., Maurer, K., Fatkenheuer, B. & Loffler, W. (1992). First onset and early symptomatology of schizophrenia. *European Archives of Psychiatry and Clinical Neuroscience*, **242**, 109–118.

Huber, G. & Gross, G. (1989). The concept of basic symptoms in schizophrenic and schizoaffective psychoses. *Recenti Progressi in Medicina*, **80**, 646–652.

Kingdon, D. & Turkington, D. (1994). *Cognitive-behavioural Therapy for Schizophrenia.* Hove, England: Erlbaum.

Klosterkötter, J., Hellmich, M., Steinmeyer, E.M. & Schultze-Lutter, F. (2001). Diagnosing schizophrenia in the initial prodromal phase. *Archives of General Psychiatry*, **58**, 158–164.

Larsen, T.K., Bechdolf, A. & Birchwood, M. (2003). The concept of schizophrenia and phase specific treatment. Psychological treatment in pre-psychosis and non-responders. *Journal of the American Academy of Psychoanalysis and Dynamic Psychotherapy*, **31** (1), 209–228.

Liebowitz, M. (1999). Update on the diagnosis and treatment of social anxiety disorder. *Journal of Clinical Psychiatry*, **60** (Suppl. 18), 22–26.

Nuechterlein, K.H. & Dawson, M.E. (1984). A heuristic vulnerability/stress model of schizophrenic episodes. *Schizophrenia Bulletin*, **10**, 300–312.

Piper, W.E. & Joyce, A.S. (1996). A consideration of factors influencing the utilization of time-limited, short-term group therapy. *International Journal of Group Psychotherapy*, **46** (3), 311–327.

Ruhrmann, S., Schultze-Lutter, F. & Klosterkötter, J. (2003). Early detection and intervention in the initial prodromal phase of schizophrenia. *Pharmacopsychiatry*, (Suppl. 3), 162–167.

Tillitski, C.J. (1990). A meta-analysis of estimated effect sizes for group versus individual versus control treatments. *International Journal of Group Psychotherapy*, **40** (2), 215–224.

Yung, A.R., Phillips, L.J., McGorry, P.D., McFarlane, C.A., Francey, S., Harrigan, S. et al. (1998). Prediction of psychosis. *British Journal of Psychiatry*, **172** (Suppl. 33), 14–20.

Zubin, J. & Spring, B. (1977). Vulnerability – a new view of schizophrenia. *Journal of Abnormal Psychology*, **86**, 103–126.

CHAPTER 12

Future Challenges

Anthony P. Morrison, Shona M. Francey and Jean Addington

Recent years have seen the development of tremendous interest in early detection and intervention for psychosis. This has been reflected in the worldwide development of clinical programmes, the establishment of the International Early Psychosis Association, and the publication of several books focusing on treatments and, in particular, psychological treatments for those in the early phases of a psychotic illness. Today, early detection and intervention for psychosis is clearly recognised as important by researchers, clinicians and policy makers alike, as data already suggests that early intervention may have a positive impact on the course of psychotic disorders.

One of the most exciting areas in psychiatry and mental health is the developing interest in what has traditionally been known as the 'prodromal' phase of psychosis. As illustrated in this book, research groups in Australia, the United Kingdom, Canada, the United States and Europe have begun to develop ways to identify individuals who may be in the prodromal phase. These young people, although they are in what may or may not be a pre-psychotic phase, are without doubt help-seeking for a wide range of mental health concerns that are already impacting on their functioning and adversely affecting their quality of life. Initial work focused on medication trials, which were not without controversy; however, major innovative strides are being made in the development of psychological treatments for these young people and their carers.

This book has presented progress to date in the identification of help-seeking individuals who are at ultra high risk (UHR) of developing psychosis. The preceding chapters have focused on a range of psychological interventions that are currently being developed, tested and used. Thus, we envisaged this book as a unique opportunity to put together for the first time an account of the work that is being done throughout the world in developing psychological treatments for those who seek help for an at risk mental state (ARMS). On the one hand it is a brief practical treatment handbook for the clinician and on the other it demonstrates how far we have come in this area (but also how far we have to go). We face many future challenges in relation to research, clinical interventions and service development.

Working with People at High Risk of Developing Psychosis: A Treatment Handbook.
Edited by J. Addington, S.M. Francey and A.P. Morrison. © 2006 John Wiley & Sons, Ltd.

FUTURE RESEARCH DIRECTIONS

Each one of the chapters in the book raises questions for research. As Lewis indicates in the opening chapter, research in this developing area of UHR for psychosis has firm foundations and is rapidly progressing. Epidemiologists are attempting to clarify the prevalence and development of the ARMS, biological issues are being studied and models of prediction developed. The role of psychological and environmental factors in transition to psychosis is also being studied, and will hopefully lead to a greater understanding of vulnerability to psychosis and to more effective theory-based interventions. At this stage of UHR of psychosis, psychological treatments are not only more acceptable but may be more relevant and helpful. However, their effectiveness must be evaluated. Each of the chapters bases the clinical work presented on existing research however preliminary and the field is clearly poised to continue with the evaluative process. Determining whether the treatments are effective and developing innovative psychological treatments for the high-risk group must be priorities for further research.

FUTURE DIRECTIONS FOR CLINICAL INTERVENTIONS

Going beyond the recent developments in the preventative treatments that have been evaluated and delivered to people at high risk of developing psychosis, many of which are outlined within this book, there are likely to be developments in the future that will increase both the efficacy and acceptability of such preventative approaches, as well as integrating different approaches more effectively. For example, it is likely that psychological interventions for the ARMS population will become part of more generic youth services, and may become integrated with work on other problems such as emotional disorders, substance use and behavioural problems. This would seem to be appropriate given the high level of axis I disorders in the ARMS population and their issues of substance use as described in the chapters by Leicester and by Patterson and colleagues. Similarly, it is likely that some of the preventative approaches outlined in this book will be adopted by health promotion agencies, and be utilised in settings such as schools and colleges; for example, using personal development or pastoral care sessions within the school curriculum to help young people to recognise and normalise attenuated symptoms may be a therapeutic endeavour in itself.

Specific, structured psychological interventions for the ARMS population are also likely to develop and evolve over the next few years. For example, the accuracy of the models upon which the case conceptualisations and treatment strategies are based are likely to improve as a result of psychological research into the basic processes involved in the development and maintenance of factors that contribute to risk of psychosis (such as attentional biases, unhelpful beliefs about self and others, metacognition, behavioural consequences and contingencies, and the role of emotion and physiological arousal). It may be that specific models may be developed for each 'entry route' to the ARMS; for example, attenuated symptoms may have a different conceptualisation to BLIPS (Brief Limited Intermittent Psychotic Symptoms) and state-plus-trait criteria, which may result in the development of specific treatment approaches. The beginnings of this process can already be seen within several chapters in this book. It may be that theoretical models for the understanding of family processes may also increase the effectiveness of family interventions, with increasing emphasis on the role of parental attributions for the behaviour of the at-risk child.

The development of normalising information specific to the ARMS population is also likely to contribute to the evolution of psychosocial treatments. For example, accurate knowledge about the proportion of the general population experiencing attenuated psychotic symptoms that meet different criteria specified by ARMS measures, such as the Comprehensive Assessment of At Risk Mental States (CAARMS) and Structured Interview for Prodromal States (SIPS), may be very useful in helping to reduce distress and stigma and promote a sense of normality for those with similar experiences who are help-seeking. Future research on what factors lead some people to initiate help-seeking contacts while others are able to cope without distress may also contribute to the improvement of treatments. Similarly, discussion with service users regarding the terminology for people assumed to be at high risk may also contribute to the normalisation of such experiences and the reduction of perceived stigma.

Newer therapeutic approaches that have developed in other disorders, such as mindfulness (Teasdale et al., 2000) and attention training (Wells, 2000), may also be extended to people who meet criteria for the ARMS. Similarly, the development of more specific group treatment approaches (such as the approach described by Bechdolf and colleagues) may lead to the implementation of group therapy as an alternative to individual psychotherapy, which may capitalise on the psychological processes that are specific to groups.

Finally, there are likely to be issues regarding the delivery and availability of such new treatment approaches. There may be issues regarding the format of intervention (such as individual, family, and/or group treatments), as well as issues relating to the level of skills and training required from practitioners. Future research is likely to enlighten us in relation to such questions, but these issues will also relate to practical issues such as funding from commissioners of services and the availability of suitable therapists. Thus, research that examines implementation and cost-effectiveness may help to answer such questions and promote rapid access to preventative psychosocial interventions.

FUTURE DIRECTIONS IN SERVICE DEVELOPMENT

As the growth in early intervention services for first-episode psychosis continues to gain momentum across the world (Edwards & McGorry, 2002), so too does the establishment of services aimed at early detection and prevention for the pre-psychotic phase. Inevitably, when first-episode services begin they are presented with referrals of young people who, despite severe, disabling symptoms and distress, do not meet the criteria established for an acute psychotic episode. The dilemma of whether and how to respond to such referrals is a common one for services that have often spent years using the early intervention philosophy to lobby for their first-episode psychosis service. Having set up a first-episode programme based on the belief that specialised early intervention for first onset psychosis will lead to improved outcomes, it can be difficult and seem illogical to refuse a service to those who seem to be imminently at risk of psychosis. However, for those services that have begun to offer treatment to young people thought to be at risk it has been important to consider a range of ethical and practical issues involved in commencing a service for 'at-risk' young people. These issues continue to be important when considering recommendations for the further development of services for this vulnerable group.

When establishing new services for young people thought to be at high risk of psychosis, it is essential that they are set up so that the benefits provided by the service to its users outweigh any risks. The benefits will be enhanced by the provision of better treatments, which both prevent transition to psychosis and alleviate distress associated with the wide range of presenting problems seen in UHR clients, often in addition to their UHR criteria. Although it may be speculated that these two are linked (i.e. that interventions that relieve the distress for which a client is seeking help will also reduce the risk of transition to psychosis), it is more usually the distress for which the client is seeking treatment. Thus, as long as clients are help-seeking and receive help for their self-identified problems, the risks of receiving unnecessary or harmful treatment are reduced. Even for 'false-positive' clients, that is those who were wrongly identified as 'at ultra high risk', treatment provided for their presenting problems is likely to be beneficial. Indeed, as the longer established UHR services have been observing reduced rates of transition to psychosis in recent years, it is possible that the proportion of false positives in the referred populations has increased, possibly due to changes in 'case' detection and referral methods. This shifts the risk/benefit ratio in the direction requiring increased caution, and this has implications for the types of interventions offered to UHR young people. The far greater risks associated with the use of powerful neuroleptic medications in young people than with problem-focused psychological therapy make their use hard to justify, especially in the face of lower transition rates. Earlier transition rates of 30–50% were thought to justify the investigation of the preventive benefit of novel (low side-effect) antipsychotic medication but only within the context of randomised controlled trials (RCTs). Now, even in the context of RCTs, it would seem that psychological intervention should be offered as first-line treatment with antipsychotic medication reserved for those who fail to recover with psychological intervention and continue to experience attenuated psychotic symptoms and distress. In addition it has been suggested that other forms of pharmacotherapy, for example antidepressants, may be useful for at-risk young people (Cornblatt, 2002), and warrant further investigation.

The other major risk associated with identifying and offering treatment to young people at risk of psychosis comes from stigma and demoralisation. It is important that services operate in non-stigmatising environments and offer users a balanced and optimistic outlook for their future. This is difficult to achieve if services are located in traditional mental health facilities that provide treatment for those with chronic mental illnesses. It is more appropriate, where possible, to co-locate UHR services with other youth-focused services and provide a range of complementary health, welfare, vocational, educational and recreational activities in a youth-friendly environment. This will offer the best opportunities for engaging young people and developing effective services to promote mental health. It may also be possible to widen the definition of ARMS and begin to examine early detection and prevention for other serious mental disorders, which would also reduce the risk of stigma associated with attending a clinic set up to address risk for psychosis.

Finally, it is well acknowledged throughout this book that research and service development for the pre-psychotic phase is in its infancy, and for this reason it is imperative that high-quality research is conducted to expand the evidence base. It is important that new services commence with an established research capacity so that the efficacy of different treatments and the accessibility and acceptability of new services are monitored. We need to know the impact of services on both short- and longer-term outcomes for young people treated by them and thus longitudinal follow-up evaluations of symptoms, functioning and well-being will be required. We also need to continue to research and refine our definitions of ARMS and our methods for selecting young people for targeted preventive interventions.

REFERENCES

Cornblatt, B.A. (2002). The New York High Risk Project to the Hillside Recognition and Prevention (RAP) Program. *American Journal of Medical Genetics*, **114** (8), 956–966.

Edwards, J. & McGorry, P.D. (2002). *Implementing Early Intervention in Psychosis*. London: Martin Dunitz.

Teasdale, J.D., Segal, Z.V., Williams, J.M., Ridgeway, V.A., Soulsby, J.M. & Lau, M.A. (2000). Prevention of relapse/recurrence in major depression by mindfulness-based cognitive therapy. *Journal of Consulting and Clinical Psychology*, **68**, 615–623.

Wells, A. (2000). *Emotional Disorders and Metacognition: Innovative Cognitive Therapy*: New York: Wiley.

Index

Note: Page references in *italics* refer to Figures and Tables. Abbreviations used within the index are: ARMS = at risk mental state; BLIPS = brief limited intermittent psychotic symptoms; ED:IT = Early Detection & Intervention Team (Birmingham); FETZ = Early Recognition and Intervention Centre for Mental Crises; UHR = Ultra High Risk.

symptoms of psychosis (*Continued*)
  see also attenuated psychotic symptoms; brief
    limited intermittent psychotic symptoms
    (BLIPS)

terminology, 1
therapeutic alliance, 41, 48–50, 158–9
  see also engagement
threat
  environmental, 134–5
  interpersonal, 142–3, 144–6, 148
trait plus state risk factors, 130–2
trans-theoretical model of behaviour change,
  102
trauma, 134, 135
  UHR group treatment targets, 78, 79, 80, 81,
    85, 86
treatment
  antipsychotic medication, 2–3, 5, 55–6, *83*,
    104, 112–13, 132, 184
  assessment and, 25–7
  of attenuated psychotic symptoms, 111–26
  for BLIPS, 112–13, 135–48
  ED:IT types, 83–4
  engagement *see* engagement
  family interventions, *83*, 84, 158–64
  formulation, 35, 36–8, 114–18, 125–6, 137–9
  future challenges, 182–5
  group therapy, *83*, 84, 85, 160, 169–78
  reluctance to attend, 42–3
  research methodologies, 2–3, 5
  service development, 183–5
  settings for, 45–6, 114, 184
  stigma as barrier to, 46–7
  substance use, 99–106
  targets for UHR group, 75–88
    classificatory systems and, 77–8

co-morbid disorders, 76–81, 82–3, 84, 85,
  86, 87
ED:IT, 81–7
emotional dysfunction, 75–81, 82, 84,
  85–6, 87–8
risk factors, 78–80
therapeutic alliance, 41, 48–50, 158–9

Ultra High Risk (UHR) for psychosis clients, 1
  assessment, 16–20, 25–35, 100–1, 104
  case formulation, 25, 35–8
  ED:IT, 81–7
  engagement in therapy *see* engagement
  family support/interventions, *83*, 84, 153–65,
    170
  future challenges, 182, 184
  group therapy, *83*, 84, 85, 169–78
  identification, 12, 13–21
  risk factors for UHR, 78–80
  service development, 184
  stress *see* stress
  subgroups, 130–2
    see also attenuated psychotic symptoms;
      brief limited intermittent psychotic
      symptoms
    substance use, 76, 93, 97–106
    therapeutic alliance, 41, 48–50
    treatment targets, 75–88
urbanicity, 134–5

voice hearing *see* auditory hallucinations
volitional changes, 9, *10*
vulnerability model
  stress *see* stress-vulnerability model
  substance use, 95, 98

warfare, stress–psychosis relation, 58